Helen Powell is a Senior Lecturer in the School of A
the University of East London. She has also worked i ____ry
and adopts an interdisciplinary approach in her teachi _____ research.

Stop the Clocks!

TIME AND NARRATIVE
IN CINEMA

HELEN POWELL

I.B. TAURIS

LONDON · NEW YORK

Published in 2012 by I.B.Tauris & Co Ltd
6 Salem Road, London W2 4BU
175 Fifth Avenue, New York NY 10010
www.ibtauris.com

Distributed in the United States and Canada Exclusively by Palgrave Macmillan
175 Fifth Avenue, New York NY 10010

International Library of the Moving Image: 4

ISBN 978 1 84885 175 7 (PB)
     978 1 78076 216 6 (HB)

A full CIP record for this book is available from the British Library
A full CIP record is available from the Library of Congress

Library of Congress Catalog Card Number: available

Printed and bound in Great Britain by TJ International Ltd, Padstow, Cornwall

This book is in memory of my wonderful Mum,
Barbara Elizabeth Powell.

CONTENTS

LIST OF ILLUSTRATIONS

Images from the Ronald Grant Archive (www.ronaldgrantarchive.com)

INTRODUCTION:
CINEMA AS TIME MACHINE

'What, then, is time?' asks Augustine. 'I know well enough what it is, provided that nobody asks me; but if I am asked what it is and try to explain, I am baffled.'

(The Confessions, Book XI, cited in Ricoeur, 1984: xi)

How might we begin to articulate what it is like to experience time? This is the challenge that Augustine faced (A.D. 354–430) and which continues to provoke thought across a range of disciplines into the twenty-first century. There are multiple points of access to this debate but I should like to consider a television advertisement as an interesting starting point. I have been drawn to the rise of mobile phone culture and its inter-relationship with all matters temporal: how we become visible, traceable at any moment when our phones are switched on but can disappear at the press of a button. How phones can alleviate concerns of being out of touch, of missing out. My students seem to have them permanently in their grasp and demonstrate the need to respond immediately when a call or text comes in for fear of severing some kind of invisible umbilical cord of communication. Yet it was the relationship between the mobile phone and its response to, or some might say generation of, time pressure that was most evident in the campaigns that followed their mass take-up. In 2007 Vodafone launched its 'Raining Time' campaign that centred on the rush hour, highlighting the amount of time we spend waiting, queuing, staring at our watches or indeed at the clock on the phone, as for many the traditional wristwatch has now been made redundant by this mobile device. The skies darken and it begins to rain. As people run for cover they become aware that it is actually clock parts that are falling from the sky and the voice-over begins. Dame Judi Dench announces:

> You might say it's like striking oil in your garden or finding gold in the loft. Except this commodity can't be bought or sold and we've all just become rich in it. From now on we all have more time. Because with Vodafone the internet is truly mobile. So you can make use of every minute of every day.

This mobile phone company is giving us something we can't buy: time. Fast forward then to 2010 and the introduction of the Sony Ericsson *XPERIA 10*, a mobile phone which promises to save us even more time. Its print campaign addresses us: 'Don't let time escape. Get it back –' where with 'a quick flick of the finger and you're scrolling back and forward through time.' Studying advertising provides us with an insight into the socio-cultural concerns of any given moment. The last years of the twentieth century identified a new temporal turn characterised by time scarcity, of individuals wishing they had more time to do what they wanted. However, this particular phase in our perception of and engagement with time and its subsequent media representation is just one perspective. This book taps into a multiplicity of other temporal trends that can be identified since cinema began.

From the outset of modernity, the clock has become inextricably linked to our conceptualisation and understanding of time. However, what the clock does not represent or communicate is its experiential dimension. For the time of consciousness, and indeed unconsciousness, contrasts starkly in shape and form with the rationalised world of mechanical measuring devices. And it is here that cinema, the subject of this book, begins to play a significant role in this temporal debate. Cinema needed to represent temporal flow visually and chose to do so boldly from the outset without the aid of a clock visible on screen to mark duration. Through the omission of this fundamental constraint many different ways to represent the passing of time in cinema followed and are subject here to documentation and discussion. Cinema became the primary modern means of storytelling: through varying degrees of a suspension of disbelief, audiences were willing and indeed thrilled to be transported to other times and indeed other worlds, as the genre of science fiction, examined here, will testify in the extreme. Yet early cinema existed without narrative. The Lumières' actualities captured life as it happened with all its contingencies. Only later did narrative come to dominate, and in one particular form, in the context of mainstream cinema. The classical Hollywood narrative embodies a specific representation

of temporal flow, rational and linear in its construction; it reflects the standardised view of time introduced by the onset of industrialisation and will function here as a model through which alternative approaches to film-making and
narrative construction might be explored in detail. Central to the success of
industrialisation was the uniformity of clock-time, functioning to coordinate
and control the mass of workers employed and represented with great irony in
Chaplin's *Modern Times* (1936). While its uniform presence took a hold on diurnal existence a counter-trend was evident throughout the early development of
cinema, specifically through a range of imaginative methods that began to be
employed in storytelling. What such evolving narrative devices had in common was a perception of time as something fluid, malleable and sometimes
even incomprehensible in the film-maker's hands. Clocks, therefore, can be seen
to function as a material expression of an abstract concept to allow for social
cohesion and inter-subjectivity. Clocks spatialise time: they mark its passing
from one moment to the next but offer us no sense of its meaning. For at the
level of the diurnal we occupy multiple temporal realities: memories, dreams
and fantasies all weave in and out of and provide a coping strategy for the more
mundane facets of any day. Simply put, cinema is worthy of study in relation
to our understanding of all matters temporal as it too has sought to grapple
throughout its history with the representation of the personal, inter-personal,
experiential and philosophical nuances of time.

This engaging and indeed enduring relationship that exists between time
and the cinema has recently been imaginatively documented in Christian
Marclay's *The Clock*, 'a twenty-four-hour movie that tells the time' (Smith,
2011: 1). Part of the 'British Art Show 7' (2011), this video installation comprises an assemblage of film and television clips of varying duration, all of
which contain some reference to time, whether that be specifically timepieces
or rather exploring how we spend our time waiting or, interestingly, trying
to get to sleep. What makes this work remarkable is that it is time-specific.
As Romney (2011: 30) explains, 'If you walk into the gallery at 5.15pm, the
time-pieces on screen show 5.15. Come at midnight and Big Ben will be striking twelve. *The Clock* is perfectly synchronised and calibrated – it is itself, to
all intents and purposes, a fully functioning clock.' However, as Zadie Smith
observes, the viewing experience is to a large degree still informed and regu-
lated by our temporal relations with the external world. For 'people even leave
the gallery following the conventions of time: on the hour, or a quarter past. No
one can seem to stand to leave at, say, 6:07' (2011: 2).

There are three layers of temporality contained within any film image: the
time of registration (production); the time of narration (storytelling); and the

time of its consumption (viewing). This book will examine all three layers. In so doing, it will explore cinema's relationship to and conceptualisation of the passing of time through a range of filmic subject matter. With the television series featuring the Time Lord, *Dr. Who* (BBC), remaining more popular internationally than ever, it is worth engaging, for example, with the persistent theme of time travel. The discourse of progress appears to have been dented by postmodern theorising and in the field of science man's quest to travel into the future continues to exist only on paper, imagined and yet grounded by complex mathematical formulae and diagrams. On screen, however, it is realised and therein lies its appeal.

The relationship between time and the viewer in the millennial era, and the new narrative forms that emerged as a consequence, are also worthy of investigation. Here questions are posed concerning how effective such narrative constructions are in mapping our own revised diurnal experiences, represented by fracture, fragmentation and, often, incomprehension. Through an examination of the domination of the 'classical Hollywood narrative' model, which draws upon the work of Bordwell, Staiger and Thompson (1996), it comes to function as both the lynchpin of modern storytelling and as an enduring format out of which deconstruction and innovation can emerge. However, it is interesting to note how developments in narrative experimentation can coalesce and produce trends. One such example, which this book will examine, is that of the 'puzzle film' (Cameron, 2008). Appearing in not insignificant numbers in the late twentieth century these films play with audiences' expectations of conventional roles and storytelling through the use of the unreliable narrator and the fracturing of linearity. In so doing they open up wider questions of belief, truth and reliability. Returning to the present, the book will also consider how the subject matter of cinema can function as a social commentary on the 'now', how it acts as a conduit through which the collective unconscious manifests itself, especially at times of heightened social anxiety such as war and the persistent threat of terrorism in the post 9/11 age. In particular it will draw on certain cinematic symbols and metaphors – for instance, angels and vampires – and consider how their representation on screen taps into the enduring theme of life, death and the world beyond.

The book concludes in the present and heralds the nascence of a series of narrative derivations characterised by high levels of interactivity. Such filmic experimentations take audiences on new cinematic journeys and in so doing the traditional subject positions of director and viewer become increasingly destabilised. With the rise of globalisation and ICTs (information and communication technologies) our relationship to time is constantly changing, producing moments of temporal fragmentation and rupture, some more intense than others. In the final chapter on time in the digital age – cyber-time – new forms of experiencing time are evidenced, brought about by a sense of global inter-connectedness. The emergence of vast communication networks function to reveal that 'clock time is not an absolute backdrop against which we synchronize and "tell" the time but a human construction that has very little to do with time other than as an inflexible way of measuring duration' (Hassan and Purser, 2007: 10). In keeping with the other chapters of the book, the final chapter charts the close relationship between points of social rupture that precipitate change in temporal perception, and how this manifests itself on screen. However, this book also seeks to position time as a highly individual, reflective experience, and while recognising particular social and cultural turns in temporal understanding, our engagement with time can also be highly personal, as represented by both *Donnie Darko* and Henry Spencer (*Eraserhead*). Sometimes subjective and objective time collides. *A Matter of Life and Death* and *Jacob's Ladder,* for example, produce multi-faceted, multi-layered distortions of both space and time as the world of the living and the afterlife intersect, provoking contemplation of our position in some grander scheme other than that represented solely by our time here on earth.

As with the earlier example drawn from advertising, an interdisciplinary approach is adopted throughout, not only to situate cinema within the context of other contemporary social and cultural developments, but also to draw together a range of work on temporality that has previously been kept exclusively within its own disciplinary framework. This approach allows for a broad theoretical church including Freud and his contemporary Bergson, along with the work of Ricoeur (1984), Deleuze (1989) and E.P. Thompson (1991). The material itself is ordered through the adoption of a historical approach taking the reader through cinema's pre-history and on to contemporary developments in the moving image, examining throughout this journey technological innovations and aesthetic developments. It must be made clear that this is not a history of the cinema. Rather it explores how time and the cinema became inextricably linked and how cinema has constantly engaged with the representation of all matters temporal. In view of this, the films have been chosen on the basis of what they illustrate about the structure of a narrative, the use of a filmic technique, or the specificity of the subject matter. Furthermore, the films selected are informed by my own specific preferences in terms of how they function as representations of these particular categories. For as Deleuze once stated: 'if you don't love it, you have no reason to write about it' (Deleuze and Parnet, 1987: 144). As cinema has consistently reviewed how it can tell stories, so both consciously and subconsciously, it is also reflecting and informing audiences' understanding and engagement with time through the viewing process. In its most acute form, the postmodern tells us there is no metanarrative to our engagement with and representation of time: it is fractured, its linearity broken down into moments, each packed with an intensity of emotion and action. Today, informed by social, cultural and technological change we live in a world of instantaneity where, as commanders of time, we stretch it, warp it and multitask, deepening each moment with maximum content. This hasn't always been so, as this book will document.

The relevance of the work of Gilles Deleuze to the questions addressed here cannot be underestimated. Deluze used cinema as a medium through which he could study time, believing that it allowed us to observe that which is inaccessible at the level of the diurnal. His interest in cinema was part of a wider interest in our interactions with technology (Colebrook, 2006). Engaging with technology enables us to see things differently and, in this case, experience time differently. While Deleuze's consideration of temporality is heavily informed by the work of Bergson, especially in relation to his concept of *durée* or duration, a central point of difference and useful starting point for this book is in relation to their contrasting attitudes towards cinema. While Bergson, as Chapter 1 will document, argued against the cinema, purporting that it discouraged the viewer to live life to the full, Deleuze posits that this new medium offers up the potential to see the world in both creative and challenging ways. In his two books on cinema he explores the means by which different styles are produced according to how cinematic images, shots and frames are connected, all of which consequently allow for differing representations of time. In these volumes Deleuze maps out the history of cinematic signs and recognises that there has been a necessary shift in strategies of signification since World War II. Such a shift emerges out of a re-evaluation of our understanding of time and subsequently is reflected in the images cinema produces. In this way cinematic practices can be described as 'thought machines', reflecting and processing the philosophy of an era through its images (Rodowick, 1997: 7). In *Cinema 1* (1986) Deleuze takes up Bergson's position of cinema operating on the basis of the spatialisation of time. Bergson posited that the eye perceives movement as though through an internal cinema projector, where movement and time become conjoined: spliced up and then fused back together to comprehend a single sense of homogeneous flow. And yet Deleuze argues that how the viewer actually perceives the cinematic image on screen is not as that of the melding together of a series of static moments but as an image 'directly and immediately in motion, a moving picture or movement-image' (Bogue, 2003: 22). That is to say compared with

Bergson he offers a different perspective on the relationship of the parts to the whole. In *Cinema 2* (1989) emphasis shifts to the time-image, 'durée images', as opposed to 'mobile cuts of durée' in the movement-image (ibid.: 28). Here 'every moment forms a crystal as it perpetually splits into a virtual past and an actual present' (ibid.: 133) and out of this conception of time, particular narrative forms arise. One particular derivation, the fractured narrative, as discussed in Chapter 5, is a reflection of this.

Deleuze commenced his study of cinema as a means of exploring 'the mystery of time'. Such mysteries began to demystify through the recognition of how image practices are representative, at any particular moment in history, of cinema's conceptualisation of the world in which it is situated. In this context, ideas about the temporal are made visible through the image, signified in the transition from one series of images to another; indirect visibility of all things temporal in the movement-image, direct representation in the time-image. Such direct visibility of the temporal presents us with a world based on disorder, uncertainty and unpredictability, demonstrated through narrative practices which derive from a conception of 'becoming', of a state of permanent insecurity in terms of what will happen next. This impacts directly on the nature of spectatorship where images engender sublime reactions, for what is often being viewed is something other than action, often difficult to commit to language, and where there is a greater level of inter-relationship between the viewer and what is viewed based on the need to 'read' a film rather than to simply 'see' it. Therefore we might argue that in these two works Deleuze examines not only our understanding and signification of time at the level of the social through cinema but how this representation itself changes over time. However, it is important to clarify that the time-image does not replace the movement-image. While the latter might still dominate, the former is still evolving and does so as society experiences different degrees of change which prompts revised responses. Cinema reflects this, argues Deleuze, by forcing us to think about the world around us. Within the time-image the central question is no longer 'What are we going to see in the next image?' but rather 'What is there to see in the image?' (Deleuze, 1989: 272). While Deleuze will be useful to this book in terms of what the time-image contributes to our understanding of the relationship between the moving-image and temporality, it is critical to recognise that all films draw attention to time, both directly and indirectly and, in view of this, films selected for analysis speak to their specific 'use-value' (Powell, 2005: 156) in relation to the topics under investigation.

Drawing therefore upon American and European productions, the films under scrutiny have been chosen for their specific contribution to our understanding of the dynamics of time in the Western world. Furthermore, selections are made based on the capacity of a film to make an aspect of temporality more accessible to a wider audience. This is realised either through the narrative device employed or through the film as a commentary on time, or indeed, as will be consistently noted, the inter-relationship between the two. In terms of how the book is structured, Chapter 1 examines the rare cinematic device of 'real time' film-making. It takes as its starting point, how, since its inception, cinema challenged the overt functionality of the clock as a mechanism to mark the passing of time, concealing the moment of registration by incorporating it into narrative. In this context cinema is always *over*, we are always watching something that has already passed. As a result this allows cinema to adopt a more complex relationship to time which distinguishes it from other more 'live' visual media such as many television programmes. Fiction cinema also tends to distinguish between diegetic time and screen time, rarely brought together except in the few attempts at 'real time' film-making. It is this engagement with 'real time' that is examined in this first chapter: how it rears its head throughout cinematic history embracing, as it does so, time on the clock and time on the screen.

Chapter 2 assesses Georges Méliès' contribution to film history. Not only is he responsible for providing the roots of continuity editing but in turning to narrative, he secured the future of cinema, and is simultaneously praised by both mainstream and avant-garde film-makers alike. His choice of subject matter, including the adaptation of Verne's science fiction, not only tapped into fin de siècle sensibilities but established a cinematic genre, the history of which embodies the development of the special effect, significant for its own contribution to the appeal of many subsequent productions, and which is discussed further in Chapter 6. The magic of Méliès particularly appealed to the Surrealists, who inform the content of Chapter 3. Here attention is turned to the impact of Surrealism on cinema history and how, through the work of Freud on the unconscious, film-makers were able to develop highly innovative practices with regards to narrative construction. The Surrealists' interest in cinema centred on the destabilisation of the dominant cultural logic of narrative illusionism, which in Dali and Bunuel's *Un Chien andalou*, and in the more contemporary work of David Lynch, is achieved through a defamiliarisation of traditional cinematic temporal markers. As Dali had explored through his paintings, in the unconscious time becomes 'soft' and subject to distortion, and it is such an approach that frames the Surrealists' stance on narrative, permeated as it is with fragmentation and a recognition of the role of chance and coincidence in life. Chapter 4 takes a very different direction, turning away from directors' more personalised interpretations of the diurnal to the ways in which filmic subject matter is able to reflect the socio-cultural mood of the moment in which it is situated. The symbolic roles of the angel and the vampire provide an alternative means to explore the experiential dimension of temporality while functioning as social indicator of people's paradoxical relationship to their life course. Coupled with the quest for immortality comes also the cult of youth, where living longer brings with it a yearning to stay young, as depicted in the character of the vampire. And yet, on a day-to-day basis, as television news reports constantly remind us, life is fragile and very short. The guardian angel buffers this frightening recognition, offering protection against the unpredictable and unknown. However, despite increasing longevity and otherworldly protection, there is always an ending to each life and this chapter closes with a consideration of how directors have sought to engage not only with the afterlife but also the atemporal space occupied in that moment between life and death.

Narratives of the 1990s, as characterised by a sense of state of fracture, dislocation and instability, are the subject matter of Chapter 5. Such developments are set against the history of the classical Hollywood narrative which, it is argued, derives its success from a representation of time that is based upon a dominating temporal discourse in the social sphere, one that is underpinned by standardisation, objectivity and uniformity. Such a model is critiqued through an attempt to distinguish what can be termed 'postmodern cinema'. While debates across a number of disciplines highlight the difficulties in arriving at a specific definition of the constitution and characterisation of the postmodern, what seems to be agreed upon, and is integral to this chapter, is the way in which narrative becomes tied to the circulation of a new set of temporal relations in the social sphere. At this point the work of Jean-François Lyotard (1991) is appropriated in terms of the recognised shift he outlines in contemporary understanding away from that of the grand narrative towards the petit narrative, represented cinematically as the replacement of the story by stories, puzzles and fractured time lines. This then provides the theoretical underpinning for the final chapter, which examines recent developments in cinema practice in the digital age. Focusing on revised viewing regimes enabled by the technological infrastructure that spans from the remote control to the introduction of YouTube, Chapter 6 explores questions that not only seek to address how the feature film is coping in an age of decreasing concentration but how it is even fighting back against other forms of screen entertainment.

So, to conclude, let us return to the dilemma of St Augustine that opened this introduction and use to it concretise some of the fundamental themes that will circulate this text. The increasing value of time as a resource permeates not only our working lives but also our leisure, and even gravitates onto the field of play. The value of time in deciding results, and the lucrative financial gains that come with each winning point, was documented in the context of a Premier League football match between Arsenal and Manchester United in 1997 where the manager Sir Alex Ferguson, near the close of play, went down to the touch line and started waving his watch at officials. As the football commentator on *BBC Radio Five Live* noted, earlier in the season Ferguson had reportedly stated that the management of time was far too important to be placed in the hands of the referee, a position he seems to have maintained to this day. However, football remains one of the legacies of modernity whereby the clock maintains its power through its ability to represent time as a measurement of minutes and seconds and where the quantifying of the amount of extra-time to be played out can be a highly contentious issue for fans, managers and players alike. 'The meaning of time, however, is not encapsulated in either the counting of units or the number system' (Adam, 1990: 54). Rather what this book purports, in contrast to the views of Sir Alex Ferguson, is that we need to recognise that time is historically and culturally relative and that its symbolisation in the form of the clock is not all-pervasive. The purpose of this book is not to chart the complete history of narrative cinema, nor does it seek to contemplate every film made around the subject of time. (Indeed, as noted, all films made are infused with time.) Rather, through the adoption of an interdisciplinary approach, it attempts to explore the usefulness of cinema in understanding the concept of temporality, in relation to both the individual subject and the social milieu in which they are situated.

REAL TIME

This opening chapter takes as its central focus an examination of the changes in our perception of time and maps these onto the development of cinema from its pre-history to its current immersion in the digital age. How we experience time as history unfolds and during the course of our own daily lives is never constant. At present many social commentators tell us that this is the age of instantaneity, that we live in the 'now'. One of the consequences of this temporal shift, it has been argued (McKenna, 1999), is that through the impact of the media and new technologies, significantly the internet, we are in fact experiencing the world in 'real time'. In this way McKenna (1999: 6) explains: 'Real time applies not to any device but to the technologically transformed context of everything we do. Real time is characterised by the shortest possible lapse between an idea and action, between initiation and result.' Time is viewed as a resource and a scarce one at that. In relation to visual culture, we now live in an 'attention economy' whereby 'time starvation also means a poverty of attention' (Lewis and Bridger, 2001: 60) and where 'human attention becomes the most important commodity of all' (ibid.: 65). Taking this a step further Gleick (1999: 9) is aware consequentially of the 'acceleration in the pace of films and television commercials.' This acceleration he notes is embodied within the concept of 'real time' which he describes as a 'now-ness intensifier' a 'perpetual present tense' (ibid.: 67). But are our social sensibilities towards time impacting media production or rather does the changing pace of media reflect and condition a concomitant change in our psyches?

Before we can begin to construct a response, we would need to engage with a consideration of how time entered the cinema in the first place. Indeed, the history of cinema is all about time. Early films were shot in real time and the eye saw events unfold before them at the pace at which they happened. As cinema began to experiment in terms of editing techniques and effects so this was accompanied by a quickening of the eye. Yet where did this relationship between the eye and the moving image begin? This can be traced through the pre-history of cinema, to the Victorians' fascination with optical toys which synthesised motion from a sequence of still images and which became of increased scientific interest in the quest for greater knowledge about how vision functions. This is complemented by an examination of Etienne-Jules Marey's chronophotography and the motion analysis of Eadweard Muybridge, examined here for the emphasis they both placed on the analysis of movement based on a series of photographs, thus allowing for sequential comparison to be carried out. In this way, both anticipate the aesthetic of cinema, the realisation that if you break movement down into its constituent parts, it is never possible to recapture the whole, unless a viewing subject is present. Therefore, in an attempt to map out the point at which the temporal entered the field of vision, it is necessary to briefly trace the development of the optical toys of the nineteenth century, to find the point at which the representation of time became a manifest challenge. Of specific concern is the contribution of these 'new technologies of representation' (Doane, 2002: 4) towards the creation of the illusion of movement, for it is at this juncture that fundamental observations have been made with regards to the nature of the toy and its relationship to the human subject, and more specifically to the human eye. An examination of the optical toy enables us to place the invention of cinema within its social context: the development of transportation that accompanied industrialisation, especially the railways; the technological innovations that allowed for the mechanisation of production and the onset of Fordism; and the scientific inventions, such as electricity. Electricity allows for the appropriate conditions of mass viewing to become realisable, turning night into day and day into night in the seclusion of the auditorium. In essence, optical toys prepare us in how to view.

The optical toy brought together the unlikely combination of irrational magic and rational science, the sort of combination that formed the basis of fin-de-siècle science-fiction writing and, in cinematic terms, the 'trickality' of Méliès' movies, both of which will form the subject matter of the next chapter. Barnes (1995: 7) argues that Dr. Paris's Thaumatrope was 'the first optical toy capable of demonstrating motion perception through sequential or alternating images', the first recorded description of such an invention appearing in the *Edinburgh Journal of Science* in January 1826. This device consisted of a two-sided disc, with, for example, the image of a bird on one side and a cage on the other, with both images coming together to form a bird in a cage when spun from the pieces of string attached to either side. This device was followed in the 1830s by the Phenakistiscope which provided the first stage in the idea of multiple individual images representing one position in a sequence of movement. The idea was subsequently developed in the Zoetrope which relied on a rotating cylinder and had the advantage of enabling several spectators to observe at once a simulated action such as boxing. In 1876 the Praxinoscope was invented and through the utilisation of mirrors created a more fluid sense of movement. Each progression sought to make the toy more phantasmagoric than the one before, the machine's operation becoming both more mysterious and effective than its precursor. In their synthesising of motion from a sequence of still images, and which eventually was to materialise in cinematography, such devices relied upon a belief in the 'persistence of vision', whereby the retina retains an image for a fraction of a second after its removal from in front of the eye.

Where such ideas have most effectively been documented is in the work of Jonathon Crary (1993). Outlining Crary's argument is useful for his emphasis on the role of the subject in the viewing process makes us ready for the cinema and acknowledges an awareness of 'the frailty of our knowledge of the world before the power of visual illusion' (Gunning, 1995: 122). Modernisation effected a 'deterritorialization and revaluation of vision' with an observer having to negotiate on a daily basis a world that was constantly changing due to the spatial and temporal innovations previously noted (Crary, 1993: 149). In order to effectively juxtapose the modern with the pre-modern viewing subject, Crary introduces the camera obscura as a metaphor for the way in which the observer had previously viewed the world, one that sets in place a specific subject–object relationship based upon a critical distance between the two. The camera obscura consists of a dark chamber into which a single, small aperture admits daylight. This aperture projects onto the wall of the chamber an inverted image of the sunlit world outside. However, from around 1810 to 1840 there emerges an 'uprooting of vision from the stable and fixed relations incarnated in the camera obscura' (Crary, 1993: 14) and its repositioning into an 'undemarcated terrain on which the distinction between internal sensation and external signs is irrevocably blurred' (ibid.: 24). Crary's analysis reveals the denial of a teleological development from the camera obscura through to cinematography, for along that route the observer arrives at a fundamental crossroads in the history of vision. In this context, what distinguishes the optical toy from the camera obscura was the necessary involvement of the viewing subject for its success, with such a notion of subjectivity 'steadily supplanting the belief in a cohesive shared, and fully rounded social experience' (Stafford, 1994: 378). In view of this, many disapproved of optical toys for the way in which such inventions ran counter to a belief in scientific progress that created universal truth. Nonetheless, what any analysis of the development of the optical toy brings to the fore is the relationship between the still and the moving image.

While the optical toy sought to take a series of stills and turn them into one moving image, the next stage in the pre-history of cinema involved the breaking down of the moving image into its constituent parts while incorporating a distinctly temporal dimension. The first analysis of movement by sequence photography was carried out by the English photographer Eadweard Muybridge, whose work and contribution to the history of cinema still remain current: between September 2010 and January 2011, Tate Britain in London paid homage to the man's work. Muybridge's experimental journey was prompted by a request from Leland Stanford, former Governor of California and President of the Central Pacific Railroad, to photograph a horse at speed; this was part of a long-standing debate among those interested in racing, as to whether a trotting horse had all four legs off the ground at any one point. By 1873 he had proved that they did, and that which had always been present was now visible for the first time in detail. At this stage his work rested on single photographs but in 1878 Stanford sponsored a more ambitious scheme. This time the project was based around 12 Scoville plate cameras on one side of the track and on the other side a white background marked off with vertical lines, 21 inches apart and numbered consecutively. Such a device was patented in June 1878 as 'Method and Apparatus for Photographing Objects in Motion'. Thin threads were stretched across the track and attached to individual camera shutters which were triggered as the horse ran past and broke the contact. For the first time reliable exposures of a fraction of a second were made possible and in so doing both time and movement were deconstructed. The following year the number of cameras was raised to 24 and the concept of the thin threads was replaced by a clockwork-driven electrical contact wheel which released the shutters at precise intervals making the whole device more accurate. These images were initially placed in a Zoetrope to reproduce the original movement but in 1879 Muybridge designed a projector, a Zoopraxiscope, a fusion of photography, zoetropes and magic lanterns, to reincarnate the original moving object. As Solnit argues (2003: 3): 'It was as though he had grasped time itself, made it stand still and then made it run again, over and over. Time was at his command as it had never been at anyone's before.' Muybridge's work was to inspire Etienne-Jules Marey, who sought to make time representable through chronophotography, literally the photography of time through the use of a single camera. Marey was to become a key figure in the technical development of the motion picture camera with his work concentrating on the deconstruction of the temporal continuum into individual units therefore allowing for the scientific study of motion.

Gunning (1997: 1) sees such work as pioneering the 'gnostic (from gnosis, knowledge) mission of cinema' due to its 'potential for uncovering new visual knowledge'. Following the development of a photographic gun, a high-speed camera capable of taking one hundred images per second, the major turning point in Marey's work came via what can only be described as a camera moving on rails. Here, with the shutter exposing a single fixed plate ten times a second, the actions of a brilliantly lit subject performing against a black background were recorded. Where such work marked a significant development from that of Muybridge is through the introduction of a 'timing clock' which enabled the accurate measurement of the gap between the images. Coe (1992: 30) makes the observation that: 'This concept of recording time intervals on the frame with the image has remained standard practice in motion analysis work to this day.' Finally, with the invention of the Kodak camera in 1888, Marey was able to produce pictures taken at a rate of 20 per second and by 1889 further improvements brought the exposure rate up to 100 pictures per second. The significance of the work of both Muybridge and Marey lay in its comparative nature, in the scientific recognition that each individual photograph formed part of a series incorporating temporal progression, a discovery which lies on 'the cusp of cinema' (Gunning, 1997: 16). These examples of motion analysis rely on a series of stills taken in rapid succession in order to analyse the phases an individual motion passed through and in breaking down motion into its constituent parts, making visible that which was hidden from the human eye. However, there is a fundamental distinction between these two pioneers. Muybridge's figures were separated out across individual frames but due to the distance between the figures 'too much time was lost': he could not accurately measure the time of these movements (Doane, 2002: 60). In contrast, in representing bodies in motion, through overlapping images, so Marey embraced time in motion if not necessarily accurately recording it.

From the optical toys of the nineteenth century to the work of Muybridge and Marey, the next stage in the development of the moving image was the cinematograph itself which again was to produce a different form of representation. As McQuire (1998: 64) argues: 'Where earlier contrivances had enabled the simple juxtaposition of a moving figure against a static background (or vice versa), the cinematic image produced a complex, articulated movement in which all parts of each image could vary in relation to all other parts. Moreover, movement was no longer restricted to a lateral plane, but objects could approach and recede relative to the viewer.' The pre-cinematic motion studies of Muybridge and Marey that focused upon the 'interaction between the fixity of the moment and the mobility of time' played a fundamental part in the transition from optical toy to cinema (Charney, 1995: 289). For Baudelaire, modernity was all about the fleeting and the transient and, in a way, film was to become an antidote to modernity's ephemerality, not only in the way it held the fleeting moments together to produce something continuous and substantial but in terms of how it stored time, allowing the image repeatability. Muybridge and Marey were the precursors to this through devices that sought to capture the moment. Furthermore, Marey brought to public attention the hidden spaces inserted inside each movement, that movement is really *movements*, and motion occurs 'only through the same series of progressive fragments ultimately allied to cinema' (Charney, 1995: 290). Thus together they anticipated the aesthetic of cinema: of the requisite tripartite relationship between the image, movement and the viewing subject. It is this principal relationship that underpins the success of the cinematic vision. Such work also hints at the potential of the visual narrative, of a structured movement that crossed space and time. In terms of seeing the cycle of a movement as constituted by the beginning, the middle and the end, they anticipated the way in which film would primarily be ordered, particularly in the narrative structure of classical Hollywood.

While the introduction of World Standard Time (1884) made an enormous impact on the lives of the masses, at the turn of the last century 'explorations of a plurality of private times were the more historically unique contributions of the period' (Kern, 1983: 313). Harvey (1990) also notes the coexistence of divergent temporal trends, that is to say, how industry's approach to standardisation stood alongside modernism's more subjective stance. It was the problematisation of this turn towards standardisation within the social sphere that Henri Bergson took as his starting point for his thesis on temporality. Bergson argued that our fundamental misconception of time is one based on our treatment of it as a form of space. Instead he forces us to think about how we experience time as something we live through. In this regard he introduces us to the concept of 'durée' to reflect a more psychological experience of time, one which is highly qualitative in nature. Interestingly Marclay argues, in specifically Bergsonian tones, that *The Clock* was inspired by a weariness for the 'fast edit' and instead he sought to create a visual collage 'more connected to the way time flows' (Romney, 2011: 31). For to think of time spatially, Bergson argues, is to quantify it. Rather, each moment is different from the next: affect cannot be measured. Interestingly, Bergson appropriates cinema to provide a metaphor for the impact of standardisation, turning to film's method of production, the way in which it reconstructed individual facets of reality and fused them together as the clock fuses seconds, minutes and hours, to denote a 'cinematographical' representation of time (Bergson, 1911: 315). Such a homogeneous perspective on time was placed secondary to a more experiential perspective in which flow was to be appreciated over fragment, an immersion in time over the counting of it. Bergson posits that a more qualitative understanding of time can be achieved through the adoption of a non-linear perspective. Firstly, he recognises a spatialised, abstract time, represented as a series of discrete points on a line which denote time's static nature. This he terms *temps*, the structural dimension of time. In contrast he speaks of *durée*, a more interior conception of time where, through duration, time is lived and where 'past and present melt into each other without distinction' (Game, 1993: 94). The past has not ceased to exist but indeed coexists with the present, revived by memories. In life we tend to prioritise the present over the past but for Bergson the present could not be what it is without the past that preceded it. This is what constitutes duration, the idea of the inter-penetrability of moments. As Bergson states:

> For our duration is not merely one instant replacing another; if it were, there would never be anything but the present – no prolonging of the past into the actual, no evolution, no concrete duration. Duration is the continuous progress of the past which gnaws into the future and which swells as it advances. (1911: 4)

Unlike Einstein's ideas on 'space-time' and Harvey's (1990) recognition of the 'space-time compression' of the postmodern period, for Bergson space and time play opposite roles in his philosophy and might even be regarded as a dualism. 'In space things exist separate and alongside each other; in time they interpenetrate and are never completely independent' (Lacey, 1989: 22). Therefore for Bergson, time could not be presented as a succession of linear instants but rather as something fluid and continuous.

In contrast with the objectification of time as represented within scientific discourse, Bergson was interested in how we lived time, 'real time': how we constantly oscillate between past, present and future, interspersed and fuelled by recollections and daydreams. Thus at the level of the diurnal we may no longer speak of temporality but a multiplicity of temporalities. The present is always informed by what has happened before and will inform what is to come. Therefore static, standardised, spatial metaphors of time will not suffice. When considering the flow of time, Bergson challenges the concept of succession and it is this premise of time that also informs his critique of the representation of time in the cinema. Writing at the moment when cinema as a leisure activity was gaining widespread popularity, he used the metaphor of film-making as a point of difference in relation to his own perception of temporal flow. Rather than perceive time as a succession of instants, as a spatial series, he argued that we experience 'real time' mentally. That is to say, through memory we move back into the past and through our own imaginings we move on into the future. Therefore the flow of time is never unidirectional but rather, like the tide on a beach, it moves back and forth and any one moment of our lives is constituted by a revoking of the past and the potential offering of the future. His work seeks to challenge massification and the possibility that through the standardisation of time in industrial practice and its transformation into a spatialised model, we could reduce its complexity and nuances. However, argues Bergson, through our own memories and the possibilities of our own imaginings, each individual inhabits their own unique temporal flow. Thus what makes time highly subjective for Bergson is that within anyone's present moment there exists a virtual multiplicity of possible pasts and futures coexisting.

Where Bergson's emphasis on the experiential nature of time can in fact reconnect with cinema is through the concept of narrative. Defined as 'an articulation of temporality with transitivity', narratives operate at many levels within society (Connor, 1996: 3). Subjectively we use them to make sense of the world, to coordinate our own activities and to relate them to others, one principal method being that of autobiography. Through narrative, isolated events are placed within a context and given meaning, not only in the configuration of our own individual life histories, but in history itself. Traditional narratives of film and literature mirror the structure of our lives and comprise predominantly three distinct parts: the beginning, the middle and the end. When such a premise is made problematic, as in the films discussed throughout this book, audience engagement and interaction becomes more challenging as the spectator can no longer rely upon the familiarity of linearity. The deconstruction of the linear narrative opens up new temporal relations and allows the visual mixing of past, present and future in chaotic ways that Bergson envisaged we encountered and lived through each and every day. It was perhaps writing so early in cinema's development – *Matter and Memory* being published in 1896 – that led to Bergson being so outspoken against the medium. Instead I would argue that cinema's illuminating relationship with the temporal is one of the most interesting facets of its development. That Bergson should be appropriated by Deleuze in his study of the 'time-image', might also suggest his hastiness in discounting cinema as having anything to contribute to the concept of 'flow'. This is discussed further in Chapter 2.

The point at which Bergson began to commit such ideas to paper was a period of intense concentration on all matters temporal. At the end of the nineteenth century we see the coming of the so-called 'Second Industrial Revolution', dominated by discoveries in the fields of travel, communication and leisure, of which cinema was a part. In tracing cinema's enduring relationship with the temporal, so inter-related that Tarkovsky defines a director's work as 'sculpting in time', it is important to look briefly at the social conditions in which such a courtship took place (Tarkovsky, 1989: 63). Set against a backdrop of fin-de-sièclism, what both the end of the century and the invention of cinema had in common was the generation of a duality of sentiment in terms of popular receivership: simultaneously incorporating a sense of excitement accompanied by a certain apprehensiveness. Above all, the defining characteristic of the fin de siècle of the 1890s was a fundamental sense of contradiction of mood, incorporating decay and progress, pessimism and optimism. The duality of feeling that characterised the period from which cinema emerged came out of a decade which had seen a depression in the United States, British industry steadily falling behind its competitors, the Dreyfus Affair in France, while in Russia two episodes of famine had been experienced. Such events were countered by a more optimistic stance underpinned by the driving force of progress, a watchword exemplified by 700,000 inventions being patented in the United States alone during the course of the nineteenth century (Laqueur, 1996: 18). Cinema seemed a more than appropriate medium to deal with these turbulent times as every 'new development in image technology has been accompanied by excitement and controversy, expectation and apprehension' (Chittock, 1996: 217).

Early cinema arrived and was characterised by spectacle. It incorporated a sense of immediacy and acknowledged the audience directly rather than seeking to absorb them within the diegetic universe of the film. Gunning terms this early cinema the 'cinema of attractions' (1994: 101) in recognition of the diverse set of traditions, including fairgrounds, variety shows and penny arcades, out of which it emerged and also because of its 'fascination in the thrill of display rather than the construction of a story'. Early modes of film presentation, which dominated screens up until 1906, consisted of single-shot productions capturing or re-enacting a live event. While such films initially had an immediate appeal, they soon initiated a recognition of the way in which the 'live' quality was lost during the process of viewing, brought about by the creation of a temporal fracture between the time of production and that of consumption. The commencement of a move towards narrative cinema had a direct impact in terms of the nature of the relationship of the viewer to the subject being viewed, for one of the fundamental aspects in the transition from pre-classical to classical cinema is a distinctive shift from film initially being based on presentation and monstration to that of representation and narration. Furthermore, as part of these developments, material being screened without a particular point of view is replaced by a situation in which the director takes control of narration through character subjectivity. The transition to narrative is of significant interest to this book as it simultaneously embodies a specific cinematic conception of time. Early narrative was sometimes based on the filming of an already familiar story, song or incident, and relied on the audience's pre-knowledge of the subject to be effective. Another type of production was the chase film where narrative drive was self-evident and acted as a primitive model of continuity. To ensure that meaning was clear, as films became longer and more complex, lecturers and intertitles were frequently used. The first use of intertitles as a linking device between one-shot scenes in an American film is believed to have been in Porter's adaptation of *Uncle Tom's Cabin* (1903). The next crucial step in narrative development was the interiorisation of meaning from within the film itself and, by mid-1907, the most advanced production companies began to move towards the creation of a seamless flow of linear temporality across the shots. The advances made by D.W. Griffith regarding parallel editing and cross-cutting are an important aspect in this phase of narrative development, as exemplified in his 1908 production *The Fatal Hour* which is based upon a race against time. The film is about the last-minute rescue of the heroine who will die when the pistol mounted on a clock goes off at noon. In this film, time was accelerated by filmic manipulation through cross-cutting with Griffith moving the hands of the clock forward whenever he cut to the rescue party. Griffith was to use both techniques again in *Intolerance* (1916) where parallel editing is used to juxtapose characters or social situations while cross-cutting draws attention to temporally simultaneous events. In the construction of the classical narrative with its emphasis on causality, cross-cutting was to become the more frequently used technique of the two.

That little has been written about the way in which time is organised in the cinema is perhaps due to the ongoing domination of a particular narrative form, namely that incorporated within the classical Hollywood narrative model which adopted a particular stance towards editing. Editing techniques provide a cinematic shorthand to move the spectator through space and time while seeking simultaneously, under the classical model, to avoid either defamiliarisation or distortion of one's sense of place within the scene. Editing functions to determine how much time a film will occupy and an early realisation of its effectiveness came in terms of how 'narrative time could be accelerated or decelerated, intensified and concentrated by trimming away "dead time"' (McQuire,

1998: 68). Editing impacts the construction of the classical narrative in several ways. Firstly it controls the temporal order of events, which predominantly takes a linear form, broken up, on occasion, by the flashback which services the provision of additional information to the audience. Secondly, editing allows for decisions to be made regarding the screen duration of events within the narrative. Ellipses allow the skipping over of dead time so that an audience need not see that which does not effectively contribute towards narrative progression. For example, the time taken for a character to wake up from a night's sleep to his arrival at the office might in 'real time' last an hour and a half, but through a series of shots whereby we see him wake, cut to him eating breakfast, cut to him running down the steps of the station, to a shot of him at his desk, in terms of screen time this need not take more than a minute. Such temporal manipulation was perfected so that the physical break between one shot and the next did not have a disruptive effect on the audience but rather movement from one shot to another came about in a seamless flow. This became known as continuity editing. In the depiction of a much longer progression of time, montage techniques can be used to indicate, for example, the passing of a year via the turning of pages in a diary or calendar, or in more imaginative ways, as in the 1960 film version of *The Time Machine* where the changing fashions in a shop window are used as a temporal marker. The domination of one discourse, however, does not lead to the silencing of all adversaries. Innovative director-ship has seen the use of editing in ways where the relationship between shots is not always causal and is used instead to subvert audience expectations and produce multiple levels of disorientation, as the ensuing chapters recognise.

Through the development of editing techniques cinema offers itself as a virtual time machine, providing the spectator with a unique experience. Once removed from the physical world outside, there is the opportunity to time-shift, to allow a repositioning of the subject within the spatial and temporal framework of the narrative itself. Time and the narrative become inextrica-bly linked, to the point whereby to conceive of a film without actors, music or even editing is more possible than to imagine one with 'no sense of time passing through the shot' (Tarkovsky, 1989: 113). As a result, time in fiction cinema is represented through two distinct modes of duration: diegetic time and screen time. Diegetic time concerns the period of time the film itself rep-resents, whether days, weeks or years, while screen time relates to the time it takes for the succession of images on the screen to reach completion, that is to say, the running length of the film. Diegetic time is rarely isochronous with screen time, but where these two facets of duration come together are in the few examples of 'real time' films. The second part of this chapter will explore some examples of real-time film-making, with a view not only to understanding their infrequency but also as a means of foregrounding the level and degree of experimentation in cinematic narrative forms post the cinema of attractions that will inform the remaining chapters of this book. It is interesting how the actualities were filmed in real time, as briefly noted in the introduction, and perhaps, as a consequence, any future appropriation of this technique was seen as regressive. As the classical Hollywood narrative took hold, not only would it allow for the sophisticated development of editing techniques but would also act as a model for narrative innovation, at the heart of which lay the reconsideration of the relationship between time and linearity. Therefore, in this context, real time film-making carries the capacity to be viewed as dated and, indeed, its potential is always limited, for its major setback is that productive techniques result in only a limited number of scenarios lending themselves to effective storytelling: interestingly, all seem to involve the foregrounding of the clock.

One of the most successful directors to adopt this real-time mode of film-making was Andy Warhol, who tapped into the potential of this alternative practice with *Empire* (1964). Here his eight-hour study of the Empire State Building is about capturing time, how time manifests itself visually through the cycle from dusk until dawn and demonstrates it impact through the changing effects it produces on the appearance of the building. *Empire* took exactly the same length of time to make as it does to watch. 'This is interesting' argues Morgan (2004: 15) 'as usually the artist must invest much more time in creating the work for the viewer to go and see.' However, the fiction films considered here that seek to operate in real time are all problematic in terms of what they actually represent. That is to say, they only ever provide a semblance of real time, not its realisation. As a result, Hitchcock's *Rope* (1948) was made as a highly experimental exercise in the use of the long take but subsequently when deconstructed is only able to offer an illusion of real-time filming. *High Noon* (Zinnemann, 1952), while seeking to sustain a sense of temporal flow, on detailed analysis displays a number of contradictions and flaws, particularly in terms of the times on the clock faces shown throughout. More recently, the film *Nick of Time* (Badham, 1996) evidences how in practice such films take much longer to shoot than their actual screen time, in this case 90 minutes. Finally, *Phone Booth* (Schumacher, 2002) is interesting for adopting the 'race against time' scenario but applying it to conditions of the postmodern age and the concept of the mediated 'live event'. However, the two are never truly aligned.

Rope, based upon the play by Patrick Hamilton, is considered as Hitchcock's most overtly experimental production. The plot centres on a party which is held

Figure 1. *Rope* – Universal Pictures

for the friends and relatives of, unknown to them, the recently murdered David who lies in a chest in the centre of the room in which the event is being held. The victim has been murdered by the hosts – old school friends – who view him as intellectually inferior. As time passes so the guests become concerned by David's absence and the morbid conversation that it generates. The title refers therefore both to the murder weapon and, metaphorically, the director's attempt to create a film seemingly without the aid of cutting. Bordwell, Staiger and Thompson (1996: 47) juxtapose the use of the long take in *Rope* with the use of editing in the classical Hollywood film whereby, via the inclusion of all events, 'duration comes forward as a system in the film and vies with causality for prominence'. In contrast, they argue: 'Time in the classical film is a vehicle for causality, not a process to be investigated on its own' (ibid.). Described as 'a stunt' by Hitchcock to Truffaut, the film was highly radical for 1948. Hitchcock chose to use the long take to preserve the continuous, real-time experience of watching a play unfold on stage. By severely limiting the amount of cutting used, a claustrophobic atmosphere is created from which there seems little relief, accentuated by a setting in which all the action takes place in a single location. Here, however, the feature film encounters and evidences new technical difficulties that posed no problem for the earlier actualities. As Hitchcock's first colour picture, and with only 952 feet of Technicolor able to be shot at one time, *Rope* is in fact made up of segments averaging around eight minutes' duration. I do not use the word 'average' lightly here, for it was not simply a case of filming until the reel ran out. Rather, the 'editorial transitions in the film clearly come at dramatically appropriate moments' (Bauso, 1991: 235). In order to maintain the illusion of a single take, Hitchcock masks transitions and, to hide the 'joins', the director carefully manipulates the positioning of the camera at the end of one take and the commencement of another. For example, he might use an extreme close-up of someone's jacket and then adopt exactly the same camera position to begin filming the next segment. Similarly, the lid of the chest itself serves the same purpose. As a result 'real time' remains an ideal worked towards through a careful consideration of technical limitations and how they might be challenged, to produce an apparent seamless flow on screen as would appear on stage in theatre.

The most famous example of real-time filming remains Zinnemann's *High Noon*, where such a technique is used to accentuate the quintessential facet of the Western genre, the meeting up of and final shoot-out between the forces of good and evil. Complemented by a compressed story line, the audience is introduced to few characters and nothing is superfluous here to the central narrative action. It is a film based on tension, on the anxiety of waiting, and it is the wait for the arrival of the noon train that both drives the narrative forward and determines the running time of the film itself. The concept of time also dominates the mise-en-scène, with clocks in abundance throughout its duration. Through their appearance they manage to create not only an inordinate sense of foreboding but also function as temporal indicators to the audience in terms of the unfolding of narrative progression. The plot is a simple one and revolves around a vendetta, the revenge sought by villain Frank Miller on the marshal (Kane) who put him away. This all takes place in the context of Kane having just one last day to serve in a community which fails to offer support in this dilemma – despite all his efforts in rallying others to join him, help is refused and he must fight alone. The first temporal marker is the clock at the marshal's wedding showing 10.35 in the morning, followed by a cut to the station where it is determined that Frank Miller will arrive on the noon train. The parameters for the action have been set. The utilisation of time is juxtaposed between those scenes in which people simply sit around waiting for Miller to arrive and those containing Kane's frantic efforts to raise a posse. As in *Rope*, such dramatic action is supported by a highly claustrophobic environment as Kane moves back and forth along the same street with repetitive shots of doors and windows signifying his position as an outsider. Moreover, the shadow that Kane casts as he walks along gets shorter, nature's way of indicating the approach of midday. In terms of camerawork, little use is made of the long shot, other than those of the railway line stretching back into the distance, hinting at the train's imminent arrival. Rather, the close-up dominates, and functions to emphasise the anxiety of all involved in the imminent encounter. Frank is alone on the street as the film reaches its climax and, as the shooting starts, only his wife comes to his aid. In disgust, he throws his badge to the floor and rides out of town. Once again the attempt to produce true real-time drama becomes problematic for 'although the ticking away of the minutes until twelve certainly heightens the film's tension, there are many ways in which its sense of time could be said to be quite out of joint' (Combs, 1986: 188). There prove to be a number of anomalies in the way in which the clocks are used as linking devices to propel the narrative forward. At one point Kane enters a saloon and, after taking part in a fight following an attempt to recruit deputies, he leaves with the clock on the wall showing exactly the same time as when he entered. At other points, while the hands of the clock do progressively move forward, the action that takes place seems to occupy a much greater time span than that indicated.

A more contemporary example of the problems of filming in real time is that of *Nick of Time*. Unsuccessful in the box office, despite the casting of a number of stars, it is perhaps the flaws embedded within its assimilation of real time that contributed to audience and critics' disapproval. As in *High Noon*, the film seeks to create a sense of urgency and tension through the insistent cutaways to clocks and, as in *Rope*, through the confinement of action to one place. Primarily the film 'fails' on the basis of a fundamental paradox in the film-making process, one concisely described by the director himself:

> If it was *real* real time, we'd have started on the morning of the first day, filmed the movie, and everyone could have gone home in 90 minutes. But it wasn't. So every time we cut and stopped the camera, we would be violating a real-time principle. (Badham in Ferraro, 1995: 25, his emphasis)

In fact the filming took around 40 days. The opening shot is of a clock and, as its chimes striking 12 underpin the score, the centrality of the premise of a race against time is established. Gene Watts (Johnny Depp) gets off the train with his daughter and is late for an appointment. The plot hinges on his subsequent encounter with two unknown people who kidnap his daughter. They state that she will be killed if he does not carry out their wishes to shoot the

Governor of California, who is currently at a hotel in the city on a political rally, by one o'clock. While cutting does take place in the film, it is used for spatial as opposed to temporal articulation. Primarily filmed via the use of a Steadicam, this technique was chosen by the director to contribute to the production of 'dramatic tension' complemented by 'the raw, almost unedited feel' of the film (ibid.: 25). This tension is built around the Bonaventure Hotel, famously documented by Frederic Jameson as a quintessential example of post-modern architecture, with its glass construction adding a sense of frustration to Depp's plight to escape from the situation in which he has been placed. Unlike in *High Noon* where the tension arises out of waiting for the expected, *Nick of Time* works conversely through the effective way in which the villain (Christopher Walken) unexpectedly appears at the point where Depp's attempts to secure help seem to be successfully accomplished. Time is constantly fore-grounded throughout the film: from the constant cuts to the digital display clock in the hotel lobby, counting down the action in minutes and seconds; to the articulations of Walken, Depp's manipulator, who challenges his procrasti-nations as 'wasting' time. In this way the narrative presents time as something commodified, as something that we only have a certain amount of to carry out the task in hand and which is not to be used superfluously or detrimentally. The temporal hold that Walken has exerted over Depp throughout the film is symbolically released at its climax. As they wrestle on the stairs Depp's watch falls and is crushed amidst the chaos that breaks out, triggered by the circulat-ing knowledge of the failed attempt on the governor's life. With time released, closure is concurrently enabled.

There have been two major periods in our history where our relationship to time and our experience of it has been radically reworked. The first occurred in the period from the mid-nineteenth century to the outbreak of World War I, a time noted, as documented previously, for its vast range of inventions that permeated everyday life. It was of course within this period that cinema was born. The second wave has been since the 1980s, where a noticeable change in our perceptions of time has become more pronounced and widespread. Characterised by what was described in the introduction as a sense of tem-poral acceleration it followed the advent of what has been termed 'the digital age'. Such acceleration can be defined as 'the process according to which the quantity of actions contained in a lapse of time tends to increase' and the out-come of which is an 'obsession with the lack of time' (Leccardi, 2007: 27). As a result, culture is inherently underpinned by a temporal paradox: that we require less time to travel, communicate, to produce and consume, but then this time 'saved' is countered by the quest to pack in ever more things to each temporally charged moment, simply because we can. As we moved towards the millennium a qualitative shift in how we experienced time and committed this to language via the watchwords of simultaneity and instantaneity was evident. So why do we experience time differently now? Simply put, there is too much to do. The availability and accessibility of what is out there overwhelms us and we want a part of all of it. Even with an increase in labour-saving devices, this simply allows more to be done in the time saved on one single activity. Multi-tasking is king. But with so much to do there also takes place the challenge for our engagement. 'Time starvation also means a poverty of attention' (Lewis and Bridger, 2001: 60).

One of the fundamental ways in which our experience of time has shifted at the level of the quotidian is in relationship to our ongoing interaction with new technology. Our relationship to mobile technology, for example, moves beyond a conception of communication based on linearity, on a delay in the response rate between sender and receiver. Now we are under pressure to respond instantly. Furthermore the drivers of simultaneity and instantaneity manifest themselves in and through technology where the dividing line between production and consumption is severely reduced. In photography, the digital picture can be reviewed moments after capture, and communication takes place in real time on social networking sites. Consumer behaviour is another manifestation of instantaneity: businesses flourish that can turn our wishes into realisations with the minimum of time passing (Harvey, 1990: 286). Open all hours; while-u-wait; Lastminute.com epitomise this culture of immediacy. We see only as far as the next moment and we aim more for short-term material gains. But perhaps it is the internet which has closed the gap most effectively between wanting and having. Search facilities mean we can trawl the globe from home for the ideal product while software such as iTunes realises an album in minutes. However, this produces a different dynamic between the self and the clock as more and more of how we experience life happens in the now. Moreover, our expectations regarding the speed of realisation consistently become heightened. But how does all this manifest itself in relation to media content?

Gleick (1999: 9) argues that the remote control has much to answer for, as 'their very existence, in the hands of a quick-reflexed, multi-tasking, channel-flipping, fast-forwarding citizenry, has caused an acceleration in the pace of films'. So we return to the initial question that this chapter posed: is the accelerated pace of life informing media representations, or does the changing pace of media reflect and condition our own psyche and our connection with all matters temporal? Or does the answer lie somewhere in a fusion of these positions? Throughout the book's chapters a critical question will be addressed, one that has challenged film-makers throughout cinema history: namely 'how can you visually communicate the passing of time?' Art historian, George Kubler (1962: 83) recognised, as Bergson before him, that history has only one means of measuring time: to turn it into numbers, hence 'calendrical time, which permits us to arrange events one after another'. However, 'calendrical time indicates nothing about the changing pace of events' (ibid.: 83). Kubler goes on to distinguish between what he sees as two types of duration: 'fast happening' which 'resembles a forest fire in its leaping and action across great distances' and 'slow happening' 'a glacier-like pace of cumulative drift' (ibid.: 95). Kubler acutely recognises in relation to his own work that 'the difficulty with delimiting the categories of time has always been to find a suitable description of duration, which would vary according to events while measuring them against a fixed scale' (ibid.: 96). Real time in cinema offers one such fixed scale against which different types of duration can be mapped.

Real-time cinema, it has been demonstrated, intermittently rears its head. In the postmodern period it can be seen to represent both the quickening of the pace of life that Gleick earlier documented and a sense of living in the now. 'Time horizons shorten to the point where the present is all there is' (Harvey, 1990: 240). Developing this theme of the experiential dimension of instantaneity, a popular television series that aligns the use of real time with contemporary cultural sensibilities is 24, starring Kiefer Sutherland as government agent Jack Bauer. The show, in its eighth season, might be underpinned by different narratives of espionage throughout, but it is always run in a real-time format. Each season takes place within one 24-hour period. The use of real time to create suspense is critical to 24 and functions similarly in Joel Schumacher's *Phone Booth* (2002) which also taps into, and draws its popularity from, a sensibility informed by a heightened recognition of the power of the present. Identifying with an audience brought up with live television and the internet, each minute of screen time in this film stands for a minute of story time in the life of a PR/publicist (Colin Farrell) who, by chance – a theme that repeats itself on many occasions in this film – answers a call in a phone booth. The caller knows the publicist has been cheating on his wife and wants him to come clean, holding him hostage on the line, sniper in hand, through his position in a building overhead. Immediately the film taps into the rationale behind 24-hour news – the idea that any happening, anywhere (in this case Manhattan) can be turned into an event – and adopts this premise as a means to allow the narrative to unfold. As a result the phone call becomes worthy of national broadcasting and the actions of the main protagonist become a spectacle for audience consumption.

Figure 2. *Phone Booth* – Fox 2000

The character of Stu, the publicist, is an interesting one and represents the kind of professions common to the post-industrial age. Armed with nothing but spin and an unpaid assistant, he earns a living out of mobilising the representation of others. Through a phone call, careers are made and destroyed; now someone wishes to destroy him. That it can all happen so quickly, indeed in real time, the time it takes to watch the film, allows the film to provoke thought around the absence of any moral discourses that circulate within the entertainment economy. Described by one critic as 'a static Speed' (Bradshaw, 2003), devoid of continuity editing the film utilises techniques such as split-screen and the division of the screen into quadrants to reflect the simultaneous activities of the various players, a technique returned to in more detail in Chapter 6 on digital time. The intensity that real-time filming is capable of producing is driven by the simple scenario stated by the unobserved man with the gun: 'Stu, if you hang up, I will kill you.' Situated just on the cusp of the ubiquity of mobile phone culture, others consistently pester Stu to use the public phone and therefore break his connection with the gunman. The unintentional generation of his own self as the subject of publicity develops during the time it takes to watch the film. In one highly reflexive shot, Stu looks out from the booth and sees his face reflected back at him from dozens of TVs in a store, evidencing the scenario unfolding on national news channels. In this way *Phone Booth* takes as its subject matter the mediation of fame and the potential for instant notoriety through 24-hour news coverage. That this film should adopt such a format is appropriate given the correlation between fame and its instantaneity within contemporary culture. In TV series such as the X *Factor* and *American Idol* we see stars materialise before our eyes, and YouTube provides another dimension in the production and consumption of overnight, if quickly burnt out, fame seekers. The gunman is potently aware of the drama as spectacle: 'People are going to be eating dinner and watching you die', he observes. Reflecting the ubiquity of the chat show cum confessional, Stu is forced to confess that his whole life and career is built on lies: even his watch is a fake. Ironically, the gunman is Kiefer Sutherland.

Phone Booth therefore taps into wider considerations relating to our current temporal sensibilities and their mediation. Through electronic communication we are now in a position whereby that which happens vast distances away can be brought almost immediately into any viewer's field of vision. The speed at which the atrocities of 9/11 were beamed around the world was testament to this and produced a sense of global co-temporality, now well documented. Our interaction with global events through such mediated encounters, argues Marriott (2007), are now so common that their workings appear unremarkable. As a consequence we perhaps forget to reflect on how events occurring simultaneously but elsewhere are brought into our own lived experiences in the real time of their unfolding. Live webcasts, the sending and receiving of moving images over the internet, are one such development. One critic has observed that these may be positioned as 'the return of actualities, in digital form, one hundred years on' (Muir: 2004: 42). However, unlike the actuality, once the camera has been set up the image can run indefinitely to the point where it can no longer be watched from beginning to end. The idea that a viewer might dip into that which is being screened takes us back to Warhol's *Empire* which allowed us, argues Muir, to begin to proffer the idea that we might say we have 'seen' something, even if not all the way through (ibid.: 43).

In conclusion, we may say that cinema became a 'crucial participant in an ongoing rethinking of temporality in modernity' (Doane, 2002: 20). As time became the subject of science to be measured, known and controlled, so others sought out its representation through optical toys, photography and the moving image. As the classical narrative of Hollywood began to take hold in the early decades of the twentieth century so it sought to reflect time of the clock in the context of industrialisation. Informed by the early pioneering work of Marey who sought to make time legible, cinema adopted the classical narrative structure to do just this task. However, some film-makers sought to make the real more 'real' than was possible through the utilisation of continuity editing. The challenges and limitations of this latter approach have been noted but so too has its return through new media formats.

So despite technological advances, why have so few real-time films been made? Bergson's writings from the beginning of the twentieth century offer a possible response. Interested in the psychological experience of time, or durée, Bergson saw time as a dynamic continuum of past, present and future. In contrast to ticks of the clock and time as the formal progression of moment after moment, he saw time as something perceived and experienced quite differently. 'Time, considered intensively, is therefore different at each of its moments, and cannot be considered as an accumulation of points or "nows" that are simply added on to each other' (Colebrook, 2006: 22). The analogy can be drawn here to music, and how each note on its own has no meaning but when presented in conjunction with a series of other notes something new emerges (Bogue, 2003). When time passes through us, the same quantity of time, the same 'time of the clock', impacts on each individual subject in qualitatively different ways depending on the situation that one is engaged in whether it be waiting, anticipating, enduring or healing. As a result this makes the concept of 'real time' highly problematic for it falls in line with Bergson's resistance to the homogenisation of time and ultimately his resistance to cinema. How can time be real, when for each of us it flows through us with a marked qualitative difference? Can there ever be a true notion of 'real' time?

FUTURE TIME

The invention of cinema as a new medium of mass entertainment engendered immense public interest at a time when in literature the emerging genre of science fiction was itself capturing the fin-de-siècle mood. That the two should come together in a way that was to hint at the potential for the infinite possibilities of cinematic subject matter is personified in the figure of Georges Méliès. *Voyage dans la lune* (1902) endures as his most popular work, stills from which are recognisable to many a non-film buff, and it is interesting to ask why this remains so over one hundred years after its production. The answer seems to lie in the fact that not only was this film adaptation of Verne's work *From the Earth to the Moon* (1865) highly in tune with fin-de-siècle sensibilities, incorporating ideas of both the future and the fantastic, but, perhaps more conclusively for the continuation of cinema itself, Méliès recognised the need for the development of narrative in order to deal with such subject matter effectively. The film can be described as a demonstration of the challenges faced by early film-makers of 'creating viable techniques by which the illusion of the passage through time and space could be visually represented' (Orgeron, 2008: 35). Commencing in embryonic form with the optical toys of the pre-cinematic years is a growing awareness of the vast possibilities that the moving image possesses for temporal manipulation. In the work of Méliès such manipulation was taken to a more sophisticated level via his discovery not only of the potentialities of editing but also by embracing subject matter which required the projection of the protagonists through space and time. In particular, through the opportunities that were opened up by playing with the malleability of time, new dimensions in the pleasure of spectatorship were identified that would become a significant cinematic legacy.

Figure 3. *Voyage dans la lune* – Méliès Foundation

Seen by many as a highly innovative magician and little else, I will argue throughout this chapter that Méliès' contribution to the future of cinema is far more widespread than the single incident concerning the jamming of the camera on the Place de l'Opera and the much documented metamorphoses that ensued. Rather, it is possible to trace back to Méliès a recognition of the importance of film narrative not only as a means of telling a story but also through recognising that the story itself, with its infinite permutations, was a lifeline for the indefinite future of cinematic productions. Linked to this, it is possible to trace in his work an early conception of genre, whereby, taking science fiction as one example, stories could be arranged into particular categories to provide not only variety, but later to develop into a model of film classification that was to become the bedrock of the studio system and is still today one of the significant modes of film promotion. Furthermore, the 'magic' in his productions was indeed a precursor of the concept of the 'special effect' central to the development of science fiction and a legacy that dominates Hollywood widely today. Indeed it could be argued that the priorities of cinema have come full circle for while for Méliès the narrative and the visual trick were always inextricably linked, many would argue that this trend has now returned with narratives being developed simply to exploit the latest developments in special effects' technology, including 3D. Méliès' *Voyage dans la lune* not only highlights the creativity of his work and his identification with public sensibilities, but also such a film brings to the fore many ideas that are central to this book, especially the significance of narrative to the history of the cinema.

As a genre, science fiction is highly reliant on the society out of which it springs. Ballard (1997: 17), for example, speaks of the way in which it acts as a 'sensitive barometer of the cultural and political climate of the day'. By extension, in the realm of scientific developments, as knowledge about space and time is accumulated here on earth, such knowledge can then be applied to new fictional visions. This is seen most clearly in the late nineteenth century whereby a strong inter-relationship is formed between technological develop-ments that were happening at a rapid pace and the fantasies that this inspired in both the intellectual and public imagination. Of primary importance is the actual rate of change experienced, since during a single lifetime an individual could note the way such innovations affected daily life. In the field of com-munication alone, the last quarter of the century had seen the invention of the telephone (1876), phonograph (1877), wireless radio (1897) and of course the cinematograph (1895). Taken together with changes in the workplace initi-ated by the mechanised factory system, the social impact of gas and electricity and the transportation revolution on the railways, the world was becoming a smaller place and a new relationship to space and time was apparent.

Science, with the impact of Darwin at the fore, flourished to the detriment of religion, envisaging people's destinies as residing in laws here on earth rather than in the hands of God in Heaven. Such changes sparked public interest in other worlds, in the supernatural and in magic, something cinema would tap into with its own uneasy relationship between the real and the unreal. If destiny was in one's own hands then this extended from the 1870s onwards towards a mode of writing which centred on prediction, that is to say, to 'delineate a world to come and the processes by which it would evolve' (Kern, 1983: 94). The predictions were not only fuelled by the new inventions of the period which provided abundant material for speculation, as the work of H.G. Wells testifies, but were rooted in a society which recognised the need for forward planning through social engineering, via emerging disciplines such as town planning. One interesting example that incorporates a number of themes encompassed in this chapter is the work of Tony Garnier, whose inspired designs incorporat-ing the principles of zoning with rational socialism came together in his *Cité industrielle*. Garnier 'excelled in organically interrelating the various compo-nents of the city' to produce a utopian vision that owes much to the writings of Edward Bellamy a decade earlier (Wiebenson, 1969: 15). Like Bellamy, and his

imaginative *Looking Backward* (1888), Garnier recognised the integral nature
of work to man but was opposed to the current organisation of labour. Thus
the world of work would mingle with 'the cult of beauty' in his new industrial vision (ibid.: 112). It is interesting that while Garnier promulgated a new
approach to industrial organisation, the standardisation of time still remains
integral to his architectural designs. Both the clock in the centre of the city and
the one at the railway station are prominent features. The former is described as
'visible for the entire length of the principal street' (ibid.: 109), while the latter
is 'visible throughout the entire city' (ibid.: 111).

From as early as the mid-eighteenth century we begin to see a strain of ideas
whereby the future is noted as something that will be distinctly different from
the present, as represented by Sebastien Mercier's (1771) prophecy of an ideal
world in *L'An 2440*. Prior to this 'the image of the future has been a blank'
(Clarke, 1979: 2). Yet it was a century later that a fascination with the future
truly gripped the public's imagination. As Kern writes: 'The impulse to look
ahead is universal, but the quantity of science fiction in this period and its
success in the market place suggest that this generation was especially eager
to do it' (1983: 98). Thus, in understanding the success of tales of the future in
the late nineteenth century, Clarke believes that this was due to science fiction
being able to effectively communicate in a popular form 'the ambitions and
anxieties peculiar to an era of ceaseless change' (1979: 167).

For 'visions of the future express the ethos of their times' and the ethos of
the approaching century's end was one predominantly grounded in ambiguity (Heilbroner, 1996: 112). As Berman argues, 'the nineteenth-century modern
public can remember what it is like to live, materially and spiritually, in worlds
that are not modern at all' (1991: 17). Indeed this 'inner dichotomy, this sense of
living in two worlds simultaneously' produced a fin-de-siècle mood fuelled by
a duality of feelings of anticipation and intrepidation, optimism and pessimism
(ibid.: 17). Such approaches fed directly into the production of distinct strands
of writing, utopian and dystopian in nature, both of which rest on hypothetical
propositions such as: 'What if . . .', 'If only . . .' and 'If this goes on . . .' One 'What
if . . .' scenario popularised by the science fiction writing of Jules Verne was the
unique stance he adopted towards the possibilities of travel. Verne appealed to
both youth and adult readers as he created an illusion of reality via scientific
explanation and detailed description and, in this respect, contrasts with H.G.
Wells who was more interested in the human impact of his fiction than scientific
accuracy. Verne's idea to journey to the moon was not original, having roots in
antiquity with Lucian's *True History* (160 A.D.), but as Hammerton argues, while
Verne was not the first to write about travel to the moon, 'he was the first to talk

about it as a great engineering problem ... he brought it from the merest fantasy to calculation' (1995: 10). It is the highly descriptive nature of Verne's writing that not only offered the reader a greater sense of the possibilities of space travel, but at the same time provided the required detail for the cinematic adaptation that Méliès was quick to realise, the personification of the Moon perhaps being the most famous example. A second significant point in terms of the contrasts apparent in the writings of Wells and Verne was that travel itself was the central vehicle of Verne's writing, and brought with it an alternative approach to temporality. For Verne, 'the future is in the present' and thus there is no sense of anticipation, of prediction (Angenot, 1979: 30). As Suvin (1984: 234) argues, Verne's interest in the relationship between science and time is not one based on ideas of time travel but rather to 'motion within clock-time', the voyage time always calculated in detailed mathematics in the text.

From the Earth to the Moon (1865) commences with members of the Baltimore Gun Club complaining of boredom now that war has ceased and there is nowhere for them to try out their artillery inventions. Impey Barbicane, President of the Gun Club, calls together a meeting of members and announces that perhaps they could all engage 'upon some grand experiment worthy of the nineteenth century; and whether the progress of artillery science would not enable us to carry it out to a successful issue' (Verne, 1965: 21). In a reflexive style, Verne has the President outlining various literary excursions to the moon but, he continues, 'up to the present day no bond exists between the earth and her satellite' (ibid.: 24). In view of this he plans to 'fire a shot at the moon' (ibid.). The ensuing chapters of the novel display a high level of research on Verne's part so as to convey proficient knowledge of the solar system and its functioning, with Verne coming up with some very accurate projections in terms of time required to actually reach the destination (ibid.: 153). His idea to use aluminium is also ahead of its time as this was exactly the metal adopted on the space programme, many years later. All America becomes 'moon-mad' (ibid.: 35) when it hears that the Moon is inhabited by Selenites, and especially when Michel Ardan steps forward as a volunteer astronaut stating that:

> We shall one day travel to the moon, the planets and the stars, with the same facility, rapidity and certainty as we now make the voyage from Liverpool to New York! Distance is but a relative expression, and must end by being reduced to zero. (ibid.: 103)

The speech he utters requesting to take the journey seems incredible in the context of the time in which it was written, but on further reflection it is merely

Verne's imaginative commentary on the rapid progress being made in terrestrial transportation in the late nineteenth century. The launch of the rocket brings about global disruption in the form of earthquakes and heavy cloud formation, and Verne's thoughts prophetically interject again, seeing it as inevitable 'since man had chosen so to disturb the atmosphere, he was bound to accept the consequences of his experiment' (ibid.: 153). However, such an experiment does not go entirely to plan for the novel closes with the projectile still circulating the moon some time after the anticipated landing date and forming a new lunar satellite, clearly visible from the earth.

That such a work should be the root of the first cinematic science-fiction production seems to originate from a number of different sources. The detailed descriptions that illuminate Verne's story make such an adaptation entirely appropriate for while Gibson (1996: 29) argues that 'visual media immediately and definitively "thicken" narrative, adding an extra dimension to it, endowing it with an unprecedented materiality and mobility', Méliès' tricks proved to be a natural complement to the spectacular mise-en-scène. Méliès understood that cinema had the potential to offer new ways of thinking about space and time. Thus, while time and time travel came to become fundamental to the genre now understood as science fiction, cinema was itself a time machine and offered a temporal experience quite distinct from the world outside and especially the world of work. In these two juxtaposed arenas, the representation of time was moving in opposing directions; one towards its standardisation, the other towards its manipulation. However, before moving on to explain in more detail the emergence of narrative in the early years of cinema, I would like to look at another influential pre-cinematic development beyond the optical toy documented in the last chapter: one that incorporates some fundamental ideas on temporality but in the much wider context of creating an illusory world that would become the linchpin of the cinematic experience. Hale's Tours would not only anticipate the Lumières' films of far-off places which sustained an interest in travel for those who could (and, indeed, could not) afford the 'real thing', but also paved the way for Méliès' more 'fantastic' journeys into a world beyond this one. Taking such developments even further, Burch (1990: 37) argues that Hale's Tours pre-empted the problem of the 'spectator's "exclusion" from the classic primitive picture' and hints at a solution in the creation of a suspension of disbelief so central to the classical Hollywood narrative model of fifteen years hence.

The history of Hale's Tours is an interesting one and brings together for a brief moment the world of science fiction and cinema prior to their incorporation into a distinct filmic genre. That it should be H.G. Wells in 1895, who, along with British film-maker Robert Paul, applied for a patent for an invention designed to simulate travel through space and time, is fascinating in the light of the idea of cinema as time machine. Such a patent was never taken to completion due to the high cost of such a venture, but was later brought to fruition across the Atlantic by George C. Hale. Whether Hale knew of the designs of Wells and Paul is not known. What Hale proposed was a car that moved mechanically (later electrically) which, in the semblance of a railway journey, saw the passenger engaging in images of wonderful scenery from Switzerland, Tokyo and Mexico. Such images were facilitated by the screens at the front and back of the car and consisted of pictures which themselves had been filmed from a moving train. Note here the predominance of the train in early cinema history. When the Lumières' included trains in their opening films, Christie (1994: 18) argues that not only did they capture a subject very dear to the fascination of the public, but also tapped into the idea of cinema as 'the metaphor of a journey or excursion made literal'. Loosely, Hale's proposition seems a very early precursor to the popular arcade video game where one steps inside a racing car and steers around a Grand Prix circuit flashed up on the screen.

Hale's Tours finally ceased to be shown around 1912, owing to a number of inherent problems. It was costly to fit out premises with such specialised apparatus and only a limited number of titles were ever available at one time. Because of this, the novelty value soon wore off for the spectator and the whole business was enshrouded in the problem of consistent diminishing returns. Its value in terms of cinematic development, however, should not be disregarded for although such an idea was short-lived in the history of popular mass entertainment, Fielding (1983: 129) sees such an innovation as acting as 'a bridge' between the screening of films at fairs and circuses and the establishment of movie theatres per se. He further argues that it represented one of the earliest examples in a long series of attempts by film producers to 'duplicate or simulate certain aspects of perceived reality' (ibid.).

While the temporal experimentations in science fiction literature and motion analysis during the late nineteenth century come together in the work of the film-maker Georges Méliès, to completely ignore the work of the Lumière brothers would be detrimental to this book's objectives. Gunning's work on the 'cinema of attractions', a term he uses to describe early cinema up to around 1904, provides a useful discourse for analysing the similarities in the work of these pioneers of cinema and finding more common ground than is traditionally articulated. For to constantly think in terms of the Lumières *versus* Méliès ignores the way in which both sets of film-makers' priorities rested on a sense of cinema as entertainment, of capturing an audience's attention through its illusory power, although their approaches in achieving this differed greatly. Gunning's 'cinema of attractions' emphasises display or exhibitionism over the expression of a narrative and as a result consideration is given to the cinematic apparatus itself in terms of what it is able to do. That is to say, there was more to cinema at this stage in its development than simply the screening of a good story. Thus, 'the attraction represents a momentary apex of attention or stimulation; it offers a mode of experience different from the dramatic storytelling that enmeshes it' (Charney, 1995: 289). Gunning argues that the 'myths' that surround the Lumières' first screening of *L'Arrivée d'un train* is evidence of the existence of the cinema of attractions, of the first audiences 'existing outside of the willing suspension of disbelief' (1995: 115). He analyses the 'shock' effect of the approaching train and argues that what actually surprised the audience 'was less the impending speed of the train than the force of the cinematic apparatus. ... The astonishment derives from a magical metamorphosis rather than a seamless reproduction of reality' (ibid.: 118). To a large degree, the work of Méliès rests on the same principles. While he does create a fictional world for his audience to become immersed in, he fuses such immersion with a constant reminder to the audience that what they are seeing is an illusion. He draws attention to his art primarily through an extension of his role as the theatre magician. However, what I want to pay particular attention to is the development within Méliès' films of a sense of narrative and how this acts as one of the primary factors that distinguishes his work from others around him. This is not to deny the approach of cinema based on 'shock', for while I will argue on the basis of Méliès as the founder of cinematic narrative, this concern was always inextricably linked to the emphasis he placed upon his magic and trickality. Indeed, as Ezra argues, 'the presence of spectacle in no way detracts from the films' narrative content' (2000: 5). Thus I would like to suggest that while Gunning's 'cinema of attractions' offers the concept of 'shock' as a means of uniting the approaches of these film-makers, I would argue that where the difference between them is most acute is in terms of the concept of narrative. While the Lumières' films were the 'singular result of an encounter between the cine camera and "raw reality"' (Burch, 1990: 33) and any sense of narrative is inherently naturalised in the context of the events that unfold, Méliès' work was no 'encounter' but rather was staged-managed in its entirety. The subject matter, editing techniques and above all the development of narrative as a vehicle served to demonstrate the increasingly high quality adaptation of his magical tricks from the theatre to the screen. What follows is an appraisal of Méliès' contribution to cinema history, especially in terms of his recognition of the potential it held for temporal manipulation. At the same time, I seek to challenge those critics who believe his work to be over-estimated and his contribution to cinema history as severely exaggerated.

'It is my view', argues Salt (1994: 40), 'that excessive attention has been devoted to early trick films, and particularly those of Méliès, in view of the fact that they proved a dead-end as far as the development of the cinema is concerned.' I would instead like to adopt the position of Ezra (2000: 21) who sees his films as 'innovative and responsible for anticipating and influencing every major current of film-making'. This can be supported from a number of different perspectives, the first being Méliès' choice of subject matter which was highly in tune with public sensibilities of the time. Méliès' films embrace an approach to fantasy that enabled collective escapism during a period of increasing temporal standardisation. Tapping into this idea of cinema as escapism, Christie argues that such films were able to 'strike a significant chord – to express in images what could not yet be said' (1994: 22). Warner, too, speaks of the way in which cinema was to become a suitable vehicle for the 'communication of internal fantasy' (1993: 14), later adopted by the Surrealists of Chapter 3, making visible on the screen that which previously had been stored in the imagination.

In an article that first appeared in *La Revue du Cinéma* on 15 October 1929, Méliès wrote: 'The cinematographic realm knows no bounds; all subjects that the imagination can provide are suitable, and it seizes upon them' (1984: 23). While Méliès was not the originator of the subject matter of his films, where his genius lay was in the way in which he drew upon the popular culture that surrounded him and, through the emerging medium of cinema, found a new outlet for its representation. Méliès' work takes its lead from a number of other sources, primarily theatre, but also from penny arcades and medicine tent shows. His films are 'compendia of the visual themes of late nineteenth-century popular entertainment' and include comedies, historical dramas, scenes from mythology, science fiction and féeries (Staller, 1989: 211). The *féerie*, centred predominantly on the theme of good versus evil and with roots firmly in the fairy tale, was adapted for the stage in France from around the mid-nineteenth century and included magical tricks as an integral part. In view of this, Kovács (1983: 250) argues that the féerie was the natural medium to take Méliès from stage to film production and was an important force in helping to construct a particular film aesthetic that would make his work distinctly recognisable. In terms of such an aesthetic, attention has been drawn to the similarities between Méliès' *assemblage* aesthetic and that which would later emerge in the art world under the heading of Cubism and how both relate to a shared approach of producing art that is something more than just an optical recording (Frazer, 1987–88: 96). That is to say, the artificially arranged fictive world of Méliès' cinema which relied on a flat screen, and the conceptual approach adopted by the Cubists which depended on a flat canvas, were both brought to life with multi-dimensional visual activity. In a similar vein, as a film-maker, Méliès drew attention to his work as fabrication in the same way the Cubists drew attention to themselves, sharing a self-consciousness of the relationship of the artist to his work. In accord with the disjunction and general upheaval of the modern age, Cubists represented this period on canvas via a rejection to imitate the appearance and coherence of nature. Méliès, through his films on dismembered bodies, for example, also adopted this stance. In the 1902 film *Chirurgie Fin de Siècle, ou Une Indigestion,* a patient with indigestion ends up having his arms and legs removed only to have them put back in the wrong place by a mad surgeon. It is important to remember that even when Méliès produced films based on the reconstruction of events such as the Dreyfus affair, the eruption of Mount Pelée and the Coronation of King Edward VII, such works were still extensively detailed staged fabrications, dramatic reconstructions, and in no way can they occupy the same conceptual space as the actualities in circulation.

Further to an exploration of Méliès' chosen subject matter comes an analysis of the way in which such stories were told. Early cinema history demonstrates that to trace a teleological development in the emergence of the cinematic narrative in the decade from 1895 to 1905 is far too simplistic. Rather, such a study of early narrative reveals its multi-faceted nature, some features of which fed directly into the classical Hollywood narrative model, while others subsequently went underground, reappearing in the work of the Surrealists in the 1920s, for example, as documented shortly. Thus it is important to consider the merits of early cinema in its own right, and in particular the contribution of Méliès to the nature of cinematic storytelling. Naturally, it is also apt to define what we mean by narrative *at this time* in cinema's history. A useful definition is provided by Gaudreault:

> We are, however, dealing with a form of narrativity quite different from that developed by Griffith and other filmmakers in the second decade of the twentieth century. Méliès demonstrates an alternative attitude toward story-telling, one less focused on the story qua story. He neglects those narratological aspects that mark the early films of Griffith, such as the development of psychological characters, the creation of suspense, and the illusion of realism. (1987: 12)

Such a period in film history has its own specificity of film language. Changes and developments within the emergent codes of early film narrative did not necessarily proceed in a chronologically linear fashion. One theorist who has done much to highlight the unique contribution of cinema's early history is Noel Burch. Burch opposes a teleological approach but, at the same time, by defining such a period as 'primitive' lays himself open to attack from critics such as Gunning (1994: 102) who feels that such a term is highly misleading – so I too shall use such a term with caution. Nevertheless, Burch (1990: 2) opposes 'theoretical and historical discourses tending to naturalise the "Hollywood" system of representation' which prioritises, of particular interest here, continuity editing. Rather, by focusing on 'primitive cinema', Burch is able to deconstruct such a naturalisation and draw attention instead to the qualities of early productions that are not appropriated in the development of the classical Hollywood narrative model, citing Méliès' work, and in particular *Voyage dans la lune*, as minor masterpieces.

Fundamental to Méliès' work is a conception of narrative that does not incorporate the idea of the suspension of disbelief. Gunning points to the way in which at the turn of the century cinema was caught up in a complex set of relationships whereby it was seen as both 'a device of mass entertainment' and 'a scientific tool' (1997: 17). In this context we can see how Méliès' primary concern was to create cinematic spectacles that led to the establishment of a relationship between spectators and the screen that was based on 'the recognition of the cinematic illusion' (Gaudreault, 1987: 113). Highly stylised sets, deeply ensconced in artificiality, emphasised the illusion as did his choice of subject matter based on something 'other' than reality. The illusion was further emphasised, as in *Voyage dans la lune*, in terms of the relationship between the actors and the audience. Actors actually bow towards the camera in contrast to the diegetically sealed universe of the later classical Hollywood narrative model which went on to produce cinematic illusionism quite different from that which Méliès practised. Thus while both Méliès and the Lumières sought to entertain audiences through what has been termed the 'cinema of attractions', their methods for doing so, as noted previously, differed remarkably. Méliès' approach led to him becoming the most influential pioneer of 'cinema as a narrative medium', based on his method of arranging things before the camera, rather than filming the world 'as it is' (Robinson, 1993: 22). There are many reasons why narrative became such an important dimension to cinematic development. For Charney (1998: 83) it was a means of 'marshalling concentration' for with so much happening on the screen at once it both ensured that the new spectator did not get distracted from the primary action and that the reading the film wanted to promote was arrived at by all. It is at this point that narrative and the temporal become entwined at both the macro and the micro level; that is to say, via the overall duration of the film, and the depiction of the passing of time within the film itself. In this foregrounding of the temporal, film-makers began taking time into their own hands and even the Lumières became aware of the entertainment value of reversing, screening such actualities as *Démolition d'un Mur* (1896) both forwards and backwards. Méliès' work incorporated a temporal dimension through the establishment of a relationship between shots and the development of methods for linking scenes together. While still adopting the tableaux format from his work in the theatre, Méliès began to join scenes, taking into consideration spatial and temporal continuity. He became aware of the concept of temporal flow. In adapting his theatre productions to the screen, the problem of scene changes was addressed via camera dissolves, fade-outs and fade-ins rather than the utilisation of theatrical devices such as the movable stage. Thus, as cinema developed and a trend becomes apparent away from the actuality and towards the narrative, what emerges is a recognition of the difficult relationship between representability and legibility, that is to say, of the successful manipulation of time to tell a story. It is important to note also that the development of narrative required the requisite technology. Increased film length came with the invention of the 'Latham loop' which, through redistributing the stress placed on the film as it ran through the camera, solved the problem of film breakage and subsequently enabled the shift away from the one-minute short.

Méliès' first encounter with the filmic potential for the manipulation of the temporal is by now very familiar. The incident of the camera jamming on the Place de l'Opera in the autumn of 1896, and the subsequent metamorphosis from omnibus to hearse, has been received by film critics in a variety of tones, 'apocryphal' and 'highly doubtful' being just two responses (Cook, 1996: 14; Hammond, 1974). Robinson (1993: 16) denies that it was Méliès who invented such a stop-action technique, stating that it had been used a year earlier for an Edison Kinetoscope film *The Execution of Mary Queen of Scots.* However, Robinson does believe that Méliès found out such a technique for himself rather than simply copying the previous discovery. To others, such as McQuire (1998: 79) and Friedberg (1994: 86), it brought about the fundamental transformation of 'real time' into 'film time'. The technique itself requires the negative to be cut or spliced and joined after each effect, since the hand-cranked speed of the camera varied on stopping and starting and the removal of a few frames at each join was required. This technique comprised more than simply stopping the camera at a pre-determined point, rearranging actors and or props and then reassuming filming. Méliès used stop-action to create a number of the tricks he is now famous for and which he adapted for the screen from his repertoire at the Théâtre Robert-Houdin. For Warner the result was important for our understanding of temporality. She writes that these movie illusions 'made a particular aspect of fantasy possible in unimaginable ways, far more consequentially than magic vanishing acts. [For their] victory over the stasis of the image meant that it could communicate time itself' (2006: 271). In Méliès' hands narrative became a tool for linking such tricks together, but in so doing he recognised that such a combination tapped into cinema's potential to manipulate space and time. As Chanan argues, 'it is precisely in the transgressive nature of trick film technique that we discover the node that links the realism and the illusion, the deception and the veracity of cinematic art' (1996: 122). But film historians who adopt a teleological approach to cinema history miss an important point about Méliès' use of editing techniques. While Méliès' contribution to the technological developments of continuity editing cannot be denied, he used his stop-motion technique for reasons other than the suspension of disbelief. By emphasising the illusion it in fact gave him an even greater opportunity to play around with space and time. Gaudreault explains Méliès' editing technique in the following way:

> Fundamentally, Méliès' films are montage films except that – and the exception is essential – many of his cuts juxtapose two 'shots' with the *same* framing: Before and after a stop-motion substitution, the framing remains the same. Certainly this editorial technique is quite different from the descriptive or narrative editing of later cinema that primarily relies on the *difference* of framing between cuts. But it remains editing nonetheless, especially when one considers that this type of operation led Méliès to consider and solve the basic problems of match cutting: cutting on movement, matching the positions of filmed subjects, etc. In fact, Méliès was one of the first to think of the cinema in terms of cuts! (1987: 117; his emphasis)

Early films sometimes stuttered in a temporal overlap as one action was repeated in one shot and then again in the next, as in the case of the rocket in *Voyage dans la lune* which seems to land twice from two different angles. While from the position of the classical Hollywood narrative model this may seem a very negative feature, at this stage in film history, chronological continuity did not dominate film-making priorities. Such temporal overlap or temporal discontinuity, providing two different points of view on a single action, was actually used 'in an effort to resolve problems of spatial contiguity' (Gaudreault, 1983: 316). It was not until 1907 that temporal continuity comes predominantly to the fore. Until that point 'spatial anchorage prevails over temporal logic' (ibid.: 322). This is illustrated through another primitive editing technique, the dissolve, used to join two scenes together, as in *Cendrillon* (1899), a technique which emerged out of the double exposure used frequently by Méliès to conjure up his imagery of the spirit world. Again, such a technique was not at this stage in cinema history used to indicate a time lapse between shots but rather as a means to separate scenes when 'there was no successive appropriate intertitle' (Salt, 1994: 32). That is to say, it acted as a spatial not temporal divide for use between different scenes in different locations.

It is only through an example of Méliès' work that we can see how his use of subject matter, narrative and editing come together, and while he did not see *Voyage dans la lune* as his best work, it is probably his most well known and the one that serves our purposes most adequately here, with the famous image of the spaceship crashing into the eye of a pastry-faced moon acting as a significant 'symbol of Méliès' aesthetics' (Usai, 1991: 11). The film is approximately 14 minutes long, around three times the average length of contemporary Edison and Lumière productions. *The Star Film Catalogue* of 1903 lists it as composed of 30 separate scenes or tableaux, all photographed from the same angle and connected by means of lap dissolves. This tale of lunar adventure sees Méliès as producer, director, scriptwriter, set designer, costumier and lead actor! The film commences at the Scientific Congress at the Astronomic Club. This precipitates the planning of a trip to the moon and the construction of the projectile in the factory. The astronomers go on board the craft, the cannon is loaded and fired and it flies off into space. The projectile lands in the eye of the moon and it is here that the temporal overlap takes place. We take up the action moonside as the occupants disembark. They look down at the earth from the moon's point of view, 'thus prefiguring the shot/reverse-shot structure that would become common currency in modern film-making' (Ezra, 2000: 124). A snowstorm takes place and the astronomers descend deep into a crater where they encounter the Selenites who take them prisoner and bring them before the King of the Moon. The astronomers escape and depart in the projectile which plummets from space, landing at the bottom of the ocean. All the occupants are safely rescued and welcomed home as heroes with a statue unveiled in their honour.

As Verne and Wells were writing fiction that was based on something other than reality, so Méliès' development of the camera trick saw him turn his back on the actuality. Through the narratives of the fantastic, the marvellous and the then un-named arena of science fiction, he explored the magical possibilities of the camera. Emerging directly out of Méliès' discovery of the stop-motion or 'substitution splicing' technique came off-shoots (Ezra, 2000: 28). These included the first multiple exposure (*La Caverne Maudite*, 1898), the first split-screen shot with performers acting opposite themselves (*Un Homme de tête*, 1898) and the first dissolve. His recognition of the potential of the cinematic trick feeds directly into the more contemporary 'special effect'. Kuhn notes their appropriateness for this newly emerging genre in the way they could enable the creation of an 'appearance of worlds which either do not exist, or cannot for one reason or another be recorded, as it were live' (1996: 148). What underpins both Méliès' 'trickality' and the special effect of the science fiction film is that 'special effects in science fiction cinema always draw attention to themselves, inviting admiration for the wizardry of the boffins and the marvels of technology that translates their efforts onto the screen' (ibid.). One example of this comes from *Voyage dans la lune* to which we can trace possibly the first use of the model in cinematic production. As Kovács writes:

> In certain scenes, shots of the standard-sized object taking off were juxtaposed with views of miniature models whirling through the heavens. ... These models, which were superimposed upon views of the stars and the sky, rendered flights through the air with greater realism than was possible on the stage. (1983: 253)

Special effects therefore incorporate contradictory visual pleasures in that we marvel at the effect, knowing that that is all they are and yet at the same time are drawn in deeper to the illusions of the filmic world in which we encounter something other than the reality of everyday experiences.

Méliès' contribution to the development of cinema as a unique and enduring medium of entertainment takes many forms. Méliès stands as a bridge between pre-classical and classical cinema but that his 'magical cinema', that which offered something other than 'the real', should also be held as a model for the avant-garde, demonstrates the more widespread nature of his overall impact. By extension, through his recognition of the role of the imagination in supplying infinite subject matter, the long-term future of the cinema was secured. Finally, in his adaptations of stage to screen he recognised the importance of the development of narrative and the incorporation of early editing techniques as a means of manipulating both space and time.

One highly illuminating exposition into this developing relationship between time and the cinema arises in the work of Gilles Deleuze who takes as his starting point the work of Henri Bergson. Deleuze believed that Bergson's misgivings about the cinema were misplaced since, while Bergson saw cinema as a reflection of a quantitative view of time, one moment following the next in succession, Deleuze challenged this and posited that 'the cinematic image projected on the screen is perceived not as a set of still photographs to which motion is somehow added from the outside, but as an image directly and immediately in motion, a moving picture, or movement-image' (Bogue, 2003: 22). The movement-image stands in contrast to the time-image and allows Deleuze to contemplate, through the medium of cinema, the changing nature of our conception of temporality. Deleuze argues that the roots of the shift from 'the movement-image' to 'the time-image' lay in the way in which pre-World War II European cinema, exemplified by the impact of Surrealism on French film-making (the subject of the next chapter), had begun to recognise the limitations of the action image that was dominating American cinema. However, the emergence of Neorealism, characterised by an emphasis on the image in its own right and evidencing a weak connection between events, was to precipitate a further significant crisis in the action image. Neorealism also heralded a new choice of filmic subject matter, dominated by characterisation, with the character depicted as one who 'records rather than reacts', a theme taken up by the French New Wave (Deleuze, 1989: 3). As a consequence, what subsequently emerges is a shift in reference point for the subject matter of film, from a representation of the external world to an emphasis placed on the creation of the interior world of the film itself. Above all, in the world of the time-image: 'Description stops presupposing a reality and narration stops referring to a form of the true at one and the same time' (ibid.: 135). This repositioning developed out of recognition that a fundamental reconceptualisation of the world was required, one in which it could no longer be perceived as an integrated, organic whole. By extension, time also became subject to revaluation.

The importance of the time-image is its ability to destabilise and manipulate traditional views about the temporal, where the time of the time-image refers to diegetic film time as opposed to the spectator's revaluation of their own personal sense of time situated in the auditorium *vis-à-vis* the world outside. It is impossible to evaluate the time-image without reading it in conjunction with the movement-image, in that much of its descriptive power comes from what it is not. In the movement-image, which underpins classical Hollywood cinema, each shot is subordinate to the organic whole of the film. In this context, time is subordinate to movement in terms of it being utilised to determine either the length of each individual shot, sequence or the duration of the film as a whole. The 'emancipation of time' in the time-image of modern cinema sees a reversal of fortunes (ibid.: 39). What now emerges is that 'perceptions and actions ceased to be linked together, and spaces are now neither co-ordinated nor filled. Some characters, caught in certain pure optical and sound situations, find themselves condemned to wander about or go off on a trip' (ibid.: 40). If the time-image refers to the narrative structuring of temporality, then time is no longer tied to a linear narrative based on a forward progression towards a point of successful resolution but rather 'the present begins to float, struck with uncertainty' (ibid.: 16). And while narrative is still dominant in modern cinema, it begins to take new forms, permeated with periods of 'dysnarrative' based on moments of repetition and reflection (ibid.: 137).

So what is the critical difference between the movement-image and the time-image? Deleuze's study sought primarily to explore in relation to an understanding of temporality not the composition of the shot per se but rather how shots are linked and ordered. In the movement-image montage becomes critical as a linking device to allow each image to become part of a temporal whole. In this respect the movement-image only represents time indirectly and can be traced back to the motion studies of Marey and Muybridge, discussed in Chapter 1, where any notion of time was subordinate to the principal of subdividing movement into individual segments or stills. As Rodowick argues: 'Time serves here as the *measure* of space and movement; it can only be 'seen' through the intermediaries of space and movement' (1997: 9, his emphasis). That is to say, the creation of the spatialisation of time occurs. Such subordination of time to movement followed through at the micro level in the dominant practice of continuity editing and at the macro level through the development of the linear narrative of classical Hollywood. As a result, Neorealism forms a juncture in that here the linking of images is no longer driven simply by action. Rather, the linking becomes a focus of attention in its own right, with cinematic practices adopting a more temporal turn. In the time-image, the cut becomes a recognition of the difference between shots, as in Godard's utilisation of the jump-cut. Each image, and the way each image is linked, has value in its own right rather than contributing towards some organic whole. Deleuze calls the time-image 'crystalline' because it is multi-faceted; in so doing he immediately performs a point of comparison with the sense of linearity that underpins the movement-image and effectively maps onto fundamental changes in how time was culturally perceived following World War II. All certainty has been removed and as a consequence temporality is reconsidered and represented differently. No one knows at any point how time will pan out, history has told us: anything is possible. So images have the potential to reflect time not as linear but fragmented, punctuated by intervals, heightening a sense of time as somewhat unpredictable. The interval becomes elevated in importance: it reflects a holding of breath in anticipation. This is where the conception of 'crystalline' emerges: of the way in which, as the light hits the face of any surface of the crystal, it has the potential to refract in a multiplicity of directions. If we think therefore of any surface as a present moment in time, so the present is always infused and informed by a past which it looks back on or refracts and, indeed, from which it has derived, but simultaneously it has the possibility to move on into a future moment, carrying the past and the present with it. Such a perception of time, one that places an emphasis on becoming over being, has repercussions on how the narrative is structured in the latter part of the twentieth century. For becoming is infused with a sense of unpredictability and results in the production of a narrative structure quite unlike the organic whole of classical cinema. A realisation that our temporal path is not teleologically mapped out before us is reflected in a narrative structure that no longer progresses neatly in a succession of images but instead is fractured, but not broken, as we will consider in Chapter 5.

Chris Marker's *La Jetée* (1962) and its 1995 remake *12 Monkeys* provide us with examples of the time-image explored in the wider context of the time-travel film. The abiding appeal of the time-travel scenario has its roots in science fiction narratives, the field of popular science and our own personal mental wanderings. 'Everyday we all travel in time in a number of ways. ... Time-travel fiction simply asks us to exaggerate some part of our everyday time travel' (Franklin, 1978: 364). In terms of narrative structure, such scenarios offer 'indefinite potentialities' as a film dependent upon the manipulation of time immediately is allowed to break free from the constraints of linearity (Eizykman, 1985: 82). Post-1970, the science fiction film becomes increasingly spectacularised through the rise of the special effect and its ability to push the boundaries of belief. Later, through the Hollywood blockbuster, it would be lucrative box office receipts that would more overtly reflect its appeal with global audiences. In this way, Roberts argues, science fiction 'always enarmoured of technology, finds in those technologies of the cinema developed in the last half of the twentieth century, not only a means of realising its vision, but of embodying its very aesthetic' (2005: 266). Indeed, Roberts argues, it is this aesthetic appeal that fundamentally enhances the memorability of films in this genre.

Science, and predominantly physics, has taken throughout its history an interest in the nature of time and in particular how it is represented. One of the most fundamental paradigm shifts in terms of the conception of time is that between the absolute time of Isaac Newton and the relative time of Albert Einstein. In his *Principia* (1687) Newton wrote: 'Absolute, true and mathematical time, of itself and from its own nature, flows exactly without relation to anything external' (cited in Whitrow, 1972: 100). In Newtonian physics, time is conceived as a quantity and conceptualised as a continuous sequence of individual moments.

It measures the duration between events and is unaffected by the transformation it describes. Such ideas were challenged in the second half of the nineteenth century following a series of experiments, including those of James Clerk Maxwell's theory of electromagnetism and those of Michelson-Morley, where it was discovered that no matter how light was affected, the speed at which it was travelling could never be altered. Einstein's subsequent theories of relativity, the 'special theory' (1905) and the 'general theory' (1916), developed out of a recognition that the speed of light is the only absolute constant and that everything else, space and time, are variable. Einstein suggested, conversely to Newton, that rather than time as something rigid and formulaic, it was something local, idiosyncratic and relative. The 'special theory' of relativity saw the introduction of a local time associated with each observer, challenging the idea of there being a common present moment for everybody. Einstein showed that two spatially separated events judged to occur simultaneously by one observer can occur at different moments for another, dependent upon the positioning of the subject relative to the object. Einstein's theories created a new model of the universe in which time and space were linked and where time became the fourth dimension after length, breadth and height. Such ideas of relativity impacted upon the arts in a number of ways: on the paintings of the Surrealists, discussed in Chapter 3, and in relation to ideas about time travel.

According to the equations of Einstein's general theory there is nothing in the laws of physics to prevent time travel into the future. What is more problematic, however, is time travel back into the past, which is fraught with inherent paradoxes. Lewis (1995: 134) defines time travel as 'a discrepancy between time and time', where the two 'types' of time referred to concern 'time itself, external time' and 'the personal time of a particular time traveller' measured by his wristwatch (ibid.: 36). Thus, when time travelling into the future the watch reads one hour later, personal time, but it is in fact much later in terms of external time. In reality, personal time and external time run in the same direction and at the same rate and there is no need to distinguish between them. Only in the context of time travel are they torn apart and it is this dislocation that gives the idea its substance. The principal time-travel paradox that Lewis (1995: 142) identifies is that of the 'grandfather paradox' which disrupts the causal analysis that the present state of the world is as it is due to events of the past. Consequently, to alter what has already happened has immeasurable repercussions. To go back in time and kill one's own grandfather immediately problematises one's own existence in the present. To prevent such a paradox occurring it is possible to turn to developments in the field of quantum theory which challenge the deterministic stance of Einstein's work. According to Einstein, the future is already 'out there' and seemingly thus beyond our control. Quantum mechanics, operating at the scale of the atom, allows for indeterminability in the future on the basis that at the atomic level, there are no certainties, only probabilities, and thus, by extension, if we cannot predict the behaviour of an atom, then it is impossible to predict the future. In terms of addressing time-travel paradoxes, it is argued that every time a quantum object, such as an electron, is faced with a choice, the world divides to allow it to take every possibility on offer. Such a premise leads to the 'many-universes idea', based on the establishment of the coexistence of 'parallel worlds' (Davies, 1995: 251). Here, travelling back in time and killing your grandfather impacts not on your existence in this present that you are now living in, but in a closely similar quantum version of the present.

So how do such scientific ideas about time feed into actual filmic examples? Firstly, let's consider Chris Marker's *La Jetée* (1962). The title of the film is the key to the protagonist's most vibrant memory. It is the jetty at Orly Airport and, as it reaches out into space, so this is a story of journeys out into time. Attention is concentrated on a small boy watching the aeroplanes. He sees a man being shot but is transfixed by the presence of a woman whose image is to remain with him for the rest of his life. After World War III, survivors live underground in Paris due to the radioactivity above. The victors conduct experiments which seek to send a man through time for: 'Space was off-limits. The only hope for survival lay in Time. A loophole in Time, and then maybe it would be possible to reach food, medicine, sources of energy' (Marker, 1992). The protagonist is chosen for such experiments on the basis of the power that an enduring image from his childhood has over him. Bound to the bed and covered with a strange surgical mask, over many days he returns to locations where he sees the woman of his memories, eventually meeting up with her. The experimenters are pleased with the success of the project, and he is now projected into the distant future in the hope that the people there might help the present and provide the vital energy sources required to rebuild industry. 'He recited his lesson; because humanity had survived, it could not refuse to its own past the means of its survival. This sophism was taken for Fate in disguise' (ibid.). Having returned to the past and been projected into the future, he is now offered a choice of where to reside. He decides to return to the past, to the jetty at Orly Airport. The woman is there waiting for him, as is the small boy from the opening stills, but they are now joined at the point of conclusion by a third person, his gaoler, who shoots him, 'for there was no way to escape Time' (ibid.). The body that he saw fall as a child was his own.

Figure 4. *La Jetée* – Argos films

This is the story of impossible love, of a relationship that is doomed on temporal grounds, exemplified by the protagonist's subsequent death as he seeks
to return to the woman he saw as a child. The man and the woman occupy
asynchronous worlds, she is of one time, he of another. To try to repair such a
disparity they spend many of their meetings together in museums in the hope
of seeking and sharing a common, but distant, past. That there was always the
potential for unification, for love, if the situation had been different, is depicted
in the briefest of movements, her smile, signifying a surreal moment in the
context of a film based on still images. Her movement also testifies to the fact
that while much that has constituted his time travelling has been fuelled by
his imagination, she actually did once exist. She moves and therefore she is real.
Finally, what such a brief moment of movement also contributes towards is as
a testament to the invention of cinema, to create movement out of that which
was once still.

Apart from this brief three-second sequence out of a total of 28 minutes,
the film is composed entirely of still images ('crystals') held on screen for varying lengths of time. The choice of black-and-white stills can be explored at a
number of levels. Firstly, like the photograph, the stills themselves seem to represent that which is past, but at the same time that which is eternal, appropriate
to a film which dwells on the power of memory. Secondly, they are a reference

to the pre-cinema experiments of Marey and Muybridge, of the breaking down of movement into the still in an attempt to see that which passes before our eyes in more detail, a principle which when reversed would be the very creation of cinema itself. Thirdly, I would argue the film's construction mirrors time travel itself, but here it is mental not physical, as through our capacity for recollection, we are figuratively flicking through the photograph album of our mind, and simultaneously moving through time. This links directly to Deleuze's earlier analysis of the time-image, which this film exemplifies, for the protagonist, devoid of movement, restrained from action, has only imagination, memory and time with which to construct his own narrative. What holds these still images together is principally two-fold; the voice of a narrator and the stills themselves linked by cuts, dissolves and fades, the requisite tools that makes this work remain distinctly cinematic. Added to these are the use of a soundtrack and variations in terms of camera position. Therefore, although 'the images seldom move, the film has duration and the impression of proceeding' (Kawin, 1982: 15). Marker thus plays with all the attributes of conventional film-making except its central aspect, the moving image. Yet what constitutes the particularly unique quality of this film is the way in which it is underpinned by a strong sense of spatial and temporal fragmentation, representative of the way in which Deleuze indicated the importance of the 'gap' in the constitution of the time-image. Bersmaïa (1990: 147) argues that what the gaps offer are certainly not a moment of 'perceptive non-vision' but rather that Marker uses the gap to indicate that often what is *not* seen has the most powerful cinematic effect. The horror of World War III is articulated by the voice-over but is never seen on screen. Instead it takes place in the space of a dissolve, emphasising the high level of interaction that must occur between the film-maker and the spectator to enable the effective reading of a modern cinematic production.

To attempt to look at the narrative structure of *La Jetée* divorced of any consideration of the film's overarching concern with time is impossible; form and content feed off each other in a symbiotic relationship. This is a film about time: of not being able to escape from time (the end of the film), of the possibilities for temporal manipulation (the theme of time travel) and of the ability of imagination and memory to create one's own timeless world (time explored at the experiential level). One of the fundamental differences between this and other science fiction films, including its remake, discussed below, is that it is the imagination and memory that act as the vehicles for transportation rather than actual physical displacement. In this context, the narrative is not driven by the actions of the protagonist but rather through his mental explorations of time, explorations that are distinctively non-chronological. Indeed, one of the central characteristics of the time-travel film is that by nature it defies the applicability of the traditional linear narrative. In *La Jetée* the film seems to be working towards an illumination of events that happened at the very beginning of the film, the identity of the boy, which only becomes clear at the point of closure. One of the predominant consequences of the 'time-loop structure of the narrative' as applied to *La Jetée* is that it engenders in the spectator a strong sense of anxiety, one precipitated by the central themes of life and death, and profoundly, the ability as a child to see one's own demise (Copjec, 1991: 37).

The plot of Gilliam's remake, *12 Monkeys* (1995), draws upon the central ideas of *La Jetée* but situates them in a more contemporary setting, underpinned by the apocalyptic overtones that are the subject here of Chapter 4. In this version, the protagonist, James Cole (Bruce Willis), is physically sent back into the past from 2035, to find the source of a virus that has resulted in man living underground. As in Marker's film, the dominating image is a vision Cole has of a scene at an airport; of a man falling, a woman screaming and a child looking on. Time travel is an inaccurate science and the initial attempts to send Cole to the year when the virus first broke out, 1996, fail and he travels back to 1917 and then to 1990. His greatest difficulty is to convince others of the purpose of his mission and his institutionalisation in a mental hospital exemplifies society's response to the practical implications of dealing with a time traveller. It is here that he meets Jeffrey Goines (Brad Pitt), the founder of 'The Army of the Twelve Monkeys'. The son of a famous scientist, Goines becomes Cole's chief suspect as the originator of the virus. It is also in the mental hospital that Cole meets the psychiatrist (Madeline Stowe) whom, when he successfully returns to 1996, he will kidnap, his attempt to convince her of his story forming the main body of the narrative. Her eventual belief in what he has to say comes via the analysis of a bullet in his leg, attributed to his earlier temporal displacement in the trenches of World War I. The climax of the film is the playing out of the scene at the airport that we have encountered in fragments throughout the main action. Cole and the psychiatrist learn that 'The Army of the Twelve Monkeys' is merely an animal liberation organisation and believe the impending crisis has been averted, only to realise in the last desperate moments that the root of the virus is traceable to Dr Peters, the laboratory assistant of Goines's father. Filmed in slow-motion, Cole chases after him only to be shot by an airport security guard and dies while observing the materialisation of the recurrent dream he has had as a child; the airport scene. Cole's mission has not been in vain for as others from the future are scattered around the airport, one 'traveller' boards the plane on which Peters is now a passenger. She tells Peters she is 'in insurance': she has indeed ensured that the source has been traced.

Penley (1989: 139) has suggested that there could never be a 'remake' of *La Jetée* due to 'its uniqueness of form'. That such a remake exists plays upon the fundamental differences that permeate Gilliam's approach. Firstly, Cole's travels are physical. From his initial journeys in the present above ground to collect specimens, we are aware of a distinct sense of history through the abundance of relics and ruins that inform the mise-en-scène. The film consistently plays with the power of memory, on the way in which its relationship to time is inextricably linked, albeit often in highly imaginative ways. When Cole's psychiatrist meets him in 1990 she states that she has seen him before, as indeed she has, but their meeting is a meeting of the future, yet to take place in 1996. Here we have the manipulation of the idea of memory, but one of an event yet to come. The physicality of the protagonist's travels is juxtaposed by his period of institutionalisation where he is seen to be temporally imbalanced. Here an awareness of time, the correct time that is, is perceived as a sign of sanity. In this location interesting ideas are played out around the impossibility of time travel, juxtaposed against the central narrative drive of Cole's attempts to convince those around him of his mission. Jeffrey Goines informs Cole of the rules of the hospital concerning television viewing: if you want to see a particular programme you must tell the charge nurse in advance. One man apparently kept requesting shows that had already been on. He must have been totally mad, argues Goines, as the charge nurse couldn't make it yesterday, she couldn't turn back time. Another major difference between the two films is a shift away from the utilisation of a narrator to that of Cole as the central point of view and voice. He speaks so that others might understand why he is here, an impossible task despite his lucidity. At one point at the hospital a doctor feels he understands Cole's position: 'Are you going to save us?' he asks. 'How can I save you? This already happened,' Cole replies, aware throughout that his purpose is not to alter the destiny of the world, but to trace the path of the virus to the point of outbreak. Therefore, while one of the fundamental challenges to any idea of time travel is that one would be forced to drop the common belief that causes must precede their effects, the narrative of both *La Jetée* and *12 Monkeys* does not in any sense break such a causal chain. In *12 Monkeys* in particular, parallel-world scenarios are not required as it is made clear throughout that cause and effect are still relational. Thus, Cole's mission is to trace a virus, not to meddle with destiny, and this rationally explains why it is Cole and not the carrier of the virus who must die.

The contribution therefore that both *La Jetée* and *12 Monkeys* make to this book and its analysis of narrative and temporality operates in essence on two levels. Specifically, the films demonstrate in a sophisticated form the application of many of the ideas of Georges Méliès explored earlier in the chapter. More generally they speak of the potential that cinema has to explore the visual representation of the manipulation of time. Another highly engaging film that takes such temporal manipulation as its subject matter, but adopting a parallel universe theme, is *Donnie Darko* (Kelly, 2001). Set at the time of the Dukakis–Bush Presidential Election of 1988, on one level national politics forms the backdrop of the film and concomitantly functions as a common denominator in the experiences of all characters involved. However, a different set of events slowly begins to take centre stage: the countdown, real or imagined, to impending apocalypse that occurs in the mind of the central protagonist, Donnie Darko. The 1980s' setting is important as it seeks to anchor the audience in the familiarity of the not-too-distant past. The periodisation is accentuated by the inclusion of leitmotifs from other '80s films including the High School setting and the theme of family angst, but the film also draws heavily upon an overt recognition of the significant role a soundtrack can play in locating an audience in a particular space and time. However, the familiar soon becomes destabilised as we encounter this world through the eyes of Donnie Darko.

As a result of the positioning of Donnie as narrator, this becomes a film about time but operating at several inextricably linked levels. Through its central character, time is experienced and articulated by someone who is in mental meltdown. This highly subjective perspective is set against an overarching plot the temporal clock of which is framed by the countdown to potential apocalypse. Finally, taken as a whole, the film functions as a digest on the idea of time travel itself: of the existence of parallel worlds, of fate and the position of the individual in the context of the infinite universe. Throughout the film time is frequently out of joint, slowed down, speeded up and is visually foregrounded, more so than the proceedings which are held within its grasp. As the film counts down the 28 days to impending doom, Donnie seeks to undo time, to alter the course of events. As a result, its appeal to audiences comes from the fundamental temporal paradox that jars the relationship between the viewer and the protagonist, for Donnie's sense of the temporal is seemingly so very different from our own. And yet, with the film released at the time of 9/11, Donnie's own personal psychosis potentially taps into a sense of wider social fragmentation and global uncertainty. This generation of insecurity speaks to, or rather questions, the metanarrative of time as something constant, standardised, uniform and linear which we might all relate to in similar ways. It problematises such uniformity of understanding and experience offering instead a time that is 'plastic, malleable, relative' (Stewart, 2007: 203), forcing us in its wake to reconsider the binaries of reality and illusion, fate and free will.

Central to the film and its narrative structure is the role of the jet engine that hurtles out of the sky to fall on Donnie's bedroom. The film allows the event to happen twice as a mechanism through which Donnie might not only ask questions about the meaning of his own life but also its role and relevance in relation to others. In so doing the film draws upon further dimensions of time travel, namely parallel universes and wormholes, as Donnie explores how he might travel through time and alter the course of history. As a consequence it ends, not as revealed in its opening with Donnie surviving, due to the intervention of Frank, a human-size rabbit, but rather with Donnie's death. As Walters (2008: 193) describes it: 'As Donnie travels back through time to the point at which the jet engine falls through his bedroom, the film dissolves one potential world, in which he survives, and replaces it with another world, in which he dies.' But this second ending also means that we as an audience must revise our reading of the film. For if one event in our lives is altered, so must a large part of that which circulates around it. Therefore the film depicts two parallel worlds with two possible outcomes for a particular set of events. As a result of this, argues Beck (2004: 56), the film's audience throughout is 'not sure of the basic ontological status of anything in this film in terms of reality, narrative, causality, temporality, spatiality and also characterisation.' The reason for this subsequent floundering on the audience's part is due to the inter-relationship of these factors for, as Beck (ibid.: 69) suggests: 'Donnie Darko, the character, is able to undo the narrative or reverse the narrative and all the user is left with is the vague remnants and signs of what the narrative actually was in the real, Primary universe.' A moment of the uncanny does arise, where the possibility of an inter-relationship between these two worlds is hinted at. At the point of closure when Donnie's mother waves at Donnie's girlfriend, Gretchen, whom she will now never know, since the resolution of the second scenario involves Donnie's death, there is an oppressing sense of déjà vu between them. However, by offering this particular ending as one of two points of closure in the film, the director draws attention to the artifice of conventional narrative summations. For by being 'taken beyond its temporal cut-off point, the repellent ethical implications of the "happy ending" in mainstream cinema are revealed' (Powell, 2007: 159). Instead, the audience must work at reaching resolution, although Kelly (2003: xxvi) realises that for many this is problematic: 'There are certain people in the audience that come to the cinema and want to know exactly what it all meant.' In a post 9/11 world knowing 'what it all means' is, perhaps, no longer as easily ascertainable.

Donnie Darko's narrative adopts a 'submerged forking-path structure, in which the end of the film returns us to an alternative temporality which invalidates everything else that has gone before' (Cameron, 2008: 176). In so doing it draws attention to a recurring theme of this book, developed fully in the later chapter on *Fractured Time*, that life is highly contingent. If Donnie stays in his room, one set of outcomes prevail. By following Frank, Donnie offers the viewer an alternative path into the future. I would argue, however, that there is a wider temporal message here beyond the concept of contingency. In offering up the possibility of wormholes as a means by which we might travel back in time and alter future events, time itself, as one of the few certainties left in the world, becomes fundamentally problematic. Unlike H.G. Wells' time machine, where the vehicle moves back and forth in time but can only be operated through human intervention, the wormhole does not move through time but rather is simply part of the 'cosmic architecture' (Davies, 2002: 103). The possibility that 'holes' in time exist provides a further layer of diurnal destabilisation. Following the death of Donnie's girlfriend, Gretchen, run over by the rabbit-costumed Frank, the film reaches its climax. Donnie wills the reversal of time which is visually revealed by a wormhole that forms above his house. The portentous amassing of clouds ensues and time-lapse photography enables the calendar's turning back to the date of the opening scene. Another layer of time is now made accessible (Powell, 2007: 160).

A fundamental temporal dichotomy is at the heart of any reading of the film. The countdown to apocalypse that underpins the narrative drive is based on a uni-directional thrusting forward of time's arrow that literally pierces through the characters in Donnie's visions. Mapped against the modern calendar which turns its pages on screen as the story progresses, we are presented with a young man who is losing his grip on the world, epitomised by lack of sleep, disturbing visions, voices and an overall sense of foreboding. Against this he struggles to locate himself within the routines and rituals of everyday life, especially those associated with the educational establishment. Yet the interest in time travel that he develops while reading 'The Philosophy of Time Travel', written by Roberta Sparrow (Grandma Death), and his discussions with his science teacher, Dr. Monnitoff, might be interpreted here not just as a narrative device but also as the illumination of a social experiment. For without the solidity of a universal temporal framework any sense of certainty would be removed and the possibility of living on and between different temporal planes would become, through the utilisation of wormholes as temporal bridges, imaginable. History and indeed histories would have the potential to be reversed and rewritten. This stands in contrast to how Rodowick (1997: 118) perceives the ending of *La Jetée*, where time is presented as a fixed and unalterable line, albeit allowing travel back and forth along it. In *Donnie Darko* parallel worlds function not only as an engaging narrative device but fill the imagination with possibilities and permutations.

In the UK the enduring popularity of time travel can be represented by the arrival on screen of the eleventh *Dr. Who,* a Time Lord who not only fights evil across time and space but has also proven to be a very valuable financial export, significantly lining the coffers of the BBC. To locate his appeal to generation after generation comes down to a large degree to both casting and consistency of strong plot lines that allow it to be both cult and mainstream viewing. Yet ultimately there is something else in circulation here that lies outside the remit of the programme: namely, that this series is able to achieve what science in practice has failed to accomplish. For many the first moon landing of 1969 was to be the start of man's domination of space, accessing new worlds and encountering new life forms. Stephen Hawking's *A Brief History of Time* (1988), with its description of wormholes and their relationship to time travel, took all this a step further, stirring up the possibilities of travelling not only through space but also through time. That neither spatial nor temporal boundaries have been pushed further now that we are well into the new millennium remains disappointing, especially in a global economic climate when investment in space programmes has been severely curbed. Science fiction, however, manages to keep the space programme alive and concomitantly the cinematic imagination flourishing.

DREAMING TIME

One of the principal requirements of narrative practice that developed under the classical Hollywood model was that it unambiguously located the viewing subject spatially and temporally. However, if such known temporal markers are removed, as in the Surrealists' construction of 'dreamscapes', how might the viewer ascertain any sense of concrete recognition of where or when events are happening? The focus of this chapter is to explore the appropriation by the Surrealists in the 1920s of Freud's *The Interpretation of Dreams* (1900) and the legacy left as a consequence of these experimentations for future generations of film-makers and audiences. Surrealism is primarily concerned with a new way of viewing the world, with emphasis placed not upon the reality that we as observers have become conditioned to see but rather by drawing upon the material of the unconscious, allowing an alternative vision to emerge that can, by extension, be applied to film. In the *First Surrealist Manifesto* (1924) Breton draws attention to the importance that the role of the imagination must play in providing this revised way of looking.

An innovative application of this Surrealist approach of how we might perceive the world differently filters through the critically acclaimed work of Douglas Gordon, winner of the 1996 Turner Prize, whose video installation, *24 Hour Psycho*, succeeds in forcing the audience to look again at something that is already familiar, this time projected at a much slower speed. Nothing is added or removed but the deceleration that takes place fragments the narrative flow; now, that which we previously felt we knew all too well produces a feeling of destabilisation as our sense of knowledge of this cult film slowly becomes undermined. The fact that the screen is suspended from the ceiling enabling the viewer to encircle the image, freely positioning themselves in any number of sites in the gallery space, immediately offers a unique approach in terms of the conventional cinematic relationship of the viewer and the viewed while at the same time the artist maintains as a constant the darkened environment of the auditorium. As with Marclay's *The Clock* (2011) the audience here must also challenge the natural rhythms of their own body clock if they are to stay awake and view the piece in its entirety. *24 Hour Psycho* forms a central place in terms of Gordon's overall project which, affiliated to the aims of the Surrealist movement, positions him as seeking to gain a greater knowledge of the quotidian but adopting alternative vantage points from which to observe. By slowing down Hitchcock's *Psycho* (1960) to approximately two frames per second, rather than the usual 24, such deceleration not only changes our overall perception of a familiar narrative but also enables the viewer to see details previously missed as the slow speed causes what can only be described as a stretching effect on linear time producing 'an exceptional impression of duration' (Barak, 1995: 45). Through such use of slow motion Gordon's work seems to reveal the 'unconscious of the film', bringing to light that which has been repressed at normal running speed (Taubin, 1996: 70). It is the choice of film that is worthy of note here as Gordon selected *Psycho* mainly for its familiarity – for the fact that most people would have some preconception of what they would be seeing. Gordon himself comments on how his approach to a familiar subject produces a temporal dislocation in terms of the spectator's expectations of what is being screened. He argues that the viewer is,

> pulled back into the past in remembering the original, then pushed into the future in anticipation of a preconceived narrative that will never appear fast enough. In the middle of this is the slowly changing present – engaging in itself, but 'out of time' with the rest of the world around it. (Gordon in Button, 1996)

In other words, what Gordon is seeking to do is to encourage the viewer to put to one side all the familiar baggage associated with such a cult movie and to focus more on the deconstruction of our familiarity with the film once the traditional linear narrative associated with it has been stretched to the point of breaking.

A film of 24-hour duration becomes the main consumer of time in the gallery space and takes over from the clock as the more traditional symbolic temporal marker. Thus while, for example, *Un Chien andalou*, one of the primary films under discussion in this chapter, originated out of an opposition to traditional Hollywood narrative cinema, Gordon's work is in opposition to accepted cinematic temporal signifiers. Here time takes on a new quality as he plays with traditional expectations regarding the length of a movie. Barak (1995: 45) argues that such work:

> could be considered an act of appropriation, but it is more like a demonstration of Einstein's theory of the relativity of time. Imagine that instead of lasting 45 seconds, the 70 camera angles used in the scene where Janet Leigh is stabbed in the shower were spread over ten minutes. The suspense is no longer unbearable, it is interminable.

Fundamental to Gordon's work is his recognition of the potential for time to be made malleable through the utilisation of the media of film and video. Video, and later DVD, enables all of us to be manipulators of time through the use of the remote control and, in so doing, problematises accepted viewing practices and experiences through the use of forward, rewind and still. It is this recognition of the possibilities opening up to the individual as controller of that which is seen which will be taken up in more detail as the book develops. Such temporal malleability also has a specific impact in terms of narrative structure, as Sinclair (1993: 22) indicates:

> In Gordon's version, there's really no way to understand the storyline (without which the film is, of course, meaningless) when it is stretched so badly out of shape. So you begin to see the details, you read between the lines. Every emotion and response is magnified to an almost comical degree. As a viewer you begin to construct meanings from the symbolic and metaphorical possibilities of each individual shot which really are not there.

This approach towards film, of 'reading between the lines', was articulated by Roland Barthes in his essay *The Third Meaning* (1977). By considerably slowing down a film such as *Psycho* we are not really seeing a motion picture but a series of stills and it is around this distinction that Barthes develops his analysis of the 'third meaning'. Here emphasis is placed upon an unintended reading on the part of the viewer from that designated by the director, comparable to 'surrealist tactics designed to reassert the autonomy and ambiguity of images' (Ray, 1995: 36). Indeed, Valentin, writing in 1927, spoke of the Surrealist practice of not actually adhering to the opening times of films at the picture houses but rather 'one enters and exits when it suits' extracting images from the film out of context with the overall narrative before moving on to the next one (Valentin in

Hammond, 1978: 59). Breton confirms such a practice, arguing that one gained more from the fragments than from the film in its entirety (Ray, 1995: 101). Such fragmentation allows for multiple and personalised readings in contrast to the privileging of a single reading as practised by the traditional Hollywood narrative. Thus, by turning attention to individual frames within a film – in Barthes' case those of Eisenstein – images become freed from the overall plot and attention is drawn to new details, such as Gordon achieves by use of deceleration of *Psycho*. In contrast to the 'obvious meaning' that a director seeks to convey, fragmentation down to the individual image produces, argues Barthes, an 'obtuse meaning' which is 'discontinuous, indifferent to the story and the obvious meaning' (1977: 61). Barthes raises and responds to the question of the functionality of such an 'obtuse meaning' which is outside 'the logico-temporal system, without which, so it seems, it is impossible to communicate a narrative to the mass of readers and spectators' (ibid.). He argues that the obtuse meaning operates as 'the epitome of a counter-narrative; disseminated, reversible, set to its own temporality' (ibid.), a fitting opening description for the Surrealist approach to narrative, or anti-narrative, construction.

If the primary concern here of both Gordon and Barthes is to encourage new ways of looking, either through returning to something familiar but viewed in an alternative way, or to view out of context, peering at the gaps in between, then as Angela Carter argues this is also fundamental to the whole Surrealist movement. For 'Surrealism celebrated the capacity for seeing the world as if for the first time which, in its purest state, is the prerogative of children and madmen, but more than that, it celebrated wonder itself as an essential means of perception' (Carter, 1992: 67). Rising out of the ashes of Dadaism, Surrealism was not a uniform movement primarily because it was underpinned by a belief in the importance of diversity and difference in terms of subject matter and practice and thus no one method was chosen for the pursuit of Surrealist objectives. For example, with regard to painting, Breton questions the fundamental basis of art as representation, of the need to reproduce something on canvas that already exists in the exterior world and would continue to exist if it were not chosen to be the subject of a painting. He argues that due to the constraining influence of rationality the imagination is curbed of its full potential, denied access to a greater reality that underlies the world of appearances. The most common of everyday objects are brought to life through the imagination, and the 'consistent aim of Surrealist art has been to show the degree to which the world is porous to the imagination' with the potential to be liberated through the theoretical and therapeutic techniques being developed at the time by Sigmund Freud (Short, 1991: 307). Breton, himself a student of psychiatry, felt that the Surrealist approach to painting might help others to look at the world in a revelatory way, one only ever encountered when in a state of mental illness or when dreaming.

It is at this point that we come to the heart of Surrealism and the common link that unites the movement with the work of Freud, that is to say, the centrality of the dream. Surrealism aimed 'not at the opposition of apparently contradictory states, for instance of dream and waking life' (Ades, 1995: 134). Rather it emphasised their 'future resolution ... into a kind of absolute reality, a *surreality*' (Breton [1924] 1994: 436, his emphasis). This fusion of a state of waking and dreaming, of the dream contaminating daily life, leads directly into the Surrealists' approach to film. Not overly concerned with technique and aesthetics, the Surrealists focused upon the film's actual content, recognising the medium's potential as a catalogue of visual imagery. As in Surrealist literature and painting, 'the startling power of the cinematic image [was] considered not in its capacity for imitation but in its capacity to create an alternative reality' (Williams, 1992: 9). The importance of the dream to Surrealist film-makers needs to be explored on two levels; firstly, on an experiential basis, the similarity between watching a film and the state of dreaming and secondly, through a consideration of the temporal impact of the dream and how that directly informs any consideration of narrative structure. Jacques Brunius ([1954] 1978) provides one of the most detailed descriptions of the relationship between the dream and the cinema. He considers being inside the cinema, with its darkened auditorium and the sense of individual isolation, as comparable to going to sleep, while the techniques film employs, the fade-in and the fade-out, and the way images dissolve into each other, mirror that of the movement from one image to the next in the dream. However, it is in terms of narrative technique that 'the dream [was] made flesh' (Carter, 1992: 70).

Where time can be seen to be used most creatively is in the application of the 'dream model' to narrative structure. Here recognition of the way in which the temporal order of waking life has no bearing on the construction of dreams is reproduced through the implementation of fragmentation, recombination and juxtaposition. Thus as Williams (1992: 17) acutely observes 'the real contribution of the dream model in the development of a Surrealist theory of film is not based on the more obvious imitation of dreams but on a more profound attempt to understand their similarities as systems of communication'. The Surrealists recognised through Freud's work that the mechanisms of the dreaming process had an artistic value and for film-makers an intrinsic aspect of that process was the identification of a radical revision of temporality that occurs when we dream. One of the most striking aspects of Freud's work is the

omission of direct references to time; this can be attributed to the way in which
the unconscious lacks such a concept as we would understand it in waking life.
Rather, the unconscious is outside of time. Any form of chronology is ruptured,
for as Freud (1991b: 422) writes 'the whole mass of these dream-thoughts is
brought under the pressure of dream-work, [and] its elements are turned about,
broken into fragments and jammed together – almost like pack-ice'. Such material is then edited and rearranged in the dream so that any indication of spatial
or temporal logic is denied through the application of the processes of condensation and displacement where,

> dreams take into account in a general way the connection which undeni-
> ably exists between all the portions of the dream-thoughts by combining
> the whole material into a single situation or event. They reproduce logical
> connection by simultaneity in time. (ibid.: 424)

The use made by the Surrealist film-makers of Freud's work on dreams is interesting, for earlier in 1899 Freud had written a paper entitled *Screen Memories*
(1991a: 316) which refers to the fusion of false and true childhood memories
between which, later in life, we are unable to distinguish. In any dream there is
both 'manifest' and 'latent' content and it is the activity of 'dream-work' which
'transforms the "latent" content of the dream, the "forbidden" dream-thoughts,
into the "manifest" dream-stories – what the dreamer remembers' (Wright, 1993:
10). For example, on waking, the dreamer might remember the image of a box,
while in the dream, due to censorship, the box image originated in thoughts of
containment and restriction circulating in the unconscious (Jacobs, 1992: 33).
Devices that enable the visualisation through pictorial arrangement of latent
elements include 'condensation' and 'displacement'. Condensation is the process
by which the latent content is compressed or fused into 'composite figures' or
'composite structures' so that as little as possible is left out and where several
people or events may be represented by a single entity (Freud, 1991a: 98). In 'displacement', censorship creates a shift of emphasis which results in the inflated
importance of seemingly insignificant elements, and vice versa. Here association
operates for the purpose of disguise. Freud's interest in dream-work, in the processes undertaken while asleep to convert the latent content of the unconscious
into manifest images, is part of a much larger project centring on the unconscious itself. Fundamental to Surrealist film-makers was Freud's recognition that
the processes of the unconscious pay little regard to reality. They are not logical
nor are they bound by time. The passing of time does not change them in any
way nor are things ordered temporally. The unconscious 'uses a picture language

that has no words at its disposal; it does not distinguish between past, present and future' (Anna Freud in Freud, 1991a: 77). Freud argued that dreams were a means of gaining knowledge of the unconscious, of accessing that which has been repressed during waking life (ibid.: 115). More specifically, they function to enable the fulfilment of unsatisfied wishes. Not only does the material become disguised during the dream itself but on recollection of the dream censorship once again becomes active, imposing on seemingly absurd images a narrative sense and coherence despite the fact that during the dream the original sequencing seemed appropriate and valid. Freud terms this subsequent reorganisation 'secondary revision', and it highlights the different priorities that the unconscious and the conscious have in terms of the constitution of a logical narrative sequence. Thus, the conscious mind prefers to put the irrational dream sequence of the unconscious into a familiar logical order. Consequently 'material is ignored in the determination to arrive at an acceptable *rational narrative:* the ready-made formulations of the dream are abandoned, and new ones are made of the very same material' (ibid.: 25, my emphasis). The construction of this rational narrative also transfers the dream into another temporal register: for 'once it has been interpreted, it dissolves into diurnal time' (Green, 2002: 14).

Furthermore, in discussing the arrangement of material in the unconscious Freud seems to depict it as a vast storehouse with infinite space available so that no memory can ever be lost. As Doane (2002: 45) extrapolates, this notion of storage is 'antithetical' to any concept of temporal flow and in this way it is time that fundamentally distinguishes the conscious, 'the site of all that is transitory, impermanent', from the unconscious, 'uncorrupted by time' (Doane, 1996: 323). While such a concept accounted for the adaptation by Surrealist painters of the juxtaposition of images on canvas it also became a fundamental principle for Surrealist film-makers, underpinning not only the choice of mise-en-scène but also the principles of narrative construction. What emerges is a radical approach to film-making and, of particular concern here, a fundamental overturning of the 'traditional' approach to narrative construction exemplified by the 17-minute-long collaboration between Salvador Dali and Luis Bunuel that is *Un Chien andalou* (1929), 'one of the most celebrated and shocking short films in the history of cinema' (Drummond, 1994: vii). Not only was this film an attack on established film-making practices but, more specifically in this context, it set up a head-on collision with previous narrative codes, replacing existing rules of narrative construction with a new set taken from the functioning of dream-work. The words 'plot', 'storyline' or 'characters' can only be used very loosely in relation to this film, even the title is a 'red-herring' (King, 2007: 26) adding nothing to our conceptual framework or understanding.

The 'plot' is now familiar. It centres on a male character who takes on three roles; as himself, as his double and as a cyclist. Its subject matter is his passion for a woman. While the thread that weaves throughout the film is that of 'amour fou', of the search for passionate love that is constantly thwarted by external agencies such as the church and general social mores, above all this film concerns a viewer, conditioned by the conventions of traditional narrative film, who attempts to attach a meaning, to seek out an understanding of the film as a whole, but fails miserably throughout. The spectator comes armed with the logic of a supposedly rational world and is then unprepared for the irrational events that ensue. It is this unique approach to narrative, one where all the acceptable tools required to make sense of what appears on the screen prove to be useless, that forges a fundamental assault on the spectator, who, having nothing of use in his armoury, is forced to view in a radical way. It is not surprising that this film is often remembered by the cutting of the eye in the opening sequence, and it is in this respect that it draws parallels with Douglas Gordon's adaptation of *Psycho* and the famous shower scene. In both films, an association has been established between the eye of the camera and the eye of the voyeur.

The fact that the slicing of the eye takes place so early in *Un Chien andalou* has a two-fold impact. Firstly, it happens so unexpectedly that the audience have 'no time to prepare' (King, 2007: 22) or to ruminate on its consequences as the matter is never revisited. In the next episode, the eye is unaccountably intact. Secondly, it can be read more broadly as a means of making the audience aware that their traditional expectations of what they are about to see are to be torn apart, ripped open. All that they are used to will be denied to them, for the adoption of the principles of dream-work means that in a dream the eye serves no purpose; both are closed as we sleep and we rely instead on the revelatory mapping of imagery by the unconscious. For Dali and Bunuel, the eye of the spectator must be figuratively 'opened' to be ready to receive something new, challenging not only the conventions of traditional film-making practice but the experience of everyday life. This assault can be divided for the purpose of further analysis into two sections: mise-en-scène and narrative construction, each of which have a direct bearing on issues of temporality.

The mise-en scène of the film draws on a wide range of Surrealist influences, including the work of Méliès. The image of the tie, a symbol of work and alienation, that magically knots itself, is surely a mark of the Surrealists' appreciation of his approach to cinema. A further example of the insertion of the marvellous into the mundane occurs as the hero erases his mouth, simultaneously replacing it with female underarm hair. The individual images of the film are striking and highly autonomous, particularly due to any lack of obligation they have to the overall narrative structure. But how were these images arrived at? A central problem for the Surrealists was the process of obtaining material from the unconscious and, like Freud, Dali searched for a means of tapping into its rich veins. His development of the paranoiac-critical method is outlined in his essay *The Stinking Ass* (1930) which also refers to one of the film's most striking images. In this essay, Dali argues that the unusual juxtaposition of representations is causally connected to the mental processes of paranoia. The resulting final images are subsequently possessed of a critical and emancipatory potential in so far as they reveal what is normally concealed by the mechanisms of repression. While these images are drawn from the external world, the mind reassembles them in new and interesting ways, as in the example of the great burden that the hero has to bear as he pulls the rotting donkeys, the pianos and the priests across the room. The image of the donkey appears in several of his paintings which precede the making of the film, including *Honey Is Sweeter than Blood* (1927), *Apparatus and Hand* (1927), *The Putrified Donkey* and *Little Ashes* (1928), where the inclusion of bristles surrounding the central image perhaps inspired the series of dissolves that starts with the swarm of ants in the hand of the cyclist. But it is through one of Dali's most famous images, that of the soft watch, that direct links can be formulated with *Un Chien andalou* in terms of the relationship employed between time and the narrative. In his paintings Dali provides a conceptual indication of the temporal through the utilisation of the soft watch, which conveys the idea of time losing its necessary structure and all sense of context. By playing around with the symbols of time, so the surrounding world becomes reconstituted, represented specifically here through the abusive use of intertitles in the film.

It is important to try and read *Un Chien andalou* not as a dream but rather to recognise in the context of the narrative structure, or rather anti-narrative, that the rules it adopts are those that hold the dream together. Finkelstein (1996: 134) draws attention to the poetry and prose pieces by Dali and Bunuel written prior to making of this film which clearly indicate parallels with the script in terms of the anti-narrative procedures employed. Examples cited include Dali's prose piece *My Girl Friend and the Beach* and Bunuel's *The Comfortable Watchword of St Huesca*. As Hammond (1978: 3) argues, 'Bunuel and Dali wanted to describe the play of unconscious thought, so they borrowed the devices it uses; displacement, condensation, disregard for time, space, syntax and causality.' Reflective of this process at work is the imaginative play they make of the use of intertitles. By the time *Un Chien andalou* was made the development of filmic narrative conventions was firmly established in the silent cinema. Film-makers had taken into consideration that it was important to formulate a logical narrative sequence, one that would clearly depict an ordering of events and it is here that the intertitle played an important part as a temporal indicator. Sopocy (1996: 123) defines the function of the cinematic intertitle as something,

> whose interaction is to make it more intelligible as narrative or to enhance its effect as entertainment or its clarity as document. Its relation to film imagery is exactly that of a caption to a photograph. It identifies, it explains. It elaborates on the image. It gives background information or points out what is significant though not immediately apparent.

If we take as a starting point the intertitle's function in making the narrative more intelligible, then those used in *Un Chien andalou* seem to frustrate any attempt to interpret them according to pre-existing patterns. The titles challenge all rational expectations and deny any efforts to try and attribute to them a sense of meaning. What emerges is a fundamental clash between a film which addresses a rational viewer and a series of intertitles firmly located in the world of the irrational. The opening intertitle 'Once Upon a Time' makes 'an ironic appeal to the conditioned response normally elicited by this kind of narrative signpost' (Thiher, 1977: 40). The irony is that a whole set of expectations are triggered by this first interaction with the audience. It is a title linked to a particular kind of story, one based in fantasy, myth or legend, so we expect that the tale which follows will be based on the simple chronological order appropriate for such a genre. However, the images that confront us immediately after the intertitle are contemporary, not myth-like at all, and centre on a sequence of shots that shift from a man's face, to that of a razor, to the blade of the razor being tested for sharpness. The man then looks away and a shot of the moon against the night sky follows. At this point, all the images seem to be driven by conventional film syntax; a man is about to shave but instead he goes out on to the balcony to look at the night sky and to smoke a cigarette. Such logic is slightly shaken when the following shot is that of a close-up of a woman's face. This close-up denies the traditional usage of an establishing shot that would place this character within the context of the film. As it is, we know nothing about her, or her relationship to the man with the razor, if there is one. Nor are we sure where to place this woman either spatially or temporally. A hand opens her eye and we cut to the night sky, to the thin cloud passing in front of the moon, and then back to the cutting of the eye itself.

It is at this point that the spectator realises that the coherence of these shots cannot be arrived at by adhering to the conventions of narrative logic in circulation at the time but rather, as Finkelstein (1996: 132) argues, what actually happens is the utilisation of 'the conventions of montage against the grain of traditional filmic continuity'. Such an image is shocking on a number of levels. Firstly, the imagery of the slicing of the eye does not tie in with the expectations one has following the intertitle 'Once Upon a Time'. Secondly, that the attempt to determine a meaning to the series of shots that make up 'The Prologue' cannot be arrived at by the application of contemporary narrative codes. Finally, at a more general level, such a scene sets up the rest of the film as one in which meaning cannot be ascertained by adhering to a rational, logical sequence. Such a denial of expectations carries through into the second intertitle, 'Eight Years Later', where the audience will realise that the woman seen earlier, wearing the same dress, now appears with her eye uncut. As this is still only the second intertitle, the viewer will try to apply rational logic to what happens next, but when the cyclist falls over in the next sequence for no apparent reason the film-makers have 'succeeded in parodying the spectator's desire for continuity, motivation and verisimilitude' (ibid.: 43). The third intertitle, 'Towards Three in the Morning', is temporally very specific and signifies the appearance of the hero's double. The double had been a central part of nineteenth-century Gothic literature and was a device which increasingly destabilised the boundaries between 'the psyche and reality, opening up an indeterminate zone in which differences between fantasy and actuality were no longer secure' (Botting, 1996: 11) and will form a central theme in the ensuing discussion of David Lynch's *Lost Highway*, where a number of characters either have 'doubles' or metamorphose into another being. In this particular vignette the doubles fight with each other and there is a false ending as the dead body of one is carried away in a funeral cortege. During this sequence the fourth intertitle is used and plays with the concept of the flashback, announcing 'Sixteen Years Before'. In the fifth and final intertitle the words 'In The Spring' conjure up a whole series of expectations that once again will be thwarted. While such a term connotes a time of rebirth, romance and happiness, the death of the couple, buried up to their necks in sand, parodies any such associations. Even the characters represented in this last sequence remain problematic, for while Drummond (1977: 72) views the man as the woman's former lover, Williams (1992: 99) believes it to be a new love that she has just met on the beach.

At the same time as the inappropriate use of the intertitle seeks significantly to undermine any conventional understanding of a sense of temporality, a second approach progressively breaks down the narrative by 'the deliberate use of inconsistent details' (Walker, 1977/8: 4). Examples of this occur throughout

Figure 5. *Un Chien andalou* – RGA

the film, including the disappearance of the wristwatch between shots in 'The
Prologue', where a mystery also surrounds the identity of the man involved in
the cutting of the eye: while logic assumes that it is the same man who in earlier shots was sharpening his razor, he is now wearing a neck tie to replace the
previously seen open collar. This same striped tie will appear again in the next
vignette, but should continuity be assumed or is the similarity purely arbitrary?
In a similar vein, Williams (1992: 68) draws attention to a 'subtle tension'
within the film, as opposed to 'total rupture', brought about by the inclusion of
imagery that does not contribute directly to the diegesis of the film, such as the
image of the hand-held cocktail shaker. She argues (1992) that our tendency to
want to embed a non-diegetic element that ultimately cannot be absorbed into
the diegesis is not only a reflection of the importance placed on the juxtaposition of images by the Surrealists but moreover of the audience's application of
the rules of traditional cinematic narrative which run contra to a film made
under the 'rules' of dream-work. The series of dissolves starting with the ants is
another temporal dislocator, this time involving a primitive editing technique
which functions once again to parody the realist narrative. The dissolve is con-
ventionally used as 'a means of moving from one image to the next in such a
way that the end of the first is superimposed on the beginning of the next. It is

also a technique with a psychological meaning' (Dulac, 1988: 311). In *Un Chien andalou* the use of the dissolve refuses to adhere to convention. Rather, argues Fotiade (1995: 406), dissolves here 'play on the viewer's frustrated expectation, on the absence of any elucidation or psychological reference to the previous and/ or following shots'. For example, we arrive at a series of dissolves where ants emerge and dissolve into the sunbather's underarm hair which then becomes the spikes of a sea urchin. The connection is inexplicable and in the context of *Un Chien andalou* as an anti-narrative, the utilisation of the dissolve fails to provide any thematic continuity across the images shown.

A final technique used in the film to produce narrative disruption is the recurring manipulation of space and time. The overall denial of the temporal logic of reality has already been discussed but what also add to the spectator's feeling of total destabilisation are the many spatial, as well as temporal, inconsistencies. One prominent example of this involves the death of the double who begins his fall inside the room and ends up outside in a meadow. While the times of these events match and hence are synchronic, the actual space occupied jumps and hence is diachronic. Such manipulation is reversed following the flashback intertitle 'Sixteen Years Before' where the shots that ensue show that neither the actors nor the setting of the room has changed in any way from their present appearance. Surely 16 years earlier would bring at least a change in the characters' physical appearances? Here, space is synchronic but now it is time that is diachronic. Another example of this happens earlier in the film when the woman escapes from the cyclist into a room exactly the same as the one she has just left. A fragment of time has passed but her whereabouts stay constant despite her movement. On a more general level, the use of cutting results in dramatic changes in geographical location so that the woman can step out from her room, which we know faces the main road, onto the seashore. Spatial relationships also become blurred, as in the scene where, out of nowhere, pianos, priests and donkeys fill a room that is obviously too small to contain them. This is certainly not the sort of logistical problem that would be confronted in a dream, where space appears to be infinite and where such a transition from the city to the seashore is unproblematic. This overall lack of spatial continuity throughout the film is fundamentally based on the premise whereby locations 'accumulate *discretely,* by a process of *simple addition* rather than by reflexive systems of re-permutation and re-cycling' (Drummond, 1977: 69, his emphasis).

Dali and Bunuel collaborated as film-makers on only one other occasion, the production of *L'Age d'Or* (1930), where once again dream-work defines the rules of the game and where mise-en-scène and a specific approach to cutting continue to frustrate narrative conventions applicable to Hollywood. After this production their relationship with the cinema was on a much more individualistic basis, and even after Bunuel left the Surrealist movement he did not abandon Surrealism per se, with the importance of dreams and the unconscious remaining influential throughout his long-standing career. Dali, however, adopted a more flirtatious relationship with the world of film, writing in 1927 in *Film-arte, fil antiartistico* of the way in which film can realise images of a kind that painting is powerless to render. Five years later he was to repudiate such a position in his *Short Critical History of the Cinema*. Dali was to write many scenarios which never reached the production stage but it was finally through another collaboration, this time with Alfred Hitchcock on the familiar dream sequences in *Spellbound* (1945), that the work of Dali, the film-maker, would once again be seen by an audience.

In the *Manifesto of the Surrealists Concerning L'Age d'Or*, published to coincide with the film's first screening, it was stated that both collaborative works of Dali and Bunuel were situated 'beyond anything that exits' (cited in Hammond, 1978: 119). As a result these films probably remain as perhaps the 'purest' examples of Surrealist film-making. Other directors, however, have adopted an approach which recognises and appropriates the innovations of these Surrealist pioneers, both in terms of imagery and narrative and it is to one such inheritor of this legacy that this analysis now turns. Interviews with director David Lynch reveal his articulation of a particular world view centred on its defamiliarisation. As a result Lynch's oeuvre is a series of films that are to be 'experienced rather than explained' (Foster Wallace, 1996: 113). In these interviews, the origins of Lynch's perspective emerge and have indeed much in common with the ideas of the Surrealists documented above. Speaking of his childhood, for example, Lynch tells of the way in which he became frightened by the obscure things he encountered in the city. 'My grandfather owned an apartment building in Brooklyn with no kitchens. A man was cooking an egg on *an iron* – that really worried me' (Rodley, 1997: 8, his emphasis). The will to document, to record mentally such observations continue throughout his life and begin to be incorporated in his work, which draws upon both the uncanny and what he defines as the specifically surreal. On his recognition of the everyday pervasiveness of Surrealism, he states: 'But I think the American public is so surreal, and they understand surrealism ... You go anywhere and old-timers will tell you very surreal stories with strange humour' (Rodley, 1997: 199). One way in which Lynch draws on the surreal is through the incorporation of the dream into his work, either directly, through a dream sequence, or indirectly through the conjuring up of a particular mood. Rodley (ibid.: ix) argues that for Lynch, the power of cinema comes from its ability to create a certain atmosphere and describes how 'The feelings that excite him [Lynch] most are those that approximate the sensations and emotional traces of dreams: the crucial element of the nightmare that is impossible to communicate simply by describing events.'

The possibilities of the dream to inform film-making practice are evident in three of Lynch's films considered here. Made approximately ten years apart, his use of mise-en-scène in *Eraserhead* (1976) and *Blue Velvet* (1986) and his innovative employment of narrative ordering in *Lost Highway* (1997) are significantly informed by the tropes and tendencies of early Surrealist cinema. *Eraserhead* draws upon the potential dystopia of family life and revolves around a simple plot of Henry, the male protagonist, and his relationship with Mary, with whom he has a baby. However, in Lynch's hands, traditional familial relations immediately become defamiliarised and the conjugal life that follows is made strange through an intense sense of claustrophobia and alienation. Indeed, this world is so insular 'that it exists apart from anything in our everyday life even as it reflects it' (Odell and le Blanc, 2007: 31). As with Joseph K. in Kafka's *The Trial*, things seem to happen to Henry. He is lonely and caught up in a situation that is taking over and controlling his life. This sense of loneliness seeps out into the spaces he occupies: the interior sparseness of his own room and the exterior bleak, post-industrial wasteland that pulses with mechanical sounds. Even in his apartment it seems as though noises encroach upon him, unsettling and unnerving him: electricity crackles, the radiator hisses and we encounter an anonymous buzzing, humming, ticking. As the camera pans around the scene placed before us we too are made to feel uncomfortable but cannot determine exactly why. The atmosphere is equally intense in the home of his girlfriend, Mary, who is expecting a baby; when the baby arrives and Mary moves in with Henry, his sense of isolation is exacerbated rather than ameliorated. The film seeks to communicate but never explain Henry's sense of bewilderment with modern life. Of seemingly pivotal importance to Henry is how, at moments of extreme loneliness, his world is punctuated by a series of dreams and visions that take over the protagonist's life. The only source of affection that Henry seems to receive emanates from the 'The Lady in the Radiator'. Whether or not she is real or a figment of his imagination does not seem to matter. Rather she shows her love and warmth, literally and metaphorically, through her dedicated song and dance routine in which she reassures him that 'in heaven, everything is fine'. The arrival of the baby allows Lynch to continue to warp expectations around domestic life. While the stable ingredients of lack of sleep, arguing parents, a father left with a constantly crying baby and, subsequently, infidelity are recognisable from any of a number of domestic dramas, the director stretches audience expectations and indeed the father's frustrations as he tries to kill the baby by piercing his heart. Such actions are accompanied by portentous flashes of light that illuminate the screen leaving Henry and the Lady in the Radiator to emerge together on a stage. The film cuts to black and the credits roll.

It is within this disturbing depiction of the family unit that Lynch's Surrealist tendencies are displayed. A couple move in together following the birth of their baby and while at the outset this seems a 'normal' and familiar scenario, Lynch challenges our expectations through the employment of an overall strangeness in relation to the cinematography and his choice of mise-en-scène. As an audience we have difficulty in identifying with the characters, something which becomes even more disconcerting when on screen the characters themselves interact with each other in what appears to be an acceptable and rational manner. A fundamental paradox is therefore evident: on the one hand, the whole scenario seems to the audience to be abstract and remote, despite having family life at its core, and yet by the internal logic of the film, all the participants act coherently. What emerges is a fundamental dislocation between two worlds; that of the characters and that of the audience. We find ourselves 'in a kind of psychological quicksand, unable to find the correct footing – emotional or intellectual – from which to view what is occurring' (Godwin, 1984: 52). It seems that our own experiences are totally inappropriate in terms of offering guidance and understanding. Resolution, argues Godwin (ibid.), comes from the adaptation of a new set of rules used to work through this film which 'are not those of our familiar material world, nor indeed of any well-defined literary or cinematic tradition, but rather those of a dream'. Once again we encounter a film that is held together not by narrative logic – although traces of that do exist – but rather by something more closely affiliated to the experiences beyond waking hours. Interestingly, the film was shot completely at nighttime and gained its initial success by playing on the midnight circuit in the United States.

The disturbing unfamiliarity of the evidently familiar seeps through into the second of Lynch's films under consideration here, *Blue Velvet*. Made a decade later, it continues to draw upon the world of the dream but this time pushes the boundaries further by slipping into the terrain of its close companion, the nightmare. Such slippage is brought about not only by chance, coincidence, but also by spatial trespassing. The plot centres on Jeffrey, who discovers a severed ear and sets out to determine the mystery behind it. This allows him to meet both Sandy, the daughter of a true detective and, more dangerously, the enigmatic Dorothy Valens, a nightclub singer. The ear is revealed to belong to Dorothy's husband who has been kidnapped by the evil Frank. While it adheres to the more traditional demands of film-making in terms of the incorporation of an identifiable narrative structure, what is far more fundamental to this film is the close attention paid to a duality of worlds that exist in close proximity, in any neighbourhood, in any town: those occupied by the forces of good and evil. Lynch states that early on in his childhood, 'I learned that just beneath the surface there's another world, and still different worlds as you dig deeper. ... There is goodness in blue skies and flowers, but another force – a wild pain and decay – also accompanies everything' (Lynch in Rodley, 1997: 8). Set in contemporary America, the saturated choice of colours in the opening shots produces an unsettling effect on the viewer. That the lawns are so green and the picket fences a brilliant white contribute towards an exaggerated representation of suburban living: a derealisation even. This is enhanced by a vivid red fire engine which drives across screen and from which a waving fireman reflexively engages with the camera. By taking such familiar signs and yet playing with audiences' expectations of them throughout the film time and space become destabilised in Lynch's hands. This plundering of familiar visual signs and their reconfiguration and assemblage in the opening shots into something hyper-real contribute towards what can be read as Lynch's rendering of a postmodern dreamscape. Rather than operating on the premise of the duality of reality and the dream, Lynch seemingly fuses the world of consciousness and the unconscious to produce his own destabilisation of the familiar, which underpins both the film's aesthetics and the creation of affect. As a result, locating an exact time period for the film's setting becomes problematic.

If periodisation is problematic then so too is the mood of the piece. The inclusion of Bobby Vinton's upbeat song *Blue Velvet* provides the audience with a warm feeling derived from a familiar tune heard in conjunction with the brightly coloured visual on screen images, which creates an overall sense of 'goodness'. However, Lynch demonstrates his art of making daily life strange as themes of surface and depth are played out and expanded upon to incorporate a series of dualities including good versus evil, light versus darkness and dream versus nightmare, all of which exist in close proximity to one another. The problematisation of such dualities are depicted through the two communities located just a couple of blocks away that are personified in the characters of Frank, the psychopathic gangster and Sandy, the detective's daughter. Both seem to occupy an unreal relationship to the everyday, with Frank's brutal violence in stark juxtaposition to Sandy's quest for happiness. Lynch's recognition of the thin line that separates these two worlds operates both diachronically and synchronically. As the dream can so easily slip into the nightmare so can Sandy's domestic world shift into danger and damage. Not only does evil exist around any corner, but seemingly familiar surroundings may also have the potential to turn rotten, if one drills down a little. The opening scene may be initially comforting but the American dream is quickly tainted as the old man suffers a heart attack while watering his seemingly beautiful garden.

The mise-en-scène of both *Eraserhead* and *Blue Velvet* convey Lynch's belief that any image is multi-faceted, that it has an internal life rarely seen except when the surface is scratched a little. As a result, the vivid colours of the opening shots of *Blue Velvet* peel away to reveal the dark seedy life of film noir. While a radiator is simply 'an instrument for producing warmth in a room', in Lynch's hands it takes on a new life (Lynch in Rodley, 1997: 64). Although not included in the original script, 'The Lady in the Radiator' was inspired on the set by an actual radiator which, on close observation, had a small chamber, like a stage, contained within it. Taking this familiar object into unfamiliar territory allows a new character to emerge, but one that only Henry is allowed to encounter. The warmth of her feelings towards him mirror the physical warmth produced by this material object. She is constantly there for Henry as a source of comfort and when they finally touch, a blinding light is generated. While an emphasis on mood and texture, on the power of the individual image, underpins both these films, Lynch's application of a sense of narrative provides a point of continuity between them, and a point of contrast with the third, *Lost Highway* (1997). With reference to Lynch's first production, Chion (1995: 41) argues that despite its 'gaps and incoherences, *Eraserhead* is a narrative film with dialogue, a hero and a linear story'; such linearity can also be traced through *Blue Velvet,* from the finding of the ear to the resolution of the mystery, albeit with a certain amount of parody at the point of closure. However, what underpins *Lost Highway,* as Lynch once again seeks to utilise the medium of cinema to create a dream-like feeling, is a denial of the specificity of a single genre and the abandonment of the conventional film narrative with its demands for logic and legibility. Here, themes of fracturing and doubling become evident and these will later be expanded upon in the figures of Rita and Camilla and Betty and Diane in Lynch's *Mullholland Drive* (2002).

Lost Highway is described by Lynch as a twenty-first-century noir horror film, a film that 'delights in contradictory or unexplained events, fracturing narrative logic at every turn' (Newman, 1997: 48). Such a denial of the rules of the classical Hollywood narrative model is encapsulated in the fragmentation of the personality of the central protagonist Fred Madison (Bill Pullman) and his emergent alter-ego who takes over the second half of the film. Rather than a single identity, mapped against a linear narrative, as Fred's identity fractures, so does any sign of narrative cohesion. The film draws upon several of the themes we have already considered, including domestic disintegration and the defamiliarisation of our accepted reality. My own particular reading of the film centres on the symbolic opening and closing shots, filmed from a fast moving car, of the broken lines that run down the middle of the road. At speed the line looks continuous but when stationary its fragmentation is obvious. At its heart is the character of Fred, a saxophonist. As he doubts more and more the fidelity of his wife, so he imagines himself as a younger, more attractive man, reinventing his wife and a relationship that is the opposite of the stasis that they currently occupy. Whether the murder of his wife is actual, or symbolic of the death of their relationship, and whether his transformation into another character in the second part of the film is due to the fact that he wants to repress being a killer, or repress being himself and the 'prison cell' of a relationship that he is in, is open to interpretation. What cannot be denied is that such permutations allow for the creation of a highly innovative narrative structure which can facilitate such multiple scenarios and readings.

One route into the narrative structure is to return to the dream-work approach of the Surrealists, whereby the narrative is much more reflective of the workings of the unconscious and where the functioning of causality and rationality are denied. Such an approach ties in with the references made to memory throughout the film, symbolised by the role of photographs and video tape that play a prominent role in plot development. At an early point in *Lost Highway*, when the police come to investigate the mysterious tapes that Fred and his wife have been receiving, they ask why he hasn't installed a video camera himself to catch the perpetrator. He says that he doesn't like using them as he likes to remember things in his own way: 'how I remember them. Not necessarily the way they happened' (Lynch and Gifford, 1997: 18). It is as though the tools of surveillance are the tools of the conscious, but Fred prefers to remember things in his own way, as the unconscious does. The video recorder figures again in the death of Fred's wife, Renee (Patricia Arquette). We never see Fred murder her. Rather we as an audience only ever see it on screen, through the video playback in Fred's mind during his imprisonment. Perhaps this is a reflexive Lynch making audiences aware that what they are seeing is not reality but rather drawing attention to the way in which the camera can manipulate and create something new, which, in keeping with the theme of this chapter, might be described as 'surreality'. This sense of disturbing the clarity of what is real is added to by the fact that the video image that runs through Fred's head is in black and white, traditionally associated with documentary footage, with a sense of 'truth'. Already Lynch has played with these cinematic codes, utilising black and white in a disturbing manner in *Eraserhead* to create a macabre depiction of the 'reality' of family life, while in contrast, the hyper-real colours that occupy the opening and closing shots of *Blue Velvet* interestingly produce a similar effect. Once again, there appear to be no rules through which an audience might make meaning, not even by referring back to previous Lynch productions. As a result, the opening section of *Lost Highway* is highly resonant of the affect achieved in 'The Prologue' of *Un Chien andalou* as attention is self-referentially drawn to the audience's role as voyeur. While Renee and Fred watch video tapes of themselves, so we, as an audience, watch them watching. The tapes provide the only sense of a linear narrative in the film, in that each video builds on what was shown in the tape previously sent. Exterior shots of the building become interior shots of the couple sleeping, and finally culminate in the screening of Renee's demise. Her death, however, offers, like the death of the double in *Un Chien andalou,* a false sense of closure, as conversely it opens up a plethora of new identities that constitute the second part of the film.

The chameleon-like tendencies of characterisation in this film can be treated under the headings of 'fracturing' and 'doubling' and help explain and support Lynch's move away from the utilisation of a linear narrative. The problematisation of identity is presented at the very opening of the film with the arrival of the cryptic message that 'Dick Laurent is dead'. Who is he? We learn later in the film that he and a certain Mr Eddy are one. But this complex and mysterious twist in characterisation, the fact that if Dick Laurent is dead, then how

Figure 6. *Lost Highway* – October Films

can Mr Eddy become such an integral figure in the second part of the film, is never resolved or explained. Indeed, we can never really identify with any of the characters since, rather than being presented as fully rounded figures, they are encountered as highly transient beings. Evidence that a fissure lies at the heart of Fred's marriage is connoted through the use of cutting techniques to convey marital breakdown. Rarely do we see the couple occupying the same spaces, rather, in the interior shots, they are placed in different rooms doing divergent activities. In terms of the mise-en-scène, this highly strained atmosphere is suggested through a sense of lack, by the sterility and sparseness of the furniture and decor, the low-key lighting and a mood supported by a breakdown in communication comprised of prolonged silences and monosyllabic conversations. The death of Renee, whether fantasy or reality, offers an opportunity for the theme of fracturing, central to the first part of the film, to shift to that of doubling in the second part. We first see Pete Dayton, Fred's alter-ego, sitting in a chair in his garden. In the background we see the same picket fence as used in *Blue Velvet*. Symbolically, a fence could be seen to demarcate the two worlds of the first and second part of the film but, because it is such a low, non-functional structure, perhaps it can be read as representing the point of their potential elision. The theme of doubling weaves through the film in many ways. Directly, it incorporates Fred's Kafkaesque metamorphosis into Pete, and Renee's Hitchcockian change of hair colour to become Alice, the blonde femme fatale. Indeed, the character(s) of Renee/Alice demonstrates a change in Lynch's portrayal of women compared with the film previously analysed. In *Blue Velvet* women were manipulated and controlled by men. Here, Lynch recognises the potential of women's desires and fantasies and the power that they can evidence in search of their realisation. Renee is possibly having an affair with Dick Laurent while Alice too is prepared to risk all in her association with Pete.

The transmutation of Fred into Pete in the prison cell is fundamental to the second part of the film and works 'along the lines of a surreal logic' (Buckland, 2009: 51). Buckland explains further how 'this sudden jolt in the film's narrative is caused by the fact that the previous protagonist, whom we were given privileged access to, and from whom the camera rarely departed, has suddenly and inextricably disappeared' (ibid.). Fred's reinvention of himself as Pete, either to deal with his failing marriage, or to cope with Renee's murder, constitutes nothing more than an outer skin, a surface appearance, as there are moments when Fred himself seems to push through. As the radio plays in the garage and one of Fred's saxophone pieces fills the air, it forces Pete to clutch his head in agony. Through such overt bodily manifestations, the new identity is suggestively presented as being incomplete. The former self seems to be struggling for reinstatement, to find an outlet for the realisation of his previous identity, representing perhaps the same way in which material of the unconscious seeks strategies for release under conditions of repression. On the other hand, on screen such a transformation is not deemed as problematic or, as in the world of the dream, something that requires explanation. This reoccurs in the later desert scenes when Pete once again inexplicably becomes Fred. While for the audience the instability of characterisation is troubling, in terms of the internal logic of the film, it is accepted.

Another means of approaching the theme of doubling is through the character of the Mystery Man. He is nameless and depicts something that is beyond the real, outside of language, and in essence offers the least opportunity for audience identification. The Mystery Man displays the ability to converse with himself on the telephone and to view himself on his own television for he is constrained by neither time nor space. 'This dual series of experiences, this access to apparently separate worlds, is repeated in my nature in every respect: I am a Doppelgänger, I have a "second" face in addition to the first' (Nietzsche, 1989: 225). Perhaps these 'separate worlds' can be read as his occupation of both the conscious and the unconscious, but his presence throughout the narrative is always highly disturbing. One of the most interesting scenes in which he is involved is his first meeting with Fred and it exemplifies the way in which the ordinary can spiral into the extraordinary at any moment in Lynch's directorial hands. 'We've met before, haven't we?' asks the Mystery Man, in one of those lines often used as a mode of introduction at a party. But here it takes an obtuse twist when the conversation progresses to the point where the Mystery Man argues that he knows him so well that he is currently in Fred's home and telephones himself, or his double, at the house to prove it.

The Mystery Man also symbolises that for Lynch the power of the image is far more important in creating an impact on the audience than in terms of its contribution to the construction of an overall sense of narrative flow. While his appearance is highly disturbing so is the house where the Mystery Man lives. Situated against the backdrop of a Daliesque desert landscape, it is but one instance of the surreal nature of the cinematography producing affect in the film as it manages to constitute 'the febrile quality of a dream' (Pizzello, 1997: 36). Peter Deming, cinematographer on *Lost Highway*, draws attention to the scene in the desert where Alice and Pete make love. Illuminated only by the white-hot headlights of the car, all that you can see is their eyes, mouths, noses and hair, an effect of the lighting which he himself describes as 'surreal' (ibid.: 40). There are other significant points in the film where the power of the image is such that it almost puts time on hold. These include Pete's first encounter with Alice as she gets out of a cab and walks towards him across the floor of the garage. Her beauty holds his attention to the point that both Pete and the audience are oblivious to anything else. Time stands still and her approach seems to last forever. The attention to detail in the selection of sounds that populate *Lost Highway* also adds a certain quality for their potential to enhance any particular mood. Lynch adopts a highly sensitive approach to sounds and seems to suggest that there exists a third space, resonant of Barthes' 'third meaning', between noise and silence, which he describes as 'room tone' (Rodley, 1997: 73). In *Eraserhead*, it was documented how the apparent silence of Henry's room is actually permeated by a variety of noises operating at a low frequency that is rarely tuned into. Developing this theme, *Lost Highway* manifests in a number of ways Lynch's suggestion that silence is rare. When Fred plays the videotapes he has mysteriously received, the script refers to the picture being accompanied by 'an eerie droning sound', while later in his prison cell Fred sits in the 'humming darkness' and in the interior of the Dayton's house the 'refrigerator's hum is the only sound' (Lynch and Gifford, 1997: 10, 42, 63).

Un Chien andalou and *Lost Highway* express the difficulties that a viewer experiences in seeking to apply the logic of traditional narrative conventions to the events that unfold before them. In *Lost Highway* any meaning that one can arrive at seems to derive from something greater than the sum of its parts, as Barthes (1974: 120) states: 'the meaning of a text can be nothing but the plurality of its systems'. That is to say, meaning is not derived through the straightforward progression of the linear narrative but by an accumulation of sound, mise-en-scène and characterisation that creates an overall mood which is difficult to quantify. In terms of the narrative itself, any analysis of storytelling might appear to be a somewhat marginal activity; in that the emphasis Lynch places on all the other composite factors would render it of minor consideration. Nevertheless, whatever place it adopts in any ordering of the film's priorities there clearly emerges a highly innovative narrative structure that complements and effectively carries forward the themes of fracturing and doubling.

In terms of genre, if such classifications can at all be applied to a work by David Lynch, the film potentially offers up a new appropriation of the concept of the road movie for the twenty-first century. Road movies, with *The Wizard of Oz* (1939) establishing itself as perhaps the first example, encapsulate ideas about progress and discovery and naturally have built into them definitive starting and ending points. Lynch states that his own fascination with *The Wizard of Oz* lies in the fact that there is 'a certain amount of fear in the picture, as well as things to dream about' (Rodley, 1997: 194). But while the yellow lines that form the opening and closing shots draw parallels with that famous yellow brick road, this is a dysfunctional road movie on many levels. In the standard form of the genre, the car acts as a vehicle of self-discovery, but in this film, based on a highly intricate interweaving of multiple identities, the main characters undergo a complex fracturing, reconstitution and even meltdown of their personalities as the film progresses. Where *Lost Highway* most radically challenges the ethos of the road movie is in its cyclical structure which in itself denies any sense of progress being either evidenced or achieved. Indeed, beginning and end are merely arbitrary markers in this film. While the narrative of *The Wizard of Oz* can be described as circular in that Dorothy returns home, gets back to her original starting point, that adopted by *Lost Highway* is cyclical. We are back at the beginning but things are slightly different. This time it is Fred who announces into the intercom that 'Dick Laurent is dead'. So who now occupies the house and thus sets the cycle off again?

The film concludes with much remaining unanswered and this disavowal of a traditional sense of closure, as witnessed in *Un Chien andalou,* frustrates audience expectations. Indeed, rather than reaching a sense of ending, we are apparently at another point of departure. So untraditional is this narrative structure that it has been suggested that the best way to screen the film would be to show it as 'an endless loop ... in which spectators could enter at any moment during the cycle and leave at any point' (Celeste, 1997: 33). This is resonant not only of how Gordon perceived that *24 Hour Psycho* should be viewed, but also records the Surrealist practice of entering and leaving the cinema at will. This foregrounding of the cyclical also 'serves to complicate the traditional notion of time as a forward progression consisting of three dimensions – past, present, and future' (ibid.: 34); a point echoed by Warner (1997: 6) who describes the plot as one which 'binds time's arrow in time's loop'. Lynch once stated that 'some things in life are not understandable, but when things in films are that way, people become worried' (Rodley, 2005: 227). Our dreams rarely make sense so, when Lynch draws attention to them and makes them the subject matter of his cinema, why do we find this problematic?

The Surrealists were fascinated by cinema, commencing with its particular environment, the dark auditorium conjuring up a dream-like state through its oscillations of darkness and light. Cinema provided a vehicle that enabled the world to be seen differently and it is this qualitative difference that unites the Surrealist vision. While heavily influenced by Freud, they were not interested in the interpretation of dreams but rather the unconscious mechanisms that allow dreaming to take place. In view of this *Un Chien andalou* was deemed worthy of revisiting 'as an ambiguous turning point between the alternatives of dominant and counter-cinema' (Drummond, 1994: xv). Yet, while recognised as highly influential, to take this a step further, to define what actually constitutes a Surrealist film is problematic for it 'is not a style, it is equally not a fixed set of principles or attitudes' (Richardson, 2006: 3). Thus we could conclude by arguing that it is nigh on impossible to delineate a Surrealist director if there is no model or template against which comparisons can be made. Even Lynch himself is somewhat ambivalent: in some interviews he uses the word 'surreal' while in others he disavows such direct references. Nevertheless, if the Surrealists succeeded in making the familiar strange then Lynch deserves to be situated in their company.

CONSUMING TIME

Every film has an ending. The majority reach an unambiguous point of closure while others leave the viewer contemplating resolution long after the credits have rolled. However, some specifically deal with 'the end', the threat or actual occurrence of a global calamity underpinned by varying degrees of optimism for the future of mankind. Blockbusters such as the *Lord of the Rings* trilogy and the tales of *Harry Potter* share fantastical apocalyptic plots while director Roland Emmerich (2009) brings the end of the world much closer to the present, using the reckoning of the Mayan calendar to locate doomsday in the year *2012*. Indeed it could be argued that we are all dealing with endings, both real and imagined, on a daily basis. In this respect Chapter 4 seeks to explore how cinema has sought to represent and manage significant temporal markers: extreme as in 'end of the world' and those located more at the level of individual subjectivity.

Although public sensibilities towards 'the end' become heightened at moments of threatened national and international security, every day of our lives we experience the inevitable progression towards our own mortality, evidenced by the processes of ageing whereby time consumes us, leaving its visual markers and embodying its progress. While our awareness of advancing towards 'an end' is complex, two specific trends can be identified as running through contemporary culture. On the one hand, at the level of the social, we are aware how fragile life is and the constant 24-hour news feeds provide a pressing reminder. As a result we wish to feel safe, to be secure. In contrast, another more individualistic approach to life can be identified. Statistics demonstrate that in the West we are living longer and concomitantly on a daily basis wish to push the boundaries of our own mortality further: to challenge the omnipotence of

time and take ourselves into the realm of immortality. Indeed, in the UK, life
expectancy has reached 'its highest level on record for both males and females'
with men living for an average of 77.2 years and women to 81.5 (ONS, 2008).
But while living longer is acceptable, looking older is not. And herein lies the
paradox, as Turner (1995: 249) observes:

> Our awareness of time is also an awareness of passing through time, but
> this consciousness must be connected with the very fact of our embodi-
> ment. The embodiment of human beings is necessarily of a limited dura-
> tion because ultimately our bodies are not endlessly renewable.

However in the media, and in particular in discourses of advertising and con-
sumerism, the cult of youth predominates, resulting in many refusing to accept
the signs of ageing that inherently come with living longer.

How the existence of social insecurity coupled with a quest for individual
immortality is represented on screen is highly engaging, especially if considered through certain enduring symbolic figures that in themselves offer both
diurnal reassurance and temporal resistance, that is to say, through the emotionally charged subjects of angels and vampires. This chapter will look at how
and why the angel has been a recurring leitmotif in cinema's history, set against
a backdrop of significant temporal dislocation including war, the fall of the
Berlin Wall, the onset of a new Millennium and the persistent threat of terrorism post 9/11. I will also investigate the vampire and consider a revised Gothic
reading for the twenty-first century, whereby 'the other' is represented through
the figure of the 'ageing self'. Finally, I will close with a consideration of a
specific ending, our own inevitable mortality, and our journey into the afterlife
where time no longer consumes us but we spend our days consuming time.

In *Time Magazine* (December, 1993) a full-length feature article on angels
revealed that in the United States 69 per cent of survey respondents were
quoted as believing in their existence. More recently, in 2009 in Great Britain,
an Ipsos MORI survey indicated that 46 per cent of Britain's adults believe in
guardian angels and three out of four of these people agree that such figures
have helped them in some way during their everyday lives. The question 'Do
you believe in angels?' strikes right at the heart of our interaction with contemporary belief systems, for such a question produces a fundamental conflict
in the mind of the respondent, one that will underpin much of the filmic
analysis explored here. On the one hand, we are frequently reminded of the
precariousness of human existence and on the other, as the survey above indicates, a belief circulates that someone is watching over us, and even protecting

us. While the recognition of the fragility of human existence has influenced cinematic productions since World War II, many of these have been interlaced with the stuff of Biblical texts and fairy stories, while today the angel manages to coexist alongside a more gritty twenty-first-century realism. A recent Lynx advertisement which draws on the motif of the fallen angel is testament to this (2011). Bloom (1996) can perhaps provide a clue to the enduring appeal of the angel in cinema, noting a marked trend towards their domestication which has diminished their spirituality and seen their adaptation towards a more aesthetic function. A high level of sentimentality is now associated with them, whereby they are consigned to a new role for a more secular age based upon reassurance and consolation in juxtaposition to the highly functionary performances displayed in traditional Christian theology. The path of their domestication and their aesthetic humanisation commences at the time of the Italian Renaissance and has subsequently developed by means of other factors: firstly, that Protestantism moved away from the need for intercessionaries and secondly, that science contributed to an overwhelming sense of doubt that not only was it impossible for angels to fly but also challenged old beliefs that it was angels who kept the universe turning. Finally, in terms of their artistic representation, a marked shift throughout the period of industrialisation saw the depiction of angelic women here on earth, untouched by the markings of toil (Gauldie, 1992: 19).

There have been angels, or flying spirits of some kind, in the culture and mythology of every civilisation, but how we actually conceptualise what it is we mean by 'angel' comes from a variety of sources. Of course, there are the testimonies of people who have claimed to have seen one but these are few in number compared with their depiction in Christian theology and later in art and literature. While it is in the Book of Revelation that angels are most frequently mentioned, they are first noted in Genesis as the guardians of the eastern gate of the Garden of Eden. Their depiction is not constant throughout the Bible but shifts with the respective representations of God, more benevolent in the New Testament than the Old. In the Old Testament interest centres more on their function, while in the New Testament their nature is more clearly defined, with Christ represented by angels at the most important periods of his life, including his birth and resurrection. In St Matthew's Gospel, Jesus speaks of the angels of children and hence the possible root of the idea of the guardian angel. As the scriptures refer to the creation of angels, it is clear that they have not existed for all eternity. The time of their coming into being is never specified, although it is probable that it occurred in connection with the creation of the heavens in Genesis 1:1 (Davidson, 1967: xxvii). In the fourth and fifth centuries the Christian Church spread its beliefs throughout Europe and angels began to appear in visual form via their incorporation into architecture. By medieval times, when death and the nature of how one came to enter heaven was a subject of much concern, angels were accepted as the means by which this transition could be made. Roofs, doorways and pew ends all depicted their image and fuelled their popularity. In art we find a visual catalogue of ideas regarding their appearance, function, movement and nature with a fundamental shift coming at the time of the Renaissance when angels began to be depicted in human form, a reflection of the wider knowledge and developed skills of the practising artists. The power of flight still remained integral to such depictions, symbolised by the angels' wings. The continued presence of wings in artistic representations is significant, for they have an important iconic quality which demarcates them from humans, indeed from mortals (Child and Colles, 1971: 119). However, with regard to the films under consideration here, it is only Clarence, the angel of *It's A Wonderful Life* (1946), who makes a significant point about earning his wings. All the other angels, while on earth, are neither represented as having them, nor recognising a need for them.

It is a psychological state, depression and potential suicide, that leads us into one of the most famous films to place the angel at the heart of its narrative, namely Capra's *It's A Wonderful Life* (1946). The story of George Bailey is well known, being one of the most popular screenings at Christmas, a time itself of birth and new beginnings. Despite the emotional state of the central protagonist, this is a highly optimistic work that operates on both the macro and micro level; a filmic exploration of the nature of human existence and of the coping strategies of individual beings. The whole film is shot from a heavenly point of view. In the opening sequence the camera tilts upward from scenes of Bedford Falls to the heavens above, offering the viewer the opportunity to ponder on the meaning of the individual in the context of the universe, a question that the film will seek to address throughout. A shot of the stars and planets is accompanied by the voices of God and Chief Angel Joseph who are aware of George's plight. A smaller star is summoned, Clarence Oddbody, AS2 ('angel second class'), who is yet to earn his wings after a period of 200 years. Clarence is told: 'At exactly 10.45P.M. earth time, that man will be thinking seriously of throwing away God's greatest gift.' The omnipotence of God is revealed and through a long flashback, Clarence has one hour to learn of the events that have brought George to this critical point in his life. As in *A Matter of Life and Death*, discussed later in this chapter, both films share establishing shots that are not of a place or a person but rather of the whole universe and all of human life.

The action takes place in Bedford Falls between 1919 and 1945, but one critic has described the setting in somewhat Lynchian terminology. Ray (1985: 179) speaks of the way in which Bedford Falls exists 'outside of time', how it is a place that contains both 'the sunny, small-town world of its surface and ... deaths, anxieties, frustration, and near-madness' (ibid.: 182). The choice of black-and-white film stock underpins the theme of good and evil in this highly moralistic tale of the precariousness of life and the fragility of fate itself. In the Book of Revelation, Satan's fate hangs in the balance; in *A Matter of Life and Death* the records of those who have died and those who have entered the 'other world' remarkably do not balance and set events in motion; here, it is the fact that the books of the bank that do not balance that sets George on his path to suicide. It is snowing heavily and we can hardly make out George in the storm. On a bridge he looks down at the icy water below but as he prepares to jump he is distracted by screams, for Clarence has dived in before him. We cut to inside the bridge man's hut, where the bridge man stares speechlessly at Clarence, who is dressed in very old fashioned white undergarments, the ones in which he 'passed away'. The bridge man swallows hard. Clarence reaches for his book, *Tom Sawyer,* which is drying out beside him. Such a text is highly significant to the story for not only does Tom consider an alternative to life when things go badly, 'for it seemed to him that life was but a trouble at best', but he also gets to see what life would be like without him as he attends his own funeral, with friends and family believing him to have drowned (Twain, 1994). At the point at which Clarence explains that he is an angel AS2, the bridge man falls off his chair and runs out of the door, doubtless any mortal's response. The rational explanation that Clarence gives for being there sounds ludicrous but, following the establishing shot of the heavens, the audience can place such divine intervention in a wider context. The workings of the world of the spiritual from an earthly point of view are not easy to understand. George, however, is at such a low point in his life that he is more than ready to listen. He flirts with the rhetoric of angels and playfully asks Clarence where his wings are, suggesting that he looks more like a 'fallen angel' than a guardian angel. The answer that Clarence gives, however, is in keeping with the seriousness of his mission: he hasn't earned his wings yet. 'Go off and haunt somebody else', is George's reply. George cannot see how the angel can be of any consequence unless he can come up with the missing money. 'I wish I'd never been born', states George, a wish that Clarence will grant him in the film's revelatory second part. Clarence functions primarily to enable George to gain a divine perspective on life, to allow him to contextualise his problems and to recognise the significance of his own life in relation to others around him.

The decline in popularity of the film blanc (of which this film is a seminal example) towards the end of the 1940s can be attributed to the way in which its Pollyanna view of the world jarred uneasily with the more pessimistic viewpoint of post-war realist cinema. The genre lay dormant until the 1970s when it underwent a very minor renaissance. On the cusp of the Millennium film blanc re-emerges, this time more forcefully, with subtle changes that take into account a marked decline in religious beliefs. Such changes are encapsulated in the way in which the words 'The End' come up on the screen at the point of closure in *It's A Wonderful Life.* That few contemporary films use the term so specifically is possibly 'indicative of today's more tentative and fragmentary understandings of how life will proceed after the credits have rolled' (Brown, 1997: 230).

What remains constant in this third wave of film blanc, and is now under consideration here, is the inter-relationship of mortal and immortal worlds as represented by Wenders' *Wings of Desire* (1987) and, a decade later, Silberling's remake, *City of Angels* (1998). The original title of the film was *Himmel über Berlin* (*Heavens above Berlin*), depicting a neutral space occupied by the angels of the city that remains untouched by political and historical discourses. For the angels the Berlin Wall forms no barrier as they can move through it as they have moved through the whole of history. To them the Wall possesses little historical significance – to a being that has been around for all eternity, the Wall's brief lifespan makes it very inconsequential. The Wall acts as a metaphor for the obstacles that exist in our lives but Damiel's symbolic transference from immortal to mortal, brought about by his love for Marion, signifies that all barriers can ultimately be overcome, providing within the film a central message of hope. The angels remain invisible to everyone except small children and spend their days amongst the people of Berlin listening to their thoughts. They occupy the National Library where apocalyptic texts are read and where Homer, an elderly gentleman, thinks about the Berlin of his youth. As the Homer of the ancients wrote of the intervention of the gods in human lives, so here this man functions as a conduit through which we might begin to understand the presence of the angels in modern times. The film is alert to the changing role of the angel in the latter part of the twentieth century, especially the decline of their role as messengers. They have indeed suffered a loss of impact for, rather than having a direct influence on individuals, as in the case of George Bailey, their new function is less interventionist, and this is powerfully depicted in the scene where the angel cannot prevent a suicide.

In this highly innovative film we learn much of the angel's perspective through Wenders' effective camera work. Not only does the camera take on the angels' point of view through a series of aerial shots, but by camera movement, sometimes at high speed, an illusion is created of unlimited motion in time and space, a technique that will later be adopted by Coppola to depict the world of the immortal vampire. What gives *Wings of Desire* a more universal appeal outside its Berlin setting is that while place and space are important, it is the temporal aspect of the film that is primarily foregrounded. In falling in love with a trapeze artist, Damiel is faced with an irrevocable choice: to continue the atemporal, spiritual existence of an angel or to take on human form and indulge in a world of sensual pleasures. The film turns its attention to Damiel's deliberation. His decision is highly influenced by his awareness of a physical world that in his present state he cannot be a part of. He longs to eat and drink, to feel the change in the weather, to be ill, to see his fingers blackened by newspaper print, to be able to guess things rather than always to know them. His decision to 'fall' is informed by his frustration at being a mere observer of history, able only to 'look, assemble, testify, preserve', rather than participate as the figure of Homer in the library does. In an early scene in the film, Damiel and his companion, Cassiel, sit in a car in a garage showroom. One takes out a notebook and records the times of the sunrise, 7.22A.M. and later the sunset, 4.28P.M. As he turns back the pages, so he moves through his past observations of the city, some 20, 50, 200 years ago. In the same

Figure 7. *Wings of Desire* – Road Movies Film

scene Damiel is frustrated by his spiritual existence, which he contextualises through temporal references. He wants to 'say "now" and no longer "forever" and "for eternity"'. Later in the film it is again his relationship to time that informs his ultimate, life-changing decision: 'I want to transmute what my timeless downward gaze has taught me.' The change in clothing that accompanies his fall, from dark coat to brightly coloured jacket, accompanied by the acquisition of a watch marks 'a trade of anonymity for expression, eternity for the moment' (Ehrlich, 1991: 243).

Wenders has described his film as a celestial road movie, not horizontal but vertical in form, in that Damiel's self-exploration takes him from immortal to mortal being, and from the skies to the earth below. Just as *A Matter of Life and Death* will explore the juxtaposition of two worlds through contrasting film stock, so similarities occur in this film. A black-and-white documentary style is punctuated by brief moments of colour at points of heightened sensual awareness: Marion's flight through the air on her trapeze; Marion undressing in her caravan; a bed with red linen, vibrant amongst the rubble of the bombed city; a lonely individual in a launderette at night. Such usage of colour mirrors the way in which underlining is used in relation to a written text, informing us to take note, to pay particular attention. But these moments are only transitory, fleeting: we should not take them for granted. Indeed, the significance of Damiel's decision to fall is represented in the latter stages of the film by the permanent shift to colour, an attempt to depict the world as experienced through the full range of human senses that the former angel now has access to. As Damiel enters into history so he enters into narrative. Marion says that their relationship will begin a new story.

A new story and a new reading of the film was produced just over a decade later. In *City of Angels* many of the themes of its predecessor are taken up and universalised with the love story forming the central driver of the narrative from the outset. The shift to colour is almost permanent, with monochrome used sparsely for the memories that run through Seth's mind at the point of his 'fall'. Tribute is paid to the original through a film that marvels at the wonders of the physical world and in the long, dark clothing that the angels wear. How they spend their time remains a constant theme. They pass their limitless days roaming the city and comforting those in need, although remaining unseen, except by children, who smile from their pushchairs as the angels pass by. They are able to speak every language, they can read people's minds, travel at the speed of thought and when photographed appear in the picture as a brilliant white light. That they remain unable to intervene is demonstrated by the death of a child in the opening scene. Though they care deeply for people, they perceive the events and emotions that go to make up mortal lives with a certain sense of wonder since celestial restraint results in them lacking access to the world of the senses. Seth, the central protagonist, reads Hemingway, relying on the descriptions of others to try to understand the nature of taste.

The use of aerial shots, as in Wenders' work, conveys their non-mortal point of view as the urban landscape is transformed through their eyes. It is not just the city that is beautiful, however. Some of the most spectacular scenes of the film come from the use of long shots as thousands of angels gather on the beach at sunrise and sunset; their black silhouettes contrasting with the orange and purple backdrop of the sky. Newton (1997: 4) states that according to the Apocalypse of Paul, certain angels travelled to earth each day to watch humanity and at sunset travelled back to Heaven to report to God all that they had seen. The library also remains a symbolic location, possibly deriving from the interpretation of the 'Sixth Heaven' as a place of knowledge where the angels went to study, or alternatively, it represents in textual form the whole of history of which the angels have been observers (Godwin, 1993: 123). However, once again it is the temporal that propels the narrative forward. Angels as atemporal beings have no sense of urgency, of expediency, and thus when Seth is forced to respond to the news that Maggie, the woman he is in love with, is to marry someone else, we encounter a fundamental jarring of time frames. His subsequent decision to 'fall' immediately accelerates the narrative and draws it to a conclusion.

Finally, *A Life Less Ordinary* (Boyle, 1997), while also situated on the cusp of the new Millennium, interestingly offers us a point of contrast in its depiction of the angel's role, bringing about a return to the earlier film blanc tradition of divine intervention, with a 'deus ex machina' solution to the problems on earth. This time, the angel is appropriated not for its spiritual role but to deal with unhappy couples and rising divorce rates. The angel now is positioned as matchmaker. That they must succeed in their assigned mission is paramount, for the price of failure is very high: they will lose their immortality. Gabriel remains in charge but Heaven is somehow 'humanised', represented in terms of the vast bureaucracy that is a contemporary New York police department. The distanciation created between Heaven and Earth is managed effectively through the creative use of colour: Heaven is all white, with direct resonances of purity and goodness compared with that which lies below. Times have changed, however, from early film blanc. God takes on a more direct role, called on the telephone at one point in the action and asked to intervene when the angels look like failing in their mission. Such divine intervention, understood in the context of a world in which religious beliefs are on the decline, is repackaged as 'fate' and 'destiny' and where the protagonist realises at the point of closure that all that has happened is 'inexplicable, unpredictable and absolutely beyond control or understanding'. On the cusp of the Millennium the enduring presence of angels on screen was clearly demonstrable, with, for example, the launch of the controversial *Dogma* in 1999. However, what was not so discernible was any sense of consistency as to their specific social role. But that there was still a shared need to recognise and indeed represent their existence is interesting and perhaps speaks to the angel as a symbol offering nothing more than a sense of comfort in what were and are increasingly uncertain times.

As the new Millennium made its calendrical mark a second cinematic theme emerged: namely the revival of the vampire genre on big screen, small screen, electronic game and in book format. These productions, however, all took a significant turn in media representation: speaking directly to and overtly celebrating the cult of youth. Across all major television channels in the UK *The Vampire Diaries* (ITV), *True Blood* (HBO/C4) and *Being Human* (BBC3) have popularised the form and, in cinema, Stephenie Meyer's *The Twilight Saga* rolled on into 2011 with *Breaking Dawn – Part 1*. The vampire, therefore, both continues not only to present itself but also to evolve across multiple outlets of contemporary popular culture and appears to be refusing to go away. We need to ask why.

Throughout contemporary culture a binary opposition of representation exists: youth versus ageing. Cinema forms a critical role in underpinning its construction, for the primary narrative of ageing in the West is one of edging towards decline, yet this is countered cinematically through that medium's obsession with the performance of youth. Here youthfulness is held up as a role model with its qualitative associations of liveliness, vigour and zealousness. Continued off screen, such performativity is communicated largely at the level of the everyday through a consumer culture that promotes goods as props, in a marketplace littered with time-resistant products. As a consequence, a body that is ageing is one that is deprived of symbolic capital and 'the proliferation of images of bodies which valorize youth, beauty, slimness, perfect body shapes and physical competence in contemporary culture is problematic for older people whose bodies, not conforming to these images, consequently become devalued' (Tulle, 2008: 3). The challenge to all, so the market proposes, is to hold onto youth, frequently embodied through the utilisation of 'celebrity as role model' in much promotional literature. However, it could be argued that there is a more interesting role model to consider: one that embraces both the realisation that not only are we living longer but also that in doing so we seek to negate any sign of the ageing process. The vampire, I would argue, gains its popularity in the context of the twenty-first-century Gothic for the way in which it uniquely performs subjectivity. Time as history might move forward but the vampire offers the fixity of self that many mortals crave. At all *fins de siècle* since 1790, the emergence and re-emergence of the Gothic brings about both a heightened sense of awareness of man's lack of control in a seemingly rational world and a deepening sense of one's own mortality as time passing becomes amplified. The Gothic's persistent revival at moments of temporal significance in either novel or film hinges on the way it 'gathers up the anxiety that is free-floating in the reader or viewer and binds it to a narrative. Thus the anxiety is displaced and brought under temporary, tenuous control' (Edmundson, 1997: 12). In the 1790s the Gothic acted as a response to the spread of industrialisa-tion and urbanisation, and in the 1890s to science and new technologies, but in the 1990s a new spectre was looming: an ageing population. While it might be argued that man's greatest fear has been always death and our own mortality, by living longer such anxieties are now circulating much later in life, and the new enemy is the appearance of age itself. In this way, the vampire begins to take hold of the collective consciousness as a mythological representation of the ability to stop the process of ageing which is inextricably linked to the concept of its immortality.

It is through the challenges that living longer brings to the population that I now turn and will discuss, not through one of the new cinematic productions noted previously that explicitly link the vampire with youthfulness, but to two earlier postmodern vampire tales that I believe not only significantly contribute towards the current appeal of the genre but also pose important ontological and epistemological questions about the drive towards immortality. Commentators have noted how two vampire films of the early 1990s, Coppola's *Bram Stoker's Dracula* (1992) and Neil Jordan's *Interview with the Vampire* (1994), inform cen-tral themes of the genre's most recent revival. In particular, as Jackson (2009: 42) argues, in the tradition of Rice's novel, 'of late, vampire fictions have been opting not merely for quotidian settings, but for aggressively bland versions of the quotidian'. On the post-Millennium screen, vampires continue to strike us as highly sympathetic figures and the trope of seeing the world, and hence all its trappings, from their point of view has evolved out of these two notable predecessors.

Francis Ford Coppola's adaptation of Stoker's novel positions Dracula as a time traveller crossing centuries to be reunited with his reincarnated wife, Mina. The densely woven narrative of the novel, in which a number of points of view are incorporated and a number of discursive fields are represented, is mirrored in the film by its use of direct speech and by having characters read from their journals. The film also retains Stoker's recognition of the way in which information can be recorded, through diaries, journals and newspaper reports, as well as through the modern technologies of the typewriter and cylinder recording, all of which are visually represented. In the novel, not all the fragments come together to form a perfect whole, and this seems fundamentally due to the omission of the point of view of the vampire himself. Rice directly reverses this in her writing and, to an extent, so does Coppola who gives the audience the opportunity to see much from the vampire's perspective, although it is possible that, by seeing events through the vampire's eyes, Coppola is not so much interested in a narrative continuity between his work and Stoker's as in creating on screen a 'maelstrom of sensation' (Dyer, 1993: 10). As in Rice's work, Coppola pays attention to the sensual world of the vampire, of a vampire that cries tears of blood on hearing of Mina's impending marriage. This sensationalism is represented by a proliferation of colour dominating the mise-en-scène through lavish sets and costumes. Red functions as the primary colour of the film: from the blood that spills from the cross of the opening scene to Dracula's cloak; to the nightdresses of Mina and her companion, Lucy, prior to their seductions by the Count; to the red blood cells seen under the microscope and to the red flowers that die instantly via time-lapse photography. Throughout the film a dense visual texture resonates, exemplified in the scene of Lucy's seduction where the screen is awash with blood as Dracula, in the guise of a wolf, attacks her. The blood rushes up on either side of the screen like waves in a storm. It is also interesting how Coppola has chosen to adapt the visual appearance of the Count from the descriptions of him in Stoker's novel of 1897. There he is described by a zoo-keeper as 'a tall, thin chap, with a 'ook nose and a pointed beard, with a few white hairs runnin' through it. He had a 'ard, cold look and red eyes' (Stoker, 1993: 179). This is not Coppola's Dracula who wines and dines Mina in the lead up to her seduction. Here the director more successfully captures the Gothic dualism inherent in the vampire: the idea of the victim being both frightened of and yet tempted by his presence.

A varied use of camera techniques also contributes to the film as spectacle: fast motion photography, for example, depicting the speed at which immortals move. Dracula himself is the embodiment of the special effect, visually transmogrifying into a green mist, a bat and a human-shaped body composed of live rats as circumstances dictate. The dissolve is creatively appropriated to explore the theme of vision in the film while simultaneously allowing for a sense of narrative continuity. The blue eye of a peacock's tail becomes the tunnel of a train; the two bite marks on Lucy's neck become the piercing eyes of the wolf; and the iris of Lucy's eye becomes the bottom of Mina's glass as she dines with the Count. Such inventiveness is at its most heightened at the fairground where

Dracula first meets Mina, a scene not included in the original text. Its inclusion here allows visual emphasis to be placed on the juxtaposition of rational science with the irrational world of the Gothic that runs throughout much of the novel. It is 1897 and Coppola recreates the period through the recuperation of cinematic techniques of the time. Dracula asks Mina the way to the cinematograph which he has heard is a wonder of the civilised world. Her response is that if it is culture that he is after then he should really go to a museum! Coppola (in Coppola and Hart, 1992: 5) stated that such a scene, which includes the screening of the Lumières' train, was introduced to emphasise a sense of 'magic', for at the time of Stoker's writing, cinema was still in the hands of magicians. Such a positioning of Dracula's arrival in London to coincide with the birth of cinema reflexively suggests that this is the original vampire film.

Sheehan (1993: 14) argues that in Coppola's *Bram Stoker's Dracula* space becomes a 'function of emotion' so that a small area may seem huge in relation to the enormity of the event going on there; we see such an effect in the garden where Lucy has her first somnambulist confrontation with the Count. In contrast, the ocean, simply an obstacle that needs to be crossed, is passed over in a few seconds of filming. The suggestive use of space communicates the ambivalent association between place and safety: although the streets of London and the terrain of Carpathia are represented so contrastingly, in both domains danger lurks. Carpathia is a desolate, eerie place, with dirt tracks for roads, where wolves howl and it is always night. Such uncomfortable geography jars with the familiarity of a city; its peopled streets lit by artificial lights and with accustomed sounds reverberating. Yet both are the lair of the vampire. Dracula defies the boundaries of space, his omnipresence derived from his command of the elements. The wind he summons turns the pages of a history of Dracula that his would-be destroyer reads hundreds of miles away. As an immortal, perhaps the spatial means more to a vampire than the temporal, which is of almost no consequence in the context of eternity? If so, any sense of time might be understood spatially where time,

> is a space belonging to the expanded present of the post-historical imagination, in which time ceases to have meaning. Within it there is no decay, no corruption and no forgetting. If the present we inhabit now could be infinitely stretched, it would approximate that space. (Benjamin, 1998: 231)

Thus if command of the spatial is a fundamental facet of the vampire's identity, its significance is derived in inverse ratio to its relationship with time. For vampires exist outside time and defy modernity's attempt to rationalise and synchronise it. While Stoker's novel opens with Jonathan Harker's temporal specificity, 'Left Munich at 8.35 pm on 1st May', pages later Dracula speaks of 'how few days go to make up a century' (Stoker, 1993: 7, 35). Like Dali's dissolving watches, in the presence of a vampire time is made to feel flexible and fluid. Lucy, on changing into a vampire, undergoes a temporal reversal with her decaying body becoming even more beautiful than she was before 'illness' struck her. The same transformation happens to the Count who, revived by human blood, returns to a state of youthfulness as represented by his portrait that hangs on the castle wall. As Jackson (1993: 47) argues: 'Chronological time is similarly exploded, with time past, present and future losing their historical sequence and tending towards a suspension, an eternal present.'

In summary, the fundamental difference between mortal and immortal worlds centres upon a specific relationship to time. In the world of mortals, temporality has the upper hand, our time on earth is short and time devours all things. As Renfield, Dracula's servant, acutely observes: 'Time presses, and in our implied agreement with the old scytheman, it is of the essence of the contract' (Stoker, 1993: 314). For immortals, however, it is they who devour time. When Van Helsing, Dracula's nemesis, decapitates the three female vampires that inhabit Dracula's castle he describes the way in which immortality has transformed their bodies into a container for time. As they are rapidly turned into dust death, at last, asserts itself as it should have done centuries ago. And now, in the twenty-first century, there has been much speculation as to whether immortality might eventually become a possibility if science can overturn the framework of ageing through the discovery that 'stem cells were capable of indefinite division and hence were "immortalized"' (Turner, 2006: 227). While attempts to create immortality are not new, with gravestones, paintings, statues and street names all functioning as long-standing memorials, work in the field of bio-gerontology has given the quest a distinctly postmodern character, as stem cell research considers the replacement of worn out parts of the body by growing genetically matched replacements.

Again we return to an essential driver of the film's content and its appeal: the jarring of time frames that we experienced in *City of Angels,* of incompatible temporal registers between mortals and immortals. In Dracula's domain any sense of linearity, of teleology, is denied, and it could be argued that the reason the vampire has become such a frequent subject of film may stem from the relationship they share to the subject of immortality, since both the vampire and the cinema display an ability to 'transcend both time and space, cross the divide between life and death, move between the invisible and the visible and travel freely within the spiritual and the material' (Bloom, 1998: 17). The presence of an actor on screen who might in real life have long been dead provides another dimension to this idea. Burch (1990: 12) sees the evolution of the cinema as descending from the 'great Frankensteinian dream', that is, that through the creation of life the power of death is vanquished.

In its appropriation of a very familiar subject *Interview with the Vampire* is sensitive in recognising a fundamental change in audience's perceptions: that they are more knowing, less easy to convince and are steeped in the scepticism of the late twentieth century. In readdressing the problem of the vampire myth, emphasis is now placed upon the vampire's subjectivity, mirrored by a narrative structure that sees the tale told entirely from the vampire's point of view. This approach destabilises preconceptions built upon previous encounters with the genre and, as a result, establishes a closer relationship between the viewer and the vampire himself. Through such positioning, the vampire becomes more empathetic, more explicable. When the original *Dracula* was written, it played with our primal fear of the dark: a world where, pre-electricity, the familiar easily slips into the strange and haunting. Today 'the dark' extends its remit; it functions as a metaphor for everything out of our control, including our obsession with ageing. Indeed, it is eternity that the vampire Lestat offers the mortal Louis: 'you can be young, always', he states. The actual transformation of Louis into a vampire is highly visceral, involving agonising changes to the body, but this is not the only pain Louis will endure. Immortality brings its own eventual penance: ennui followed by despair.

As Wenders' angel wished to become a part of history as opposed to simply being an observer and recorder, so Louis wishes to re-enter history, to belong to something from which he is now detached. The telling of his story is his way of doing this, while simultaneously his extended autobiography provides the narrative path. Throughout this narrative it is the journalist, as mortal, who makes us aware of the passing of time in the present, glancing at his watch, telling Louis that it is still early, merely ten o'clock. Such temporal specificity jars awkwardly with a story that is told from the viewpoint of eternity. In this late-twentieth-century rendition of the vampire myth many of the traditional norms of the genre have been deconstructed. Here there are no dark alleys, crucifixes or garlic. At one point, as Louis tells of his travels to seek out other vampires, the journalist asks, 'So there are no vampires in Transylvania, no Count Dracula?' Louis replies, 'Fictions my friend. The vulgar fictions of a demented Irishman.' Instead, Louis defines himself as follows: 'I'm flesh and blood, but not human. I haven't been human for 200 years.' In this vein the mise-en-scène, resonant of the sumptuous approach taken by Coppola in his

Figure 8. *Interview with the Vampire* – Geffen Pictures

vampire tale, concentrates not on the darkness but on light, on the minutiae of daily existence. For while vampires play the piano, shop and go to the theatre, over time their immortality creates a very low threshold of boredom and they are constantly seeking out new avenues of enjoyment. Thus in a highly reflexive moment late in the film, Louis comments on the pleasure that the invention of the cinema has brought, enabling him to see the sun rise once again, albeit on screen. The world around them changes: new inventions, new technologies, new political struggles arise but they do not age. In this context the challenges of immortality are interestingly brought to the fore. Louis' loneliness is temporarily filled by the vampire-child, Claudia, but she eventually dies, showing that vampires too may cease to endure, through fire, dismemberment or exposure to sunlight. Claudia also personifies the detriments of an immortal existence for, while in humans the body is important as a site that marks our passage into adulthood, she is a child who can never grow up, her physical form remaining consistent as the years pass by. At a point of utter despair, expressing her frustration at constantly being dressed like a doll, she cries: 'Can't I change like everybody else?' In fury she cuts her hair but it immediately grows back. The trade-off for never growing old, she realises, is that she will never grow up. Even Armand, the oldest vampire in the world at 400, sees immortality as a 'penitential sentence' (Rice, 1996: 306).

As Wenders used angels to comment on the fears and anxieties embedded within contemporary human nature, so the vampire is Jordan's vehicle for such ontological questioning, this time specifically focusing on the drive for immortality. In order that this might successfully be attained, Louis is fundamentally humanised and, as we noted earlier, his character attracts empathy and engagement with his plight. Unlike Dracula, who recreates himself as mist, wolf and bat, in Louis the distinctive character traits that should define him as a vampire become fundamentally problematic. He never truly renounces that which defines one as human, and this is epitomised in the telling of his story and articulation of personal memories, often underpinned by high levels of emotion. Becoming a vampire is accompanied by the agonising death of the human body and with it the supposed trappings of mortality but for Louis such a transition is never totally complete. So is immortality to be striven for? The journalist thinks so: 'What I wouldn't give to be like you!' Louis feels that the purpose of his narrative, to highlight its dangers, torments and tragedies, has been severely misunderstood.

We have discussed the reassuring figure of the angel, appearing at moments of historical uncertainty and anxiety, cinematically evidencing a belief that circulates within the collective unconscious that someone is watching over us. That this figure has taken an increasingly secular turn demonstrates that while our religious faith might have dwindled we do still believe in 'something'. If angels represent a controlling influence at times of temporal discord then the vampire functions as master of time itself. As the population lives for longer but refuses to let age leave its traces on the body, so the vampire's popularity circulates as a figure not only of possibilities but also of lamentations. That we all must die, that the guardian angel's work is not absolute and that immortality, despite scientific progress, remains a fiction takes us into consideration of the domain beyond this world: the afterlife.

The affective journey towards the afterlife is dramatically depicted in Adrian Lyne's *Jacob's Ladder* (1990). Here the space beyond this earth is not simply a void but becomes an active site, a battleground for the forces of good and evil in determining the passage of the deceased to either a heaven or a hell. That such a battle should be taking place at the point of each person's death makes the film highly disturbing. In Lyne's hands the state of transition to the next life forms the whole of the narrative drive and stands in contrast to its deft symbolic representation in the form of a tunnel in *What Dreams May Come,* discussed next. *Jacob's Ladder* was made in 1990, the same year as *Ghost* (Zucker) and *Flatliners* (Schumacher), films that also deal with the afterlife. However in contrast to these softer renditions, here 'death is a frightening experience only so long as one clings to life; when one finally makes peace with the inevitable, then what appeared to be malevolent demons are actually angels guiding one to the other side' (Biodrowski, 1991: 52). Jacob's refusal to accept death informs the plot of the film and, as the protagonist's point of view is the only one we have, this, along with a highly fragmented narrative structure, creates an overall sense of temporal instability. This is the time of dying. In this highly destabilising narrative, the audience is never sure what is real and what is not; one moment we are in the jungle in Vietnam, Jacob blinks and when his eyes reopen he is on a subway train at night. Through such an effective use of cutting, Jacob's movements are made highly confusing and the choices he makes seem arbitrary and irrational. Only at the end of the film do we realise that rational activity as a driving force is inconsequential, when we learn that much that was inexplicable needs to be recontextualised in relation to Jacob's dying. Jacob's visions are fuelled by his existence in a transitory state positioned somewhere between this world and the next. Throughout the film, visions of heaven and hell are located firmly within this world, and demons are subliminal images on a screen which the audience peers at to try and make out a significant form but which are never visible long enough to ascertain their true identity. Hell has many guises: a burning car, a subway train station that you cannot get out of and, in one of the most horrific scenes, a hospital in which Jacob is on a trolley being pulled by demons along a dismal, dirty and dark corridor. Lunatics and people with contorted bodies line the route while bloody human body parts litter the floor and impede the trolley's movements.

The flashback is an important mechanism throughout the film to produce temporal destabilisation as the past constantly invades the present. It has been used throughout cinema history and is clearly signalled to an audience to indicate past events that have a bearing on the unfolding of the narrative. However, as Anna Powell (2005: 175) argues, used here they have a much more disturbing effect as they 'are not distinguished by their difference from a solid level of fixed reality'. As we only have access to the world through Jacob's point of view, we struggle to locate what is real from what is a dream, fantasy or hallucination, what was then and what is now: Jacob in Vietnam; Jacob at home playing the family man; Jacob the postman. Consistency of characterisation is rendered problematic as a consequence of these factors, and Powell continues: 'viewed through the prism of Bergson and Deleuze, *Jacob's Ladder* is a journey through sheets of past that undermine the authenticity of the present' (ibid.: 180).

It is Jacob's guardian angel, his chiropractor, who rescues him from the demons' permanent grasp. The choice of occupation is significant as the chiropractor physically contorts Jacob's body while at the same time Jacob's visions push and pull the narrative into a similarly contorted form. A series of overhead shots of the patient, accompanied by a brilliant white light which illuminates his face, provides the atmospheric setting in which the chiropractor works. With his white gown and the light shining, celestial imagery is resonant. Even Jacob says to him that he looks like an 'overgrown cherub'. Such exaggerated and yet imaginative use of lighting consistently suggests Jacob's state of transition. In an early scene where Jacob is on a subway train, the lights go off and on intermittently, enshrouding him in temporary blackness. This is juxtaposed with a later image in which, as he stands on the platform, Jacob is lit up like a ghostly spectre by the dazzling lights of an approaching train. It is in the closing scene, however, that lighting, and the effective symbolic use of the staircase, suggests that Jacob's transition to the next world is being finally realised. Bright sunlight fills the room and Jacob is encouraged by the presence of his dead son to climb the stairs that lie before him. As he ascends so the light becomes brighter, so bright that it fills the screen only to dissolve into a light above an operating table which, when switched off by the doctor in charge, represents the death of the patient, who has, we are told, put up a very strong fight for his life.

As opposed to the use of lighting, it is the juxtaposition of colour and black-and-white stock that is employed to depict the differences between two worlds in another landmark 'film blanc', Powell and Pressburger's *A Matter of Life and Death* (1946). It was made at the end of World War II and speaks to the uncertain times that lie ahead, so it is easy to understand its popularity. With so many lives lost or unaccounted for, the idea that some form of afterlife might ensue was not too remote a concept. The attention to detail in this film, the consistent juxtaposition and indeed close proximity of this world and the next, would have made such a belief all the more 'real'. Film blanc can be defined as 'almost the mirror image of film noir' (Johnson, 1997: 71) not only in terms of their contrasting styles of darkness and light in the lighting techniques used, but also in their approach to the human psyche. Valenti (1978: 295) believes that a film can be classified as 'film blanc' when it is characterised by the following scenario: 'a mortal's death or lapse into a dream', followed by a 'subsequent acquaintance with a kindly representative of the world beyond, most commonly known as Heaven', often accompanied by a 'budding love affair' concluded by the 'return to the mortal world'. Such films centre upon the juxtaposition of altered states of existence between that of mortals and a world beyond which involves both spatial and temporal displacement. In view of this, these films rely on the cinematic principle of the suspension of disbelief taken to the extreme. *A Matter of Life and Death* remains the quintessential film of this genre.

The establishing shot is unusual in that it is a still of the heavens with the following inscription on the screen:

This is a story of
two Worlds
the one which we know
and another
which exists only in the mind
of a young airman
whose life & imagination
have been
violently shaped by war

A voice-over introduces us to the universe, providing the viewer with a number of scientific facts as the camera weaves us in and out of stars and planets. A close-up of the earth follows, then Europe, and then the English coast covered in fog. It is World War II. We have problems determining what exactly it is we see before us as the fog encircles the frame. Confusion continues and the voice of a woman interjects. We cut to an aeroplane on fire with one dead body already on board and with Peter Carter (David Niven) reciting poetry as the aeroplane goes down. At this stage Peter tells the radio controller, June, that he plans to jump, but that he has no parachute; it is as though the film should end at this point as the odds of survival are surely not in his favour. As he prepares to jump he jokes about his lack of parachute, playing with traditional angelic imagery: 'I'll have my wings soon anyway, big white ones. I hope they haven't gone all modern, I'd hate to have a prop instead of wings.' As he falls through the sky a series of cuts then take us from a body lying in the water, to black-and-white imagery of rows and rows of white wings that mirror the foam of the waves in which the body is enshrouded.

The shift to black and white is more permanent as we encounter Bob, the dead co-pilot of the mission, awaiting the arrival of his colleague in an entrance hall with soldiers and airmen passing through. It seems that what has saved Peter Carter from death, argues Christie (2000: 10), is a 'bureaucratic mistake of the kind only too familiar to those who had lived through the war with uncertain news of loved ones' fate'. The clerk explains the administrative procedure as they peer over a vast labyrinth of records, one for each person currently alive on earth. We cut again to the earth, and back to Technicolor, as Peter opens his eyes and a low-angle shot presents a view of the sky, the first of a series of linking shots that connect this world to the one above. Peter thinks he is in Heaven with an angel as he sees a young, naked shepherd boy playing a flute. This image turns out to be more representative of traditional angelic imagery than any others encountered throughout the film. As we cut again to the 'world above' we become aware of a monumental problem. The records do not balance as Conductor 71 has lost a person in the fog, complicated by the fact that during this 'borrowed time' the person in question has fallen in love. The Conductor is to go to earth to explain his error and escort the missing person back with him. Matters, however, do not prove to be that simple.

Michael Powell, in his autobiography, draws attention to the exactness of terminology used on set, with the word 'Heaven' to be avoided (1986: 487). In another clever linking shot of the two worlds, the Conductor looks down at the black-and-white flower in his lapel that dissolves into a close-up shot of a pink rose on earth. As the camera tracks back, he reflects how 'one is starved for Technicolor up there'. The Conductor is in a garden full of rhododendrons. This will be his first meeting with Peter and time is frozen while they converse. Nothing moves, nothing changes and, above all, no one else is aware of the events taking place. 'We are talking in space not in time', says the Conductor – the temporal frame of immortality. In contrast, he explains, Peter should be dead as 'your time was up'. On the second occasion that a meeting takes place, June and Peter's doctor are playing table tennis. The camera moves

Figure 9. *A Matter of Life and Death* – ITV Global Entertainment

quickly in a series of shot/reverse shots, followed by a long shot of both players visible at either end of the table when suddenly the image is frozen. This
situation astounds Peter as he observes the ball suspended in the air. As Sutton
observes:

> The table tennis sequence is an uncanny illustration of the difference
> between the organization of time and our experience of it. The tick-tock
> sound of the ball as it is passed from player to player is abruptly stopped,
> ball in mid-air, as if a clock were stopped. Time itself appears to be inter-
> rupted and the present exists only as internal experience. What is left is the
> time of Carter's mind as he argues and debates with his conductor. Time,
> no longer governed by movement or sound, is simply duration: as long or as
> short an impression of being as it needs to be. (Sutton, 2005: 52)

While the differentiation between the two worlds centres predominantly on
contrasting film stock, how these two realms are brought together is symbolised by a moving staircase, the central motif of the film. The significance of
the staircase was emphasised in the United States where the film was released
under the title *Stairway to Heaven.* The staircase is a physical link between
worlds, one that Peter rides up as preparations for his trial take place: a trial
that he needs to win to secure his future in the world of mortals. Further links
between these worlds are then made through the simultaneous sets of activities
in advance of Peter's trial. On earth he undergoes an operation to remove what
is possibly a brain tumour. Angelic nurses surround his bedside and a low angle
shot of Peter looking up at the bright single light of the operating theatre gives
the scene an ethereal quality. The camera is inside his eyelids as they close and
the image of the light is replaced by the colours of the eye's interior, reds, pinks
and then white which dissolves into the clouds as we rise above them to witness
thousands of ant-like figures walking towards the trial. In the third meeting
of the Conductor and Peter on earth they are at this operating table, building
evidence for Peter's trial. June, standing at the window, is perceived as frozen,
as are Peter's body and the medical staff that surround him. Peter eventually
wins his trial, his operation is a success and a new date for his arrival 'above' is
ascertained.

The film originated from an invitation in 1944 by Jack Beddington, the Head
of the Ministry of Information's film division, to make a movie which would
engender stronger Anglo-American relationships. Powell and Pressburger rose
to the challenge in a quite extraordinary way but the film was received harshly
by British critics on the basis that it did not adopt the common currency of

the time, realism. However, what is identifiably real is the overall message of the film. By depicting earth in Technicolor and heaven in black and white, the message is about seizing life: that despite evident difficulties, the mortal world is the place to be. In a wider context, Powell has been fashionably dismissed by critics as a '"technicians' director", a virtuoso of the special effect, with a joltingly uneven story sense, for whom a narrative was only an invisible thread permitting the startling juxtaposition of visual beads' (Durgnat, 1978: 65). Interestingly this is the same criticism that had earlier been launched at Georges Méliès and indeed there seem to be many parallels in their work, such as the emphasis that is placed on fantasy and spectacle, and especially the debt that Michael Powell pays to the influence of Surrealism over realism in his autobiography. However, I would argue that the narrative at the centre of this film is hardly an 'invisible thread' but rather, from the opening sequence, it posits a very firm world view. That is to say, the documentary style adopted as we tour the universe sets the tone for the rest of the film: that there is an order and structure over and above anything that goes on in this world of ours which if disrupted requires immediate resolution. In his autobiography Powell emphasises how he did *not* want to depict the 'Other World': 'I threw out all the double-exposures and ghosts waving curtains' and instead attempted to 'make each world as real as the other' (1986: 497). The documentary style used to depict this other world, accompanied by the monochrome film stock for all such sequences, sets up a certain detachment between the spectator and what is visible on the screen, underlining the orderliness of the organisation of the other world as something beyond human intervention. This can then be contrasted with the use of colour for events here on earth where a 'strong emotional response' is engendered (Ellis, 1978: 94).

In order to successfully contain the narrative across two worlds, the selective use of Technicolor and monochrome is not the only device employed. Rather, significant characters in the film complement this linking strategy. The Conductor's role is obvious, but more subtle is the character of Dr Reeves, whose premature death enables him to represent Peter at his trial. Thus, what is presented as the greatest challenge in this film, and is successfully achieved throughout, is the negotiation of the visual representation of two very different worlds: that of the mortal and that of the spiritual, while at the same time sustaining a high level of narrative continuity that enables both worlds to be depicted as equally real. Therefore, rather than being subservient to technical wizardry, a strong, highly complex narrative is present. On the one hand there is a linear narrative running throughout, that Peter must win his trial in order to stay on earth and be with June, yet at the same time this narrative is consistently fractured by the Conductor who personifies the intervention and interruption of one world by another. Such interruptions have significant temporal consequences as the meetings take place in the fourth dimension. Powell has said that in researching for the film he called on the assistance of a surgeon who explained how pressures on various parts of the brain can produce highly organised hallucinations which can be comparable to real-life experiences, illusions which can 'take place in space but *not* in time'. Therefore what occurs is a highly detailed incident but taking place in 'the thousandth of a fraction of a second' (Badder, 1978–79: 12, his emphasis). This has been termed TLE or temporal lobe epilepsy.

A Matter of Life and Death is interesting for the figure of Peter Carter and the specific condition he finds himself in. Positioned between two worlds uniquely allows for an exploration of alternative representations of time. The time of the social, of chronological time, is allowed to stand in contrast with a much more personal, experiential dimension of time thus presenting 'the two simultaneous actions as separate, where they would normally interpenetrate' (Sutton, 2005: 60). For much of the film Carter is in limbo, but what of cinematic representations of those who pass over into an afterlife, a world distinctly beyond this one? In Greek mythology, Hades is the abode of the dead, taking its name from its ruler. The dead descended to Hades as shades or phantoms, mere semblances of their living selves, deprived of bodies and consciousness. In Christian theology, the word 'Heaven' denotes a sense of physical location, the dwelling place of God and the angels, although as the Old Testament acknowledges the Heavens cannot actually contain God as he is omnipresent. Another commonly cited conception is that of a 'seven-layered heaven', deriving from both Sumerian and Hebrew scholarship. Features of this hierarchical structure include the 'Third Heaven' where Hell is believed to be situated, and the 'Seventh Heaven', the abode of God. With such a variety of material to draw upon it would seem that there need be no consistent depiction of Heaven on the screen, but in fact there emerges a high degree of consensus. One characteristic feature of Heaven is that film-makers have seemed to overplay the idea of its bureaucracy although the fact that God is both omnipotent and omniscient results in there being no real need for him to adopt the role of head of an organisation. That angels have most frequently been depicted throughout the history of art as messengers of God is possibly where such a bureaucratic conception originates. *What Dreams May Come* (Vincent Ward, 1998) takes eternity as its subject matter and in this film we learn as much about life as death, in that our visions of Heaven and Hell feed off what informs our daily lives. However, in contrast to the consensus of representations of the afterlife in the post-war period, here we create, on death, single or shared universes formulated out of our most precious thoughts, memories and fantasies. Reflecting perhaps a more secular vision of the afterlife, nothing is pre-ordained. Age and identity are interchangeable in this version of Heaven, allowing us to be whoever we want to be: avatars, indeed. Personal creativity becomes the watchword of daily existence and whatever brought us the most joy in our lives forms the basis of all that surrounds us in the afterlife.

A more recent depiction of Heaven to reach our screens is *The Lovely Bones* (Jackson, 2009) which tells the story of the afterlife of Susie Salmon. It centres on her experiences following her brutal murder and how she tries to come to terms with what has happened to her, especially in relation to arriving at a sense of permanent detachment from her former life on earth. As an audience we sympathise with Susie's frustrations to 'get through', to connect. That no one can see or hear her is something she struggles to deal with in the initial stages of her transposition. Yet this is no ghost film. At no point does Susie come back to earth in spectre-like form. On death, Susie's spirit runs back home but it is still embodied. However the streets she runs through change; a menacing blue glow indicates an altered relationship to the spaces she previously occupied and indeed the imaginative use of lighting will once again become a central leitmotif. The film is of specific interest to this chapter for the way in which the director, Peter Jackson, seeks to visually portray the stages that one might pass through on death. He considers the representation of transitional spaces as 'the in between'. The first such space is the bathroom of her killer, Mr Harvey, which is permeated by a brilliant white light. On the floor lie heavily bloodied clothes. As Susie aggregates the signs assembled before her she lets out a piercing scream. Sound morphs into colour and the screen is suffused by whiteness. The initial idea presented around this journey to the afterlife is that once the body has stopped functioning, one's spirit needs to review and adapt. This can take some time.

Against this brilliant white backdrop we now see shooting stars and fireworks and an outline of a body bathed in and effusing an energising glow. The body falls and lands in beautiful green fields, with mountains and cornfields drenched in hyper-saturated colours. To guide her in this next phase she meets a companion, Holly, who informs her that the ultimate place of rest is 'wide, wide Heaven' but we can only reach there when we have come to terms with our own demise and severed all links with earth. Much of the narrative is made up of Susie trying to connect with those that were closest to her, thereby forfeiting the opportunity to move on. Her greatest success is with her little brother, Buckley, and with Ruth Connor, who has extraordinary visions of what happens in the afterlife but whose character is much more developed in the original novel by Alice Sebold. How Jackson perceives this 'in between' space is as follows: 'It's a very surreal world made up of elements of her life and memory, things that she saw on television, things she experienced, and things she was looking forward to but never got to do. It's not some universal viewpoint of what heaven is like' (*Empire*, 2009: 30). The fact that each transitional space is unique marks its function. We each have to come to terms with our passing in our own individual ways, so to represent it with any sense of uniformity would omit the nuances involved in this process of detachment. As a result the 'in between' space functions for the deceased in the same way as mourning does for the living: 'we rely on it being overcome after a certain period of time, and consider interfering with it to be pointless, or even damaging' (Freud, 1917/2006: 311).

As her moods change so does the backdrop of her creation: grey, dark and barren, for example, as she observes her father's beating as he goes in search of her killer. Here Jackson illuminates the complexities of the spirit: that it has feelings and responds to events it sees on earth but is frustrated through the impossibility of intervention. In terms of the temporal dimension of this limbo she occupies we learn that 'The days were unchanging and every night I dreamed the same dream': that is to say, she relives her death. But while she does not age and time appears as an enduring loop, an eternal return, on earth life progresses in linear form. A significant moment comes towards the end of the film when all of Harvey's victims gather together in the radiant cornfield, the location of her death, ready to transport Susie to 'wide, wide, Heaven'. But Susie is not ready: she turns her back on them because she still has two things to do before she can finally accept closure. Occupying the body of Ruth Connor she fulfils her desire to be with her first love, Ray. Secondly, she witnesses the eventual demise of her killer. Poignantly Susie articulates that, 'Nobody notices when we leave, I mean the moment when we truly choose to go.' The screen fades to white and Susie moves on. However, it could be argued that while Jackson is sensitive to Sebold's adaptation, to the nuances of the personalisation of the afterlife, therein lies the rub. For in seeking to visualise what each individual's transitional journey might be like so it becomes more spectacle than spiritual.

One of the most remarkable insights into the power of cinema early in its history was its capacity to transcend death. This occurs at several different levels. Firstly, via mechanical reproduction, we are able to see a film over and over again and secondly, those that appear on screen do not age despite the passing of time. Thirdly, that which has ceased to exist in the real world can continue to be viewed in its spectral form on screen. For the Surrealists the cinema put us directly into contact with 'an occult life' produced in a 'trance-like atmosphere' (Artaud, 1972: 66). This highly 'spiritual' sense of cinema emerges directly out of the spirit photography of the 1880s. Spiritualism shares in common with the cinema an ability to disrupt the temporal continuum by bringing the past into the present through the summoning up of the deceased. As the work of Marey and Muybridge demonstrated, the camera has the ability to show that which the human eye cannot see and, while deemed as a scientific instrument in this context, its use by spirit photographers demonstrated that it can also be allied to the highly irrational. Spirit photography was welcomed by spiritualists as 'scientific proof' that the afterlife existed. Méliès' subsequent adaptation of these principles through films such as *The Spiritualist Photographer* illustrates the complex relationship between photography, the spirit world and the development of motion pictures. That many still believe in a spirit world, of someone or something guiding us through life, is documented in the films considered here, although it is interesting to note both the change in form and ambition of the contemporary angel represented. While some identify with these symbols of protection, others seek to embrace more of life's possibilities. As Dorian Gray, over a century ago, showed the price to be paid in pursuit of immortality nevertheless the quest remains enticing. The contemporary Gothic takes the body, rather the house or the castle, as the site of danger, its violation coming not from an outside source but from within, challenged by disease, illness and, most significantly, age. 'We are resistant to the thought that we might become old, and have difficulty consequently forming an empathy for the aged ... in fact we might say that we find difficulty empathizing with our own process of aging because we subjectively cling to an image of ourselves as unchangingly young' (Turner, 1995: 250).

FRACTURED TIME

In tandem with the standardisation of time across the railway network during the 1870s was the quest to realise a universal measure to coordinate working patterns following the spread of industrialisation. Clock-time was adopted as a functional standard in that it could be adapted to any mode of work. Fundamentally its appeal lay in the fact that it engendered precision while denying interpretation. In *Time, Work-Discipline and Industrial Capitalism* ([1967] 1991) E.P. Thompson argues that the current Western approach to time, quantitative in nature, was fuelled by the Industrial Revolution which saw a shift from agrarian to factory-based industry. Inextricable from this was a reconceptualisation of the perception of work's relationship to temporality, as 'tasks to be completed' were replaced by an idea of 'time as currency'. Thompson commences his analysis by problematising the impact of the appearance of the clock: 'how far, and in what ways, did this shift in time-sense affect labour discipline, and how far did it influence the inward apprehension of time of working people?' (ibid.: 354). As individuals began to work for others, as opposed to working for themselves, 'time-discipline' became a requirement (ibid.: 388). Such temporal standardisation was not only to impact upon film form but also upon the pastime of cinema-going. As trade unions began to take up the issue of the number of hours in the working week, this simultaneously had an effect on the number of hours left for leisure time. And leisure could not escape the pervasiveness of clock-time, either, as the birth of mass entertainment, firstly theatre and later cinema, became structured around a definitive set of screening times. In conjunction with this development, as we saw in Chapter 3, the Surrealists adopted subversive tactics to deny such organised viewing by running between cinemas at will.

In this seminal essay on time, Thompson (1991) documented how our relationship to work had fundamentally changed with the introduction of the clock instead of the completion of tasks being based on available light. So the introduction of the factory system, made efficient through the findings and implementation of time and motion studies, saw productivity measured on the basis of the completion of a certain amount of work per hour. Bergson also highlighted the negative impact of industrialisation: how standardisation led to the spatialisation of time and in so doing negated any sense of the nuances of time as experienced by the individual subject. Man experienced depersonalisation and de-humanisation through engagement with conveyor-belt technologies. As the twentieth century progressed, this temporal regime intensified and continued relentlessly despite the change to the economic base and the onset of the post-industrial age. Somehow, a relationship to time centred on the intensification of activity has continued. 'We now try to pack every moment full of activities as experiences – at work, at home and at leisure. In the process, the ways in which we think about time as well as use it are being warped into new configurations' (Florida, 2002: 144). Now, in the twenty-first century, I would argue, how we perceive and engage with time has reached new qualitative levels: our sensitivity towards time has become heightened and our responses to it, more emotionally charged. Fundamental in terms of influencing these changes is the introduction and proliferation of ICTs (information and communication technologies). As a result, the adoption of specific strategies has arisen to allow for time management in the seemingly extended present. Florida draws our attention to one of these strategies known as 'time-deepening' (ibid.). Here, if we cannot elongate time then perhaps we can deepen it, intensify it. Essentially this involves engaging with activities that take less time to complete or where more than one task can be done at the same time: we operate in life as we would on screen, keeping multiple windows open to enable effective multi-tasking. Increasingly people are configuring time to suit their own requirements, drawing on virtual culture considerably to do so. This Lash and Urry term 'social desynchronization' and categorise it as follows: 'There is a greatly increased variation in different people's times. They are less collectively organized and structured as mass consumption patterns are replaced by more varied and segmented patterns' (1994: 246). In summary, we are witnessing the acceptance of new temporal strategies. While appropriating a sense of temporal deepening from the era of early mass production, practices have now become more individualised as we struggle to negotiate life, work and play. As a result, I would argue, this has produced specific challenges to the representation of time on screen, leading to the espousal of high levels of innovation in narrative practice, representing a sense of time that is more personalised and nuanced. In the first part of this chapter, I will consider how these more varied timeframes are realised in cinema and will adopt a highly interdisciplinary approach to reach some answers. In the second part, I will discuss specific examples of films that demonstrate how cinema reflects this rupture in temporal experience whereby flow is replaced by fracture.

Cameron (2008) has drawn attention to what he terms the 'puzzle film' which suddenly populated cinematic discourse in the late twentieth century. Such films are worthy of study not only in terms of considering why such a cluster of films structured in similar ways should appear at a specific moment in cinematic history, but also for the way in which they were characterised by the fractured narratives that constitute them. The puzzles emerge, I believe, as a reflection of the ways in which Florida documented how we are beginning to not only think differently about time but also about how we use it, warping it into new configurations. These films derive their popularity as they offer 'more entertainment value per unit of time' (Florida, 2002: 180) as the puzzle film requires that we work while we watch, opening up the possibility for new forms of spectator engagement. Our concentration remains heightened as each shot is loaded with potential: every sign could be a clue, every piece of dialogue potentially critical to the narrative's unfolding. We are not simply consuming a film but an experience. As Lash and Urry demonstrated, time is now fractured and experienced in a highly subjective manner. The variations in how people manage and coordinate time, frequently with the assistance of ICTs, offer up the potential for stories to be told in a multiplicity of ways. Furthermore, through the adoption of non-linear structures, as appropriated in the films discussed in this chapter, a second dynamic filters through our reading. Ultimately, the narrative is no longer perceived as omnipotent; as in life it is subject to many contingencies, consistently informed by the role of chance and coincidence. On the one hand, such films speak to a generation brought up on non-linear media like video games, but the films under discussion also have the potential to speak to a broader church: 'if you look at such works by old criteria, these movies may seem more fragmented, but the fragments exist so that consumers can make the connections in their own time and in their own ways' (Jenkins, 2008: 121).

Many critics have noted a turn within popular cinema since the 1990s that centres on the increasing complexity of the narrative presented. Cameron (2008: 1) refers to such films as offering a 'database aesthetic in which the narrative is divided into discrete segments and subjected to complex articulations'. A central feature of such films, which Cameron groups under the heading of 'modular narratives', is the foregrounding of the relationship between 'the temporality of the story and the order of its telling' (ibid.) as represented by *A Night on Earth* (Jarmusch, 1991), *Pulp Fiction* (Tarantino, 1994) and *The Usual Suspects* (Singer, 1995). Other films, such as *Jacob's Ladder* and *12 Monkeys,* discussed previously in this book, also have the potential to be considered under this heading. So why this specific narrative turn at this moment in cinema history? The influence of television on cinema is significant as we have been conditioned to a viewing experience punctuated by advertising and the mobilisation of the remote control. Cameron suggests that such films tie in with the wider dispersal of computers and digital consumer technologies and, as a consequence, 'digitality has arguably shaped the cultural landscape in which these films are produced and make meaning' (ibid.). Our intervention with hypertext places emphasis on narrative construction based on individual choices. The user becomes master of time and, as a result, this database approach to storytelling has now been embraced by cinema. The films under consideration here derive their appeal from the need to navigate the narrative, a recognition that we must work at meaning following a breakdown in narrative sequence. Such an approach maps onto a sense of uncertainty in our own understanding of the recognised temporal order which in itself is informed by the rise of online global communications. Therefore, it can be argued, these films reflect a new projection of time and watching them, and working through their narratives, allows for the literal and figurative provision of a space in which we can begin to make sense of this new temporal regime. Innovations in narrative practice present the viewer with an opportunity to reconsider their own experiences of time. They arise at a point in history when our sense of temporality is in a state of flux and provide a vehicle through which such concerns can be represented and subsequently discussed within both a cinematic and broader social context.

Characterised by what I term 'fractured narratives' the films that populate this chapter challenge Aristotle's demands for a structure with a beginning, middle and end but, more fundamentally, take as their starting point a departure from the norms of the traditional Hollywood classical narrative. The concept of 'classical Hollywood cinema' began to receive theoretical attention in the 1970s in journals such as *Screen*, but was given greater substance in two significant works: David Bordwell's (1995) *Narration in the Fiction Film* and Bordwell, Staiger and Thompson's (1996) *The Classical Hollywood Cinema: Film Style and Mode of Production to 1960*. Both texts refer to the domination of a highly specific mode of cinematic representation, established firmly in the Hollywood studio system and incorporating a specific set of cinematic codes through which narrative is constructed. These codes have their roots in the experimental period of cinema history, pre-1917, when developments in narrative construction saw no single model dominating storytelling, but which began to become standardised with the rise of the studio system. A common structural process in narrative construction therefore arises and is underpinned by a model consisting primarily of three stages which can broadly be defined as a state of equilibrium; a longer period, in terms of duration, of disruption; and a new state of equilibrium achieved at the point of closure. Prince (1973 cited in Mulvey, 1989: 170) identifies the three phases as providing the minimal framework for the successful construction of a narrative:

> A minimal story consists of three conjoined events. The first and third are stative, the second is active. Furthermore, the third is the inverse of the first. Finally, the three events are conjoined by three conjunctive features, in such a way that (a) the first event precedes the second in time and the second precedes the third, and (b) the second event causes the third.

A number of theorists have sought to describe the large-scale symmetries that draw together and unify the parts of a narrative. Vladimir Propp's ([1928] 1968) seminal study of the narrative construction of the Russian fairytale, *Morphology of the Folktale,* emphasises its linearity, its transformative processes linked like a chain from function to function and its essential symmetry between the beginning and the end. Tzvetan Todorov (1971: 39), like Propp, argues that narrative in its most basic form is a causal transformation of a situation, in this case through five stages, whereby the changes of state are not random but are produced according to principles of cause and effect and derive out of the need to repair the disruption brought about in the opening state of equilibrium. Such 'classical' models impacted the formation of the Hollywood narrative and have subsequently had a determining effect on much seen on screen. Many of Hitchcock's films, *North by Northwest* (1959), for example, centre on a misunderstanding, a false identification, which destabilises the world of the hero but which achieves a new state of stability at the point of closure, often involving a new love interest. The 'happy ending' becomes a predominant 'fixture' in films adopting this narrative format (Bordwell, 1982: 2).

This model of narrative construction is supported by a style of filmmaking dominated by continuity editing, used to efface the moment of transition between shots without disrupting the narrative flow and allowing for the suspension of disbelief by removing the artifice of the means of representation (Bordwell, Staiger and Thompson, 1996: 46). Such codes and conventions of editing articulate a particular representation of time, one that is flowing, coherent and essentially linear (ibid.: 22, 43, 65). Time is subordinated to the cause-and-effect chain of events and only happenings of causal importance are shown, while all 'dead time' is simply cut away. As a result, continuity editing contributes towards the construction of a specific illusion of time while simultaneously creating the conditions for an audience's suspension of disbelief. That is to say, the representation of time as embraced by the classical Hollywood narrative model helps to support a standardised way of perceiving time as introduced during the last decades of the nineteenth century and which peaked in the industrialised setting of Fordist production techniques on which the studio system was founded.

The above analysis has surveyed the way in which it is important to recognise that time, 'at least as we understand and use it, has been modelled by humanity and is, in effect, a human creation' (Mandelbrote, 1996: 338). Filmmakers tapped into the constructed nature of time, recognising that through the use of editing, it had the potential to be controlled. In so doing, a particular approach to film-making practice, namely the adoption of the classical Hollywood narrative model, reinforced the idea of a standard time governing and uniting simultaneous events. O'Malley (1992) parallels such developments in editing techniques to those developed by Taylor in his time-and-motion studies. Where wasted effort was cut out in the production process, so editing omitted that which was superfluous to the cause-and-effect logic of the narrative structure. One interesting observation on this changing relationship between the visual and the temporal is provided by Miriam Hansen (1987) in her analysis of the concept of 'aura' in Walter Benjamin's seminal essay of 1935, *The Work of Art in the Age of Mechanical Reproduction*, which considers the way in which art is produced, distributed and received. Hansen approaches Benjamin's argument through the concept of 'confrontation', that is to say, of his recognition of 'the transformation of experience in industrial society (of which the cinema was both symptom and agent) against traditional notions of art, in particular a belated cult of *l'art pour l'art*' (1987: 182). Here the status of art is affected by reproduction techniques which specifically result in the loss of aura that accompanied an original and gave it a cult status, with Benjamin defining aura as 'the unique phenomenon of a distance, however close it may be' ([1935] 1992: 216). It is around the concept of distance that Hansen's work on the decline of the aura concentrates, but where the relationship between the visual and the temporal, rather than any conception of spatial distance, is foregrounded. Embedded within the concept of aura is a certain experiential dimension of the temporal which undergoes fundamental changes following the birth of cinema. For Benjamin cinema reproduces temporal experiences that are qualitatively mirrored in the new spatio-temporal relations of modernity engendered by industrialisation, where editing becomes the aesthetic equivalent to conveyor-belt production techniques, and where time is treated in a standardised way. By reducing such a comparison to the workplace, not only is 'the bourgeois cult of art' subverted but also a sense of temporal distance embedded within the concept of aura is removed (Hansen, 1987: 184). Importantly, however, Hansen argues, there are suggestions in Benjamin's essay of a remaining auratic presence which takes new forms via certain modes of cinematic production such as time-lapse and slow-motion photography which engender alternative modes of temporal understanding. Friedberg (1994: 48) also points to the way in which Benjamin recognised how cinema could transform time through the technique of slow motion, leading to temporal distension. This brings about the 'discontinuous return of an auratic mode of experience through the backdoor of the "optical unconscious"' (Hansen, 1987: 212), first introduced in Benjamin's 1931 essay, *A Short History of Photography* (1979).

While 'the classic narrative is a historically contingent form, one road out of several that could have been taken' (Lapsley and Westlake, 1992: 130), I would argue that as O'Malley and Hansen have indicated, the industrialised nature of film-making, as embraced by the Hollywood studio system, is a significant factor in accounting for its domination. Both Fordist production techniques and the classical narrative model incorporated a specific standardised representation of time that had gained widespread significance throughout society following industrialisation. Standardisation in film-making practices came via script-writing manuals, trade papers and the studio system itself which combined to set up an institutional discourse as to the correct way a story should be told. However, following the shift to horizontal integration and the adoption of post-Fordist film-making practices, one of the central innovations to emerge was an increase in the number of directors who began to challenge these standardised representations of time through the utilisation of experimental forms of narrative structure which slowly began to encroach upon mainstream cinema. Indeed, Cowie (1998: 178) draws attention to the way these innovations actually began to take shape much earlier on in Hollywood history. She questions, for example, the way in which Bordwell, Staiger and Thompson (1996) fuse together 'classical narrative' and 'classical Hollywood', with the former being only one possible feature of the latter rather than being synonymous with it. Cowie argues that classical narrative is only one aspect of classical Hollywood, the former relating to a mode of storytelling, the latter to a mode of production. Not all films, she argues, made during the time of classical Hollywood demonstrate the characteristics of the classical narrative form, and some in particular display distinct evidence of narrative fragmentation. Through her analysis of the Hollywood musical she outlines a genre characterised by stars such as Judy Garland who frequently burst into song, thereby disrupting the logic of cause and effect that dominates the narrative drive.

While early film-makers sought to capture an image of life on the screen, to preserve all the qualitative detail of that which passed in front of them, what they failed to capture was the exact temporal moment. A train arriving at a station can be projected again and again but the original moment of filming has been lost, time has moved on. The moment of production and that of consumption are not simultaneous. With the development of narrative, from Méliès onwards, cinema has sought not to capture the moment per se, but rather took a temporal turn in an attempt to represent the passing of time in the context of storytelling. That is to say, the spectator may be simultaneously aware of both narrative and temporality. One theorist who has turned his attention to this relationship, although not specifically addressing cinema, is Paul Ricoeur. Ricoeur (1980, 1984) provides a comprehensive theory of the relationship between language, narrative, discourse and temporality, which, I would argue, when applied to film has much to contribute towards new perspectives in narrative innovation. Ricoeur is particularly interested in how time is configured through the creation of narrative, how material is arranged into a narrative form not only to make sense of it but also so that in the process an experiential dimension becomes inscribed. Through his use of the term 'configurational narrative' he offers more possibilities for engaging with a multiplicity of times than through a more limited mode of representation depicted in the conventional 'arrow of time', with time flowing from the past into the future. In agreement with Heidegger, he dismisses the representation of time 'as a linear series of "nows" [which] hides the true constitution of time' (Ricoeur, 1980: 170). Rather, it is through 'emplotment' that Ricoeur sees the key to understanding the relationship between time and narrative, as the plots we invent provide an opportunity to 're-configure our confused, unformed, and at the limit mute temporal experience' (Ricoeur, 1984: xi). This process of reconfiguration converts time into human time via narrative construction while simultaneously allowing for the representation of time as something which is distinctly non-linear.

Therefore we might argue that traditionally fundamental differences have existed between the narratives we construct in our everyday lives and those represented in the fiction film, based on the premise that 'it only ever happens like that in the movies'. That gap however is slowly being eroded by alternative strategies which consistently encroach upon the mainstream. As a collective, these seek to counter a particular model of narrative that takes on board neither the 'experiential' dimension of Ricoeur's analysis nor the film-making practices described by Deleuze in relation to the 'time-image'. Such alternative models exist in opposition to the dominant, more widely utilised mode of storytelling, 'classical narration', whereby 'classicism in any art is traditionally characterised by obedience to extrinsic norms' (Bordwell, 1995: 164). In contrast, the fractured narratives under discussion here destabilise the temporal code embedded within this classical model. Temporal flow gives ways to discrete temporal units characterised by an overall sense of non-linearity. However, it is important to point out that this is not a completely new phenomenon, as I will show. Rather, what is distinctive to the 1990s is the number of these playful narrative constructions that permeate mainstream Hollywood cinema. For at particular moments in the history of the cinema a consensus arises in terms of temporal representation. This cannot be identified as collusion, as the films come out at the same time and therefore cannot be influenced by each other. So it could be argued that there must be something operating in the wider collective consciousness that informs how this consensus is derived. In the past decades, such alternative practices in relation to narrative composition have gained a more consolidated voice having been taken under the wing of the theoretical position of 'postmodernism'. I will discuss three categories of film that seek to counter the representation of time as conveyed by the classical Hollywood narrative model. In so doing, I shall foreground debates that show how innovations in narrative structure reflected perceptual changes towards the nature of temporality on the cusp of the last Millennium.

The recognition of a qualitative shift from dominant to alternative forms of narrative cinema may be said to take place where the underlying narrative structure no longer conforms to the classical model. Indeed, the pervasiveness of the classical model is in fact noticeable mainly through its violation (Bordwell, 1995: 37). As Ricoeur (1980: 69) similarly argues, we only notice innovation due to the establishment of narrative norms: 'Innovation remains a form of behaviour governed by rules. The labor of imagination is not born from nothing. It is bound in one way or another to the tradition's paradigms.' Thus innovation always works in relation to tradition, with tradition providing the framework for subversion and a context for new experimental developments. Alternative cinema contains a number of structural features that set such films apart from those based upon the classical narrative. These can include the organisation of the story along a non-linear basis permeated by unexpected turns and digressions, and the role of chance and coincidence having significant parts to play. Narrative closures can become problematic with an audience often left hanging.

Endings frequently fail to reach a point of resolution: this may be due to a weak causal chain which lacks the necessary human agency to move the narrative along or alternatively, the narrative may be centred on characters that do not seem psychologically well-rounded and hence prove difficult in terms of audience identification. Whereas classical narrative is based upon the principle of unified subjectivity and alternative practices which/that tend to treat human beings as perpetually in construction. Narratives such as these are frequently based on the creation of a fictional world assembled according to principles other than those based upon spatial and temporal verisimilitude. Finally, we can identify what might be called an anti-narrative, that is to say, one effective because of a negative dependence on the classical model, demonstrating an overt transgression of our knowledge of established narrative practices.

As we saw in Chapter 3, Dali and Bunuel had already destabilised audience expectations through their manipulation of early temporal indicators, namely intertitles. A more significant challenge came with 'modernist cinema' which 'self-reflexively seeks to estrange the viewer from the illusion of reality in order to make the viewer critically self-conscious of the values narrative logic would posit as "natural" and absolutely given' (Self, 1982: 33). The French 'New Wave' of the 1960s established itself as one tranche of the attack on the classical film language of Hollywood, in an offensive against 'the whole body of conventions which constitute the illusionist aesthetic' of narrative cinema (Hillier, 1992: 3). Film-makers appropriated the literary works of the nouveau roman in an attempt to overturn conventional modes of storytelling. One ground breaking example of this was Alain Resnais' (1961) adaptation of Robbe-Grillet's *L'Année dernière à Marienbad* which deconstructs the classical Hollywood narrative model in a number of ways. Firstly, it is embedded in ambiguity. As in Deleuze's description of the 'time-image', this film's effectiveness resides in the individual images themselves rather than any causal logic that binds them together. Throughout the film, the idea of the 'game' acts as a central metaphor, a game which in diegetic and extra-diegetic terms, no one but the initiated can win, for it is an intricate conundrum that mirrors the labyrinthine structure of the narrative itself. As individuals in the film repeatedly attempt to win the game, the spectator views the film again and again, seeking to unlock its central mystery.

From the outset Resnais' film destabilises how the audience traditionally builds a relationship with what appears on the screen. For example, there is no clear establishing shot. Rather, as we are plunged into the maze-like architecture of a building's interior, we hear a voice to which we cannot attach an identity. The use of the flashback is also manipulated to the point where we are not even sure if the events of the past ever really happened. As well as the challenging use of the flashback, there is constant temporal displacement. Time here is subject to construction in the same way as a plot or character might be constructed. Thus, by juxtaposing supposed events of a year ago so close and so frequently to those in the present, both time frames begin to merge, to the point where the only sense of time which is truly applicable is the time of viewing. Screen duration, the unfolding of events happening now in front of us, is the only temporal indicator we can be sure of. Thus what is created is an internal reality for which time and space have no referent in the outside world. No objective reality nor any sense of standardised time exists that the audience can relate to. Fundamentally, there can be no agreement on what actually happens on screen, as chronology and causality, the traditional linchpins of classical storytelling, have no part to play. And herein lies the weight of the film's impact for, as Robbe-Grillet himself states, to spend time on questions as to whether or not the couple really met last year is meaningless: 'The man and woman don't start to exist until they appear on the screen for the first time; before then they were nothing and the moment the film is over they are again nothing' (1965: 149).

If this film is characteristic of modern cinema, then what specific turn in cinematic storytelling constitutes 'the postmodern'? If we briefly consider the field of literary criticism, an area in which there has been much activity to define this term, it provides us with an insight into a series of debates which are useful in a comparative sense for the cinematic analysis of the term. Firstly, not only is the chronology deemed problematic but also which specific writers should actually be included under this heading is a challenge. Of even more interest, in terms of a comparative study, is the attempt to determine the essential features of postmodern writing. These seem to be essentially threefold: that it is a highly experimental literary form; that it is 'referential to literature itself rather than to human experience'; and finally, that it requires the reader's active participation as it is a self-conscious mode of literature that encourages the reader to think about the status of fictional things (Dipple, 1988: 9). However, when these criteria are taken separately, they are not so unique in the annals of literary history.

Firstly, the notion of being a highly experimental form is actually rooted in modernism. Waugh (1993: 21) sees a firm relationship established between the modern and the postmodern on the basis that both recognise a 'sense of crisis and loss of belief in an external authoritative system of order' and it is this sense of loss of rubric that opens the floodgates for high levels of experimentation. Indeed, Virginia Woolf wrote in her essay *Modern Fiction* ([1925] 1966: 110) that what was required was innovation with regard to the structure of the novel, that 'no "method", no experiment, even of the wildest – is forbidden'. In particular she challenged the idea of the supremacy of the linear narrative, remarking that life 'is not a series of gig-lamps symmetrically arranged' (Woolf, 1966: 106). Experimentation regarding an anti-linear style had appeared earlier, for example, in Raymond Roussel's *Impressions of Africa* (1910). Here we are presented with a highly fractured narrative of two parts: the first, a detailed series of spectacles performed by artists and magicians, the second, a flashback as to why all of this is happening. Fundamentally this is a novel in which progression is denied by a narrative which wraps around itself. But it is with the 'nouveau roman' that the term 'experimental' comes collectively to the fore. In *Towards a New Novel* (1965) Alain Robbe-Grillet, one of the pivotal figures of this movement, argues that writing is not about trying to attribute meaning to the world, for there is no universal objective reality, but rather it is about invention, about the production of a world that refers only to events in the novel itself. This allows for high levels of experimentation with regards to temporality for the denial of a universal conception of reality also denies any sense of a standardised conception of time. Such an approach to the writing of fiction becomes a collaborative project between writer and reader: if the work is a product of the imagination rather than a description of an external reality, then the reader must 'read' the book accordingly; one cannot simply draw upon events in the external world as a referent. The implications this poses for practices of viewing in relation to the films considered here are significant.

The two other most common distinguishing features of the 'postmodern' novel are deemed to be self-referentiality and the positive engagement of the reader in the production of the work. Both of these facets permeate the writing of Italo Calvino, whose work *If on a Winter's Night a Traveller* ([1979] 1992) provides a more definitive account of postmodern fiction, with Dipple citing it as 'the best example available' (1988: 107). It is a novel that subverts the traditional sense of narrative, if one considers 'traditional' in this context as the unfolding of a story around the tripartite structure of beginning, middle and end. Rather, this is a tale that keeps unravelling and restarting, a series of beginnings of other novels in a mixture of eclectic literary styles with no overall sense of progression or resolution. It is highly self-reflexive in that it is a book about books, about the reading and writing of books, even to the point where the characters are themselves readers and writers. Another highly self-referential and inter-textual novel about books is Arturo Pérez-Reverte's *The Dumas Club* (1996). Here, Corso, the central protagonist, finds it increasingly difficult to distinguish between his 'real' life and the events in books.

We too, as readers, constantly seek to demarcate which characters belong to which sphere, when in fact such demarcations are unnecessary as both worlds are the work of fiction. What might have appeared as a Diderot-like digression into literary analysis has in fact been for a purpose; namely to indicate that, in a discipline where there has been significant classificatory activity in seeking to define the postmodern, the results are far from conclusive. Thus when trying to assume the same approach to filmic texts, the problems encountered are similar, although it must be noted that film-makers themselves do not strive to make a 'postmodern' film, rather it is theorists who seek to apply such categorisation post-production.

While in the field of architecture Charles Jencks (1981) claims to be able to specifically define the emergence of postmodernism as commencing with the destruction of the Pruitt-Igoe housing project in St Louis on 15 July 1972 at 3.32P.M., such temporal specificity is certainly not transferable to film theory. Maureen Turim (1991: 182) is interested in the problematics of defining postmodernism *vis-à-vis* modernism in relation to cinema. She argues that to try and adopt a historical 'time line' along the basis of such categories as primitive cinema, classical, modernist and postmodernist immediately problematises any conception of the avant-garde. A similar point is made by Friedberg (1994: 167) who believes that to try and espouse some sort of chronology of film traditions is difficult and focuses instead on links that can be made between the avant-garde and the postmodern through the work of Andreas Huyssen (1988), who defines the avant-garde as accepting mass culture as opposed to modernism which rejected it. As a result, it is more advantageous to accept an approach to postmodernism not based on any sense of dislocation with what has gone before but rather to see it as the coexistence of forms, as opposed to the replacement of one by the other. There subsequently emerges a view of postmodernism not as a dominating discourse but rather,

> what distinguishes the postmodernist context is the simultaneous presence of that style alongside modernist, pre-modernist, and aggressively non-modernist styles, all enjoying significant degrees of popularity with different audiences and institutions. (Collins, 1987: 12)

In summary, we can argue that any conception of the subversion of the linear narrative as being unique to postmodernism is unfounded. Rather, the uniqueness lies in the number of texts, both literary and filmic, that are appropriating such techniques at a particular point in time.

Waugh (1993: 70) argues that one of the central tendencies of the post-modern is indeed its manipulation of time via experimentation in the area of narrative structure. During the 1990s a body of work emerged around a distinctive conception of 'postmodern time', especially in the journal *Time and Society*. A number of writers suggested the emanation of a new culture of time in Western societies exemplified by global media 'simultaneity' and accompanied by a more local, consumer-driven trend towards 'instantaneity' (Heise, 1997: 25). Heise argues that while temporality is a concern for both modern and postmodern theorists, how they deal with that concern is highly divergent (ibid.). In postmodern theory the conflict between the public and the private, so central to the moderns, is no longer a priority with new media such as the internet problematising what exactly constitutes a distinct public and private sphere. Furthermore, new technologies, and our engagement with them, produce revised responses to time based on short attention spans and limited engagement with any one aspect of life on the screen. This is reflected via the postmodern narrative and the recognition of a fragmentation of temporal coherence, for as Calvino writes: 'Long novels written today are perhaps a contradiction: the dimension of time has been shattered, we cannot love or think except in fragments of time each of which goes off along its own trajectory and immediately disappears' (1992: 8).

I want now to progress and suggest that in the last decade of the last century a qualitative shift can be witnessed, specifically noticeable in mainstream cinema, towards alternative forms of narrative composition, informed to a significant degree by the changes in temporal perceptions outlined above. Such narrative innovation displays an awareness of the complexity of human life; that events do not necessarily happen one after the other in neat succession, but simultaneously. This is reflected in a move away from the linear narrative of the classical Hollywood model, perceived as a predominantly artificial mode of storytelling, while concomitantly attention is turned in terms of subject matter, to the small intimate moments of human interaction, as later analysis will demonstrate. Further, innovations include a move towards a more open narrative structure that denies any sense of closure, and a shift towards multiple diegesis in the sense of films telling stories rather than a story. Embedded within these new narrative forms are more complex time frames which challenge a simple sense of causality and instead play upon the interaction between multiple persons and their worlds, creating a temporal sense that is not uni-directional but multi-directional.

This fundamental challenge to the perception of time as a linear flow makes the arrow no longer a suitable metaphor for our understanding of all things

temporal. Ballard, in his introduction to the novel *Crash*, gives us some indication of what changes in our sense of temporality inform us at the end of the
twentieth century where, 'Increasingly, our concepts of the past, present and
future are being forced to revise themselves' (1995: 4). In this context, not only
does postmodernism problematise the linear narrative but also its relationship
to our sense of history. For what is demonstrated in such narrative innovations
is a move away from 'historical time', where time is conceptualised as a linear
construct, reaching out into eternity, unfractured, to 'rhythmic time', 'the time
of experiment, improvisation, adventure [which] destroys the historicist unity
of the world by destroying its temporal common denominator' (Ermath, 1992:
27, 53). Accompanying any disassociation with the arrow is a significant shift
away from narrative conceptualised as the perfect symmetrical curve, plotted in
terms of the tripartite structure of equilibrium, disruption and a revised state of
equilibrium. New spatial models can subsequently be mapped out, based upon
the incorporation of fragmentation, destabilisation and rupture. Moving away
from a geometric model, the postmodern narrative turns towards 'exchanges
and interferences, connections and disconnections between space ... It must
concentrate on perturbations and turbulences, multiple forms, uneven structures' (Gibson, 1996: 13). While the classical Hollywood narrative model still
informs much of what is screened, the following examples visually illustrate an
inclusion of a theoretical awareness of the changing perceptions in our understanding of time that are encroaching on mainstream cinema.

   The first idea to be considered is that of cinema as 'a waste of time'. *The Usual
Suspects* (Singer, 1995) is a highly self-reflexive film which forces the audience,
like the detectives involved, to consider how we put a story together through
the collection of clues. As with many 'puzzle' films, it foregrounds narrative
construction through the introduction of a narrator, in this case a highly unreliable one. And yet it is also about the pleasure of narration; how we like to tell
our story and how we enjoy listening to the tales of others. This film, which
won two Oscars, despite being turned down by all the major studios, opens
up a series of interesting notions regarding fiction and truth, considered to
date to be diametrically opposed. In this case, however, when we learn at the
point of closure that all we have been told by our trusted narrator is a series of
lies, we feel cheated and misled. The film draws its inspiration from Gesualdo
Bufalino's *Night's Lies* (1990), a literary example which also explores the concept of engagement as a waste of time. In this book, we methodically take in
all the details that the narrative has to offer us in the form of a series of tales
within a tale, only to realise at the point of closure that all we needed to know
was contained in the novel's title. The whole substance of the narrative has

been misleading. But why should we feel cheated when both film and novel are grounded in fiction anyway? Is it due to the fact that we seem to have been punished for adopting a suspension of disbelief, a primary viewing require-ment? Or as Elsaesser observes, we feel 'cheated' as it overturns 'the common contract between the film and its viewers, which is that films do not "lie" to the spectator, but are truthful and self-consistent within the premises of their diegetic worlds' (2009: 19).

The protagonist of *The Usual Suspects* is the crippled narrator, Verbal Kint, who is under police custody following the explosion of a cargo ship, leaving 27 dead with only one hospitalised survivor. Through Verbal, detectives and the audience learn of the events leading up to the explosion; how a group of five men meet on a police identity parade and later realise that such an event was a set up by a crooked lawyer in order that the gang should form in the first place. The group, including Verbal, are subsequently blackmailed into performing an 'attack' on a ship, the contents of which remain highly questionable through-out the investigation. The film seeks to piece together the exact happenings of that night via a series of flashbacks and the intervention of US Customs Agent, Dave Kujan. The film's pacing is effectively mobilised through the contrasting uses of space: the claustrophobic atmosphere generated by the confined, intense environment of the interview room where the stationary but babbling Verbal is located, juxtaposed with the sweeping panoramic shots of external locations. This is complemented by contrasting cutting speeds: between the slow, inte-rior sequences of dialogue compared with the action of the heist itself. Yet it is in the way that the film challenges traditional narrative expectations that its interest for this chapter lies. Indeed, it is possible to analyse the film's narra-tive structure through the primary figures involved in the investigation. Kujan can be seen to represent the classical Hollywood narrative model, where, as a detective, he wants Verbal to provide him with as much information as possible in order that he might fit all the necessary pieces together to form a coherent whole of the events that have taken place. Verbal, however, is symbolic of the challenges that such a model faces. The dialogue between Kujan and Verbal builds on Verbal positioning himself as a 'stupid' cripple, a line that Kujan feeds off to ascertain his superiority in the situation. The irony and trickery of such positioning is revealed in the closing shots. As the camera tracks Verbal as he leaves the building, he shrugs off both the signs of being a cripple and his sheer stupidity, in the rapid transition he makes from a limp to a run as the bad guy gets away.

Another challenge that this film makes to the classical Hollywood narrative model is through the role that hindsight plays. Due to the realisation that we have been misled throughout, the audience needs time to re-read the film, to reinterpret all that has been seen. Such is the weight of revelation on reflection that a number of significant visual clues only later demonstrate their primacy. In one of the final shots of the opening scene on board ship, the camera tracks in on a tangled pile of ropes. A close-up of one strand of rope dissolves into a close-up of Verbal as his interrogation begins. The metaphorical association between Verbal's story and the tangle of ropes will only be realised on reflection, although the clue has been discreetly positioned right at the start. A further example of the necessity of reflection, of being able to discern the correct clues only at the point of closure, is that of the choice of angle used to film Kujan drinking his coffee. In the first instance we see him drinking, it is through a close-up shot of the underside of the mug, its significance later demonstrated as the producer of the mug is one of the fictitious characters in Verbal's own constructed story. Finally, early on in the interrogation we have a series of shot/reverse shots, not of Verbal and his interrogator, but of Verbal and a noticeboard positioned directly opposite him. The same sequence of shots is later used when Kujan becomes aware of the source material that lies at the heart of the deception. It is not only the detective who has been tricked but the audience too, based on three principal methods: the destabilisation of any sense of temporal reference points; the over-provision of information; and the denial of the rules of conventional filmic analysis. The tale is told not in the form of a single flashback but rather the story shifts constantly between past and present. McQuarrie (1996: xxiii) specifically indicates in the introduction of his screenplay how 'time jumps around and gets so mixed up'. He further explains how this temporal manipulation provides additional problems for cinema audiences compared with the same effect being carried out in a work of literature for 'when you're reading, you can go back and double-check everything. When you're watching a film, it's different' (ibid.). This sense of temporal destabilisation impacts upon the second means of effecting the trick: with so much information to digest the audience are denied the opportunity to question anything which is presented to them. Engagement in terms of the complexity of time frames and narrative detail requires such levels of concentration that the possibility of an alternative, subversive reading cannot be entertained on first viewing. Narrative analysis is concerned with the extent to which those things that we see make sense, that the various parts come together to form a whole, as Kujan believes. If a film draws attention to something then it is deemed to have a significance in the overall realisation of the story. However, in *The Usual Suspects* attention seems to be drawn to everything and as an audience it is only at the end that we realise that our accumulation of information has been both meaningless and futile. The frequent use of the close-up hovers between clue and bait and it is only on reflection that we are able to discern which was which. Even in terms of characterisation, the information that we have on the other four gang members is only ever a product of Verbal's rhetoric. The characters are introduced to us seemingly all at once and the complexity of the information on offer is demonstrated, for example, by the fact that most of the characters' names begin with 'K': Kint, Kujan, Keaton, Keyser Soze, Kovash and Kobayashi.

The primary source of the deluge of information supplied comes to the audience via the appropriately named intra-diegetic narrator, Verbal. He forces us to adopt a position whereby we feel we have to trust him as we will not gain access to details that enable us to construct a story in any other way. If we base our assessment of Verbal upon the role of the narrator in the classical Hollywood narrative model, then he is to be received as a 'voice of truth' whose function is to direct the audience towards a particular reading of the film, discouraging any alternatives. By using a single narrator, the viewer's process of picking up the all important clues is governed by what the narrator does or does not tell

Figure 10. *The Usual Suspects* – Polygram

us. Verbal seems to be doing his job magnificently in terms of the amount of detail on which his own narrative is based. But all of this rests on a very much taken-for-granted belief: that we should trust the film's narrator. The significance of the final scenes serves to destabilise this sense of trust, but the warning signs are far too late for us to reassess our judgement. Verbal's story ties together so neatly that the police can pin nothing on him and they let him go. Parallel to these events, the one, badly-burned survivor in hospital is giving a description of Keyser Soze, a figure of mythic proportions described by Verbal as the initiator of proceedings. As Verbal leaves the police precinct, two events happen simultaneously: Kujan stares at the littered noticeboard behind him to discover the sources of Verbal's story while a fax arrives with the image of the wanted man. The face on the fax is that of Verbal. Not only has the audience been deceived by complying with traditional narrative expectations, but so also has Kujan for, in his attempt to outsmart Verbal and ascertain the identity of the mysterious Keyser Soze, he has in fact been staring right at him for the last two hours.

The construction of the narrative itself was inspired by 'pulling ideas from my environment' in the same way that Verbal constructs his own story (McQuarrie, 1996: ix). The bulletin board forms not only one of the central aspects of the film's mise-en-scène, described in the screenplay as a 'breathtaking catastrophe of papers, wanted posters, rap-sheets, memos and Post-its', but the owner's assessment of it correspondingly supplies an acute analysis of the film's narrative construction (ibid.: 42). When Kujan comments on the mess, Rabin, in whose office the interview is taking place, replies: 'It all makes sense when you look at it right. You just have to step back from it, you know?' (ibid.: 130). As Kujan continues to stare at the board, the expression on his face changes. He drops the coffee mug and Eisensteinian influences are evident as the slow-motion shots see it shatter on the floor. Another way in which filmic narrative traditionally operates is through the tension created between our anticipation of likely outcomes drawn from genre conventions and the capacity to confirm, surprise or frustrate those expectations. Bordwell (1995: 31) shows how a spectator generally comes to the film already tuned, prepared to focus their energies toward story construction and to apply sets of schemata, 'organised clusters of knowledge' derived from the film's content and their own experience. Rarely do we feel totally cheated. However, one possible feature of what can be described as 'postmodern cinema' is film-makers' awareness of a more knowing audience who, recognising long-established conventions on how to read a film successfully, begin to play with such conventions, to twist the expected into the unexpected via the manipulation of the rules. In the case of *The Usual Suspects* the tools we have traditionally utilised to read a film have not been appropriate, as exemplified by the film's ending.

Arriving at an ending is an essential part of narrative construction. For the individual spectator, the interpretation of the film's conclusion must bear a relation to the interpretation of the text as a whole. In this context, 'the ending is the final product of all the narrative's labors – the end is privileged both during and after the viewing as a source of validation of the reading process. The spectator is prepared for a certain degree of resolution and closure and given to expect a possible termination point' (Neupert, 1995: 32). However, when that termination point is reached it might defy the viewer's expectations, as in the case of the murder-mystery film, so the viewer is forced to rethink earlier scenes. In the case of *The Usual Suspects*, the spectator is forced to rethink the whole film. Thus, such a film alerts us to become more critically aware of the tools of narrative construction as a central aspect of filmic innovation. As Currie argues:

> As story-telling evolves, as new narratives piggyback on the communicative breakthroughs of their predecessors and as new and more complex narrative intentions become common knowledge in the community of tellers and hearers, these inferences will become more complex, with the most inventive tellers always operating on the thin boundary between surprising the audience and having the audience completely miss the point. (1995: 278)

Where such innovation may detract from the viewing process is that these films contain within them the seeds of their own limited 'shelf-life', for their effectiveness to repeat is lessened as, once seen, the trick is realised and the initial impact created is reduced a second time around. Therefore we might say that overall this film produces a particular reaction fuelled by recognition of the heightened sense of the value of time within contemporary culture. To be misled in such a way not only has emotional repercussions for the viewer but somehow makes us feel that we have wasted something precious: time itself.

The second series of films considered here in no way rely on misleading the viewer in order to precipitate temporal reflection. Rather their significance derives from the way in which their narrative structure demonstrates a new sense of temporal awareness realised, not through a single linear narrative, but rather through a series of stories that gather together multiple temporal regimes. Jim Jarmusch's *Night on Earth* (1991) offers a series of vignettes that take, as their subject matter, a single night shift of several taxi drivers who are spatially dislocated but temporally united. While these stories are happening simultaneously, Jarmusch chooses to tell them sequentially rather than through intercutting. Resonant of Joseph Kosuth's conceptual piece *Clock (one and five)* (1965), the opening shot is of a series of clocks displaying the time at various places around the world. Throughout, the film seeks to explore the minutiae of human life and human interaction which, in this context, is foregrounded against that which cinematically is usually omitted. That is to say, a taxi ride, or rather a series of rides, becomes the subject matter of the film when frequently such journeys are abandoned on the cutting room floor. The film comprises very little action, its essence being the dialogue that is struck up between drivers and passengers in their own brief encounters. In the first story, a young female taxi driver picks up a talent scout for potential movie stars. She chats away throughout the ride and this chance encounter leads to her being offered a film part. This she refuses as her life's ambition is to become a mechanic. *Night on Earth* draws on something common to human beings all around the world: the need to talk, the overwhelming need to avoid silence to the point of detailing our most intimate secrets, as the tales in Rome and Helsinki reveal. Filmed in such a confined space, the film exudes voyeuristic tendencies: the audience feels that they are actually in the car as the intimacy builds, but which terminates on payment of the fare. The fragmented narratives are held together by the theme of chance encounters rather than any sense of linear causality, and this is accentuated in New York where a passenger is turned down by a series of cabs before one actually stops, allowing the narrative to recommence. If another cab had stopped for him, another story would be there to be told, as is the case with the other four combinations of drivers and passengers. In this context, the irrelevance of the traditional omniscient classical narrative form is detailed through an emphasis on life's contingencies on a global scale.

Again in vignette fashion, Robert Altman's *Short Cuts* (1993) offers a cross section of a dysfunctional society in the last decade of the twentieth century. The relationships that form the drama are all problematic: husbands argue with wives and they cheat on each other; children get caught in the crossfire; even the domestic pet does not escape the conflict. The constant cutting between these domestic scenes is reflective of the imperfections in people's lives. Life is not one long take but a highly complex affair, demonstrated in the way in which characters appear in more than one context, their actions in one scene indirectly impacting upon the lives of the characters in the next. It is here that the power of the film lies, in the way in which each story, seemingly independent, interacts with all the other stories that surround it. As in Jarmusch's work, *Short Cuts* plays upon the randomness of life and 'what if ... ?' scenarios abound.

The causal structure of the linear narrative again proves ineffective in a world comprised of chance, coincidence and simultaneous happenings. The influence of Godard reverberates through an emphasis on narrative intransitivity, on interruption and digression dislodging any sense of narrative flow. General themes of domestic disorder unite and organise the film more than the actions of any central protagonist. Indeed, there *is* no central protagonist. Neither an individual story nor character is allowed any sense of overall prominence. Of the twenty-two characters involved, we do not stay long enough with any one of them to gain an insight into their inner lives; their unhappiness remains as surface, not depth.

Macnab (1994: 50) has used the word 'tapestry' to describe the narrative structure of *Short Cuts* and others have illustrated the way in which 'it weaves together simultaneously developing story lines into a complex fabric stronger than the binding of its threads' (Deemer, 1997: 11). In all the affairs that take place, someone else other than the two principal participants is always involved, an example of how one life impacts on the lives of so many others with ripple-like consequences. Images and sounds too form the narrative 'threads' that weave in and out of the film as a whole, for as a glass of milk is placed at the bedside of a child that has been hit by a car, so we cut to an image of a glass of milk in an advertisement on the television belonging to the waitress whose car actually hit him. In a similar fashion diegetic sound from one story, a cellist practising, a jazz singer at work, spills over to form the extra-diegetic sound of another story. Telephones and televisions also constitute significant common denominators in people's lives, as will be further explored in Figgis' *Timecode* in the final chapter. Raymond Carver's original short stories on which this film is based are completely self-contained. The characters do not meet and there is no indication that any of them know each other. Here, however, the director seeks to make connections in a number of ways as 'Altman plays with an illusion of order by framing the narratives between two urban catastrophes during which all the characters are effectively united simply by virtue of being in the same boat' (Romney, 1994: 9). In the opening sequence a strong sense of place is created as helicopters are seen spraying an area with malathion to fight off a medfly infestation. At the point of closure, that same geographical space is struck by an earthquake, which acts as a metaphor on a macro scale to draw together the sense of instability and chaos that has permeated the lives of each individual character. In this way Altman is able to introduce an overall sense of closure that would not have been possible in the context of the individual stories presented. In themselves they remain as discrete entities; snapshots, fragments of lives lived.

Willis (1980: 11) has argued that the 1960s 'do seem, in retrospect, to have generated a cult or cults of fragmented thought'. By extension, I would argue that the 1990s has seen the commencement of the cult of the fragmented narrative, and it is this that links together the films under consideration in this chapter. In the case of *The Usual Suspects*, it was not the narrative itself that became fractured, but the spectator's relationship to the narrative, a relationship that became severed due to adherence to a set of rules that were no longer relevant to the current situation. The dislocation between what we have been led to believe and the events revealed at the point of closure require an overall reassessment of the film *away* from the screen. The concept of narrative flow is thus disrupted by the fundamental requirement in this case of hindsight, a remit outside the rubric of the classical narrative. *Night On Earth* and *Short Cuts* centre around what Romney (1994: 10) terms 'micro-narratives', where narrative drive comprises not the logic of cause and effect but rather centres on working through the points of similarity and difference between the stories told. One theoretical approach that can account for an increase in this fractured turn, is the work of Jean-François Lyotard, whose book *The Postmodern Condition*, originally published in 1979, acted as a cata-lyst for debate across disciplines around all things postmodern. While not a text for film-makers per se, it concerns the status of knowledge in the late twentieth century and the shifts that have occurred in the way in which that knowledge is legitimated. This becomes contested, Lyotard argued, follow-ing the collapse of the 'grand narratives' and here he distinguishes between two forms of metanarrative of legitimation; one is rooted in the philosophi-cal tradition of German idealism, the second in the political treatises of the French Enlightenment. The former recognises the importance of knowledge for its own sake, whereby every small contribution made will eventually lead to advancement in the totality of knowledge. The latter sees knowledge as ultimately leading to emancipation, that all research is justified on the basis that it will produce an improvement in people's lives. However, both narra-tive forms gloss over differences and temporal disjunctions. They suppress the incommensurability of the 'now' by arranging events on a teleological basis and seek to homogenise and totalise various stories, seemingly objec-tively, to create just one. In so doing, it is indicated that unfolding events lead to the revelation of a meaning or the realisation of a goal. In this way all contradictions are subsumed. According to Lyotard, grand narratives can no longer be used to justify scientific research, producing a legitimation crisis. Legitimation, including all that is scientific, now takes place in a different format, which he terms 'paralogy', legitimation through the arena of language games, operating at the local, as opposed to the universal, level (Lyotard, [1979] 1991: 10). As Bertens describes them:

> These language games range from Wittgensteinian 'models of discourse', that is, various forms of utterance – denotative, performative, prescriptive, etc. – that all follow their own specific set of rules, via the discourses that are employed by social institutions and professions, to full-scale narratives [for which he also uses the term 'petit récits' or little narratives]. (1995: 124)

Speech acts now formulate the field of play and to utter is to make a move as one would in a game of chess, and where such moves, comprising of questions and statements, according to Lyotard, form society's new bonds. Indeed, 'language games are the minimum relation required for society to exist' (Lyotard, 1991: 15). The postmodern subject is constituted at the 'intersection' of and interaction between these petit narratives adopting different strategies in the participation of language games depending upon the surrounding environment (ibid.: xxiv). Lyotard recognises a shift in emphasis towards the petit narrative, 'the quintessential form of imaginative invention' (ibid.: 60). As opposed to the grand narratives which seek to totalise knowledge, petit narratives are basically incommensurable so that no single narrative can be in a position to subordinate other narratives. That is to say, contradictions are allowed to circulate.

One film that seems to cinematically exemplify Lyotard's approach is Quentin Tarantino's *Pulp Fiction* (1994). Constructed on the basis of 'petit narratives', it defies the grand narrative of the classical Hollywood model, devising its own unique structure appropriate for the material it wishes to present. Furthermore, it is possible, through mapping the highly different attitudes towards our life course presented by the underworld hitmen, Vincent and Jules, to trace an outline of the previous academic debates surrounding the collapsing of grand narratives within a particular social setting. *Pulp Fiction* operates on the basis of a series of interweaving stories and characters and draws upon well-rehearsed 'noir' themes: a hold-up in a restaurant; taking a gangster's moll out for the evening; a boxer, Butch, who sets up a deal and then refuses to throw the fight. The familiarity of the storylines allows other areas of the film to be accentuated, to draw audience attention to the experimentation being carried out in relation to a narrative format that particularly seeks to highlight the role of chance, coincidence and contingency. The freezing of the action in the Prologue, which is only eventually returned to in the Epilogue, makes it clear

Figure 11. *Pulp Fiction* – Miramax

from the outset that this complex narrative structure sets out to challenge both a sense of linearity and chronology.

It is in relation to the challenges posed by the film's temporal ordering and the labour involved in the viewing process that allows Polan (2000: 26) to describe the film's structure as 'a puzzle'. However, I would argue, taking this a stage further, that life itself is represented as 'puzzling'. Rather than being presented as preordained, events seem to materialise on screen to the amusement and amazement of both viewer and indeed the characters involved. Through identification with the point of view of the lead character in each of the vignettes, the audience becomes aware that those on screen seem overtly surprised by the plot's twists and turns. We look to the film's characters to make sense of what we are seeing, but they seem just as bewildered as we are. The audience's experience of watching the film can be conceptualised as a serious of jolts, both between and during the individual stories conveyed. In the Prologue we are introduced to Pumpkin and Honey Bunny, who are about to hold up a coffee shop, but as they commence their robbery we cut into the credit sequence, the soundtrack of which is itself fragmented as the needle seemingly slides along the record and moves from one track into the next. When the credits have finished we are no longer in a coffee shop but in a car alongside two hitmen, Vincent and Jules, who are dressed in black suits with white shirts and black ties. The rest of the film proceeds in this fractured fashion. When we next encounter the hitmen their suits have been traded in for shorts and T-shirts, yet no explanation is given for the drastic change of clothing and, from the audience's point of view, there is no causal logic to account for it. Causality is also challenged across the stories which seem to be held together only in that they are presented as essentially 'battles against time': the attempt to save Mia's life; the boxer, Butch, getting his watch back before being found out; and cleaning a car splattered in blood before Bonnie, the wife of a friend helping the hitmen, returns home from work (Chumo, 1996: 17). In terms of the film's lack of temporal specificity, Burger King and body piercing make it seem contemporary, yet Vince's car is a 1974 Chevy Nova, the music belongs to the 1960s and the overall dress code denies any specific periodisation.

The tale of Butch in particular is riddled with temporal references. Butch and his girlfriend are to escape to Mexico, requiring his girlfriend to speak Spanish, which she does by primarily learning to tell the time. They are to meet up with his brother on arrival when they all will be united under 'Tennessee time' (Tarantino, 1996: 95). Their plans, however, are put on hold the next morning when Butch asks what time it is as he can't find his watch, his father's watch, which formed the substance of his pre-fight memories. He returns to his apartment to find it and, as he makes breakfast there, he notices Vincent's gun. Trigger and toaster explode simultaneously as Vincent is killed; the ordinary and the extraordinary collide in an unexpected fusion of sound and vision perpetuated by the search for a lost watch. Time again permeates the final story, 'The Bonnie Situation'. Here Jimmie, played by Tarantino, is a friend of Jules and Vincent and helps them out in their dilemma when they have unexpectedly killed someone in their car. He is framed to the right of the screen with a clock up high to his left. There is only an hour and a half to clean the car and dump the body before his wife returns, offering a postmodern reflexive take on the previously discussed *High Noon*.

The relationship of one story to the next produces a complex narrative structure. Tarantino's rationale can perhaps be traced to comments made by Robbe-Grillet in *Towards a New Novel* when he argued that there is no single objective view of reality. In a similar way, Tarantino seems to be arguing that a story does not need to be told in a definitive manner; we can start and end at any given point, thus his parodic use of the Epilogue. Bordwell (1982: 4) defines its traditional use as functioning 'to represent the final stability achieved by the narrative' but in fact Tarantino takes up the use of the Epilogue to bring us back almost to the point of commencement. It is an 'episodic, circling narrative structure' which challenges in many ways the 'grand narrative' of classical Hollywood, the trajectory of which is no longer seen as a suitable model for an individual's assessment of how life operates (Brooker and Brooker, 1996: 44). The grand narratives that previously legitimated knowledge resulted in the presentation, Lyotard argues, of a single world view. The 'petit' or fractured narratives that weave in and out of each other in Tarantino's vision, and we return again here to the tapestry metaphor, reflect the complexity of everyday life. In this way, *Pulp Fiction* can be seen to articulate the two sides of the debate regarding the applicability of the grand narrative in the late twentieth century, as Jules and Vincent respond to the failed attempt on their lives. Unaware of a gunman hiding in the bathroom they stand there unscathed despite a shower of bullets. The screenplay indicates that Jules is 'shaken', while Vincent 'shrugs it off' (Tarantino, 1996: 137). For Jules, this is evidence of 'divine intervention' and leads to a fundamental transformation in his life whereby he will reform himself as the good shepherd (ibid.: 139). Protecting the weak, rather than harming them, becomes his new goal in life, exemplified immediately by letting Pumpkin and Honey Bunny walk away with the money – including his money – in the coffee shop raid. Vincent, however, remains untouched by the incident. Less philosophical, more pragmatic, he challenges any sense of event as sign. He recognises that 'shit happens', that events occur which cannot be explained as part of some master plan and which certainly do not require deep reflection or life adjustment.

In terms of characterisation, Tarantino challenges the idea of the psychologically rounded individual through the chameleon-like and highly vulnerable Vincent. As a gangster he plays a part whereby he seems firmly in control of his life but when faced with the unknown, self-control demonstrably succumbs to overt panic. And yet how, as an audience, should we respond to a character such as Vincent? How can we make a judgement in the context of a film where characterisation itself is an unstable entity and where our emotional viewing responses are continually played with to the point where we laugh at death? As a result *Pulp Fiction* exemplifies an 'attempt to renegotiate and reanimate the immediacy and affective qualities of the cinematic experience within commercial Hollywood' (Gormley, 2005: 8). That we seek to identify with Vincent reveals much about how the learned pattern of the classical Hollywood narrative model and the associated identification with a central protagonist remain constant, despite the inappropriate context.

Overall the film represents a world view in which there is recognition that events do not happen in a neat, sequential order but are often messy, prone to simultaneity and also, through Tarantino's technique of returning to previously screened scenes, susceptible to multiple readings and interpretations when explored from alternative points of view. *Pulp Fiction* 'reproduces the everyday experience of living in a fragmented society in which each of us must stitch together a coherent narrative out of the bombardment of information and drama that is our daily passage through a market culture' (Dowell and Fried, 1995: 5). Often, however, the narratives we construct to make sense of the world fail to function as intended. Vincent's bathroom monologue as he prepares to leave Mia is significant not only in providing a highly acute observation of the way in which we use narrative to deal with and reflect upon our own daily experiences but also in highlighting the unpredictability of life; how such narratives, even the ones we construct ourselves, are susceptible to fracture at any moment. 'One drink and that's it. Don't be rude, but drink your drink quickly, say goodbye, walk out the door, get in your car, and go down the road' (Tarantino, 1996: 68). Outside the bathroom Mia overdoses.

CONCLUSION:
TIME IN THE DIGITAL AGE

Movies at a theatre take FOREVER to watch – no fast forward. And VCR
rental movies take forever to watch, even using the FFWD button.
Douglas Coupland, *Microserfs* (1995)

This book has charted the evolving paths of two important facets of modernity:
time and the cinema. As industrialisation utilised time of the clock to standardise our conception of time and organise our diurnal activities, so throughout
cinema's history film-makers have challenged the clock's authority, consequently engendering an imaginative playfulness in the art of storytelling. While
Marey's chronophotography, the photography of time, was tied to the concept
of time and motion studies, the pioneering work of the Lumières centred on
how people spend time, predominantly in the activities of work and leisure.
However, in so doing, an interesting dynamic of their enterprises was made
transparent, how, through their recording of the diurnal, they were able to capture the contingent: to record the unexpected, the fleeting, the unprovoked. It
is this representation of the unpredictable dimensions of life within the context
of an increasingly rationalised world which, this book has argued, brought the
Lumières brothers and Georges Méliès closer together in their approach to cinema. It was a moment of unpredictability that allowed the magician to conjure
with time. His camera jams, yet later reveals the malleability of time on film.
While dismissed by many as simply a producer of trick films, Méliès' work cannot be discounted in terms of the impact it had on the history of the cinematic
narrative for it enabled the film-maker 'to create the illusion of linear mobility'

(Orgeron, 2008: 32). The further potential of editing to act as a means by which we can control time opened up a gamut of possibilities for film-makers, as examined through the concept of 'future time' in Chapter 2. Here we saw how consistently the narrative adopted a linear, but non uni-directional format, as the protagonist moved back and forth in time. This linearity then breaks free in the new Millennium through the concept of 'the loop', as we saw in *Donnie Darko,* where the same event happened twice, but with different outcomes, and again in *Lost Highway,* where the specificity of entry and exit points in relation to the film's over-arching narrative seem to be devalued.

Made possible by editing, movement of the protagonist through time, and indeed to time travel, allows the film to acquire its own temporal logic 'separate from the experience of lived time or the industrialised linearity of production time' (Harbord, 2007: 72). However, before examining the development of such 'temporal logic', the opening chapter considered a second contribution of the actualities: 'real' time. Here the cinema demonstrates its ability to capture and present duration. Narrative developments that ensued beyond the actualities, those of classical Hollywood, would go on, in contrast, to trim away dead time in the name of entertainment and therefore, subsequently, only ever mimic a true sense of experiencing the time of daily life. As modernity sought to manage time, to use the clock as a mechanism of order and control nowhere is this more overtly witnessed than through the regimentation of the factory system. The time-and-motion studies of Taylorism were a distinctive facet of capitalism, of the emerging relationship between man and time, executed in the name of increasing efficiency within the labour process. It was against the dehumanisation of temporality and its appropriation within cinematic practice that the Surrealists, the subject of Chapter 3, rebelled. Still recognising the potential of the medium, this chapter documented how the Surrealists put forward their contrasting vision of an atemporal order, a 'surreality'.

In Chapter 4, I provided an insight into another way in which cinema is able to construct and visualise alternative points of view. Attention was drawn towards that which might lie under the surface, repressed in society's unconscious while concomitantly seeking some form of outlet. Through a consideration of the representation of angels and vampires in cinema, I sought to demonstrate how film can provide a commentary on time at the level of the social whereby concerns and anxieties, both known and yet lacking articulation, are visually made manifest. Nowhere was this more evident than in relation to the preoccupation of film-makers in the run up to the Millennium, with images drawn from the Book of Revelation. While the angel has remained symbolically significant at moments of specific temporal uncertainty, the vampire re-emerges on the cusp of the twenty-first century and enters a consumer culture with a supporting promotional infrastructure marketing to us the currency of youth. Yet, while increased standards of living in the West result in us all living longer, turn on any news bulletin and we are constantly reminded that life can also be precarious, fragile and short as the events in Norway, July 2011 testify.

In this book I have documented the persistence of the classical Hollywood narrative as it sought to 'stabilise the image flux by creating logical connections and associations' (Harbord, 2007: 25). But this initiative to stabilise became highly problematic in the late twentieth century as the narrative quest became dislocated from the social environment in which it was situated. As we struggled to make sense of the world around us, Chapter 5 realises, so narrative began to adopt alternative structures, 'fractured' forms that were more in tune experientially with how we lived through time. Not everything makes sense; nor does every event neatly reach resolution. Furthermore, how we perceive time is changing, largely informed by digital technologies. The future is no longer remote, abstract, rather 'it is drawing closer to the present' (Nowotny, 1994: 50). Indeed, the future seems to encroach upon us and potentially is being usurped and replaced by the category of the 'extended present'. Through our engagement with digital culture comes an increasing awareness of how our relationships online are informed by a revised sense of temporality that is fundamentally attached to a sense of 'liveness', 'grounded in the capacity for electronic media to represent something at roughly the same moment it occurs' (Williams, 2003: 163). Through the frequency by which this happens, in contrast to the 'live' event on television, we come to experience this act as seemingly 'unmediated' (ibid.). Such a position consequently problematises a model of time based on linearity and informs the ongoing experimentations in filmic narrative practice that were examined in this chapter.

It can be argued that today we live in a culture of simultaneity which replaces the concept of modern progress. Here, temporal differences have become reduced to ever shorter durations in the quest to keep up, let alone get ahead. On a daily basis we seem to share time with others, but inextricably linked to this is the knowledge that we all live in our own temporal worlds. How we reconcile the two is both challenging and illuminating. Indeed, previous productions that opened up the temporal possibilities that operate at the level of the subjective have an important influence on, and a striking relevance to, representations of life in the digital world. Today, to rely on a monolithic representation will not suffice. As Odih argues: 'Instantaneous communication and consumption mean that we no longer experience a common time "in" which we all live in more or less mutual relevance, but, on the contrary, events in convergent electronic media are simultaneously global and local, representing a unique and unrepeatable period of time' (2007: 6). Time becomes a finite event, its relevance local, not universal and previously accepted categories of past, present and future become more visibly problematic, as Bergson suggested long before any digital revolution. As a consequence, and as I documented in Chapter 5, a new relationship is set up between the viewer and the viewed. Clusters of films emerge, the central characteristic of which lies in the way temporality itself is foregrounded and, in particular, the temporality of the story and the order of its telling. Cameron (2008) has described such films as having a 'database aesthetic' because of the way in which the linear narrative is deconstructed, broken up into segments or modules, and innovatively reordered. Furthermore, the wealth of information contained within such films allows conflicting positions to arise more easily, so that work must be carried out by the viewer to create their own version of events. As a consequence, films such as *Pulp Fiction* were informed by the way in which we experience time achronologically in contemporary culture, mediated through digital technologies that thrive on short-term engagement and on user interaction that enables resequencing and repetition. Today we are used to accessing portions of time through technologies that allow us access to a segment of an image or text through fast and highly effective search mechanisms. This is realised on screen through the role of flashbacks and flashforwards, Borgesian 'forking paths' and the temporal simultaneity of the split screen or even quadrants, as Figgis will employ in *Timecode*, which we will examine later in this final chapter. Above all, what united the films explored in Chapter 5 was their degree of experimentation in relation to narrative form and its relationship to the effective representation of diurnal experiences. I also considered how such innovations themselves functioned as a reflection of the problematisation of the central relevance of the homogenising public temporal structures of modernity and their decreasing relevance at the end of the twentieth century.

Indeed, in the run up to the Millennium, popular culture became epitomised by increasing instantaneity and simultaneity. As time seemed to be speeding up, forcing us to multi-task and time-juggle, so the twenty-first century saw the emergence of a counter-trend encapsulated in the title of Carl Honoré's book *In Praise of Slow: How a worldwide movement is challenging the cult of speed* (2004). As we have the potential to do everything faster, so the consequences immanently materialise: transportation developments lead to more and more traffic jams and ecological disaster; rapidity of change in fashion cycles results in the further exploitation of many workers in underdeveloped countries; and greater choice in every market sector and the mantra of immediate gratification produces individual financial crisis and global economic meltdown. As we expect more at an accelerated pace, so we are beginning to pay the price, recognisable in our own lifetimes. Research has indicated that while we may feel plagued by time scarcity and desperately crave more leisure time, the amount of time Europeans have to pursue personal interests has actually more than doubled since 1961 (Future Foundation, 2005; Gershuny, 2005). In response to these alternative movements cinema also offers itself as a platform 'in praise of slow'. Challenges to the speeding up of everyday life come, directly and indirectly, through a counter culture of deliberate slowness. While Tarantino is representative of directors who embrace an approach in which 'slo-mo has become a standard feature of action sequences, stretching the moment, allowing you to admire the details' (Gitlin, 2001: 112), a more noticeable trend can be identified. Here the possibility of a new genre is opened up whereby 'slow cinema' is characterised and defined through its offer of 'a certain rarefied intensity in the artistic gaze' (Romney, 2010: 43). Commencing with Béla Tarr's *Sátántangó* (1994), Romney argues that there has been an increasing demand in the last decade for films that are 'slow, poetic, contemplative – cinema that downplays event in favour of mood, evocativeness and an intensified sense of temporality. Such films high-light the viewing process itself as a real-time experience in which, ideally, you become acutely aware of every minute, every second spent watching' (ibid.). As a consequence, in changing our aesthetic sensibility, allowing us to adopt a more contemplative approach to what we see, so we are enabled to immerse ourselves within the world, catching sight of that which normally we are too rushed, too hurried to notice.

While the films under consideration have been discussed under specific chapter headings, in several cases their positioning could have been more fluid: *Donnie Darko, Lost Highway* and *Jacob's Ladder*, for example, could all have been discussed in the chapter on fractured narratives. Each has at its heart tempo-rality and its representation through non-linear forms, whether that be the opportunity to present alternative readings of narrative closure; the denial of closure through the employment of a cyclical 'looping effect'; or the embedding of flashbacks so tightly within the storytelling that we become too confused and disorientated to discern any sense of temporal positioning in terms of the past and the present, as exemplified by Deleuze's 'crystal image'. This tempo-ral disorientation and its representation on screen remained a common theme throughout the history of cinema. Influenced by the Surrealists, intertitles, for example, are used to a disorientating effect in *12 Monkeys* and *Donnie Darko,* as the projected mental instability of the central character leaves the audience questioning the reliability of traditional calendrical markers. The intertitles in these films also function as a point of contrast to a subject in crisis whose psychological state is mirrored through the lack of diegetic coherence in the film itself.

While offering a point of summary and reflection, this final chapter also seeks to bring the debates on temporality into the twenty-first century, by raising the question of time in the digital age and how it impacts on the production and consumption of cinema. In considering the new digital technologies available to film-makers, it is necessary to situate them in relation to the ever-evolving technological infrastructure that emerged at cinema's inception, if not its pre-history. As Mulvey (2007: xv) has acutely observed, not only does 'technological change bring with it changes in human perception and understanding' but any consideration of digital media should also allow for reflection on the relations between old and new technologies. For new technologies are not only 'new' for a very short time, but also emerge out of and indeed reconfigure and reconstitute what has gone before, both functionally and aesthetically. Thus we might wish to reconceptualise the 'history' of cinema not as a linear narrative but rather as a Möbius strip, since current developments within digital culture take us back to the pre-cinematic toys of an earlier chapter. Gunning (in Williams, 2003) suggests that in exploring such possibilities one might draw upon the analogy of the rope, in that while the various strands of pre-cinematic development would come together in a dominant model, now, in the digital age, the strands are once again unfurling. While we may speak of old and new media, it is not about the replacement of one by other but rather about resistance and adaptability. We do not, despite earlier prophecies, live in a film-less age, but the digitisation of cinema is nevertheless a reality and its development throws up fundamental questions around, not only its production and distribution but also the experiential dimension. The term 'digital cinema' will be addressed here through three specific points of reference: firstly, we will consider the technical phenomena, how films are produced and edited through digital media; secondly, how they are consumed, not only in terms of the diversity of points and modes of consumption but how this impacts on the relationship between the film and its audience, which in itself produces new ways of seeing and new readings of what is seen. Finally, we will look at the kinds of films being produced that are informed by this technological change, and which are in themselves a product of the social and cultural changes that inform living in a digital age.

But what do we mean by the digital age? Digital technology extensively informs contemporary culture in terms of how we work, communicate and spend our leisure time. Such technologies also enable us to have control over time, allowing us to time-shift, to function in a virtual temporal world defined as operating on 'cyber-time' or 'network time' (Hassan, 2007). The argument here is that we now spend so much of our lives online that perhaps we should reconsider 'time-of-the clock' as the primary means by which we understand and communicate time. A central argument of this book has been that the clock, as a means to standardise and regulate, has become less relevant. Hassan, however, stresses the importance of demarcating cyber-time or network time from 'real time' (ibid.: 49). They are not the same, he argues, for real time is underpinned by a sense of something occurring immediately, and this is not what happens when working online. He hints at the formation of a new times-cape for the digital age, one that is formed outside, or rather marginalises, the influence of clock-time; one that allows chat rooms to comprise a global membership and where interaction is not limited by temporal barriers or time zones. As participants experiencing this new timescape we recognise the augmentation of temporal control, a theme that will be developed further in this chapter in relation to increased levels of interactivity in terms of viewing practices.

To say that we live in the digital age resonates at the level of the individual through our ongoing interactions with new technology and digital media. Gere (2008) dates this new age as commencing post-Y2K, with its fears of the so-called 'Millennium Bug'. While the concerns of the public and media did not materialise, the most significant outcome of this moment for Gere was the 'almost total transformation of the world by digital technology' (2008: 13). Digital, for Gere, refers here to more than the storage of data in binary form: it is 'to call up, metonymically, the whole panoply of virtual simulacra, instantaneous communication, ubiquitous media and global connectivity that constitutes much of our contemporary experience' (ibid.: 15). The relationship between technology and culture is an interesting one for such technological innovations not only inform contemporary culture but also reflect and embody ways of thinking and doing in the twenty-first century. For example, technology supports a shift from the viewer as passive observer to interactive manipulator of media, controlling the temporal flow and customising the content of what they see to suit their tastes and lifestyles; BBC iPlayer being one such example.

How we understand time in the digital age is inextricably linked to our daily practices. So bombarded are we with choice that we will only select to engage with that which interests us and time itself is perceived as a resource to be spent on that which is deemed worthwhile, with the result that the way in which we acquire knowledge has changed. From its progressive, horizontal accumulation it now metaphorically builds vertically, known as 'stacking' (Eriksen, 2007), enabling us to access exactly what we want to know, as quickly as possible. As a consequence, Eriksen argues, this impacts the way in which

narratives are formed for 'when growing amounts of information are distributed
at growing speed, it becomes increasingly difficult to create narratives, orders,
developmental sequences. The fragments threaten to become hegemonic' (2007:
150). Gere develops Eriksen's argument stating that this sense of 'speeding up'
is informed, to a large degree, by the development and accessibility of Web 2.0
which encourages collaboration and reciprocal communication. The proliferation of social networking sites such as Twitter and Facebook, emblematic of our
highly participatory culture, not only allows for and represents the personalisation of communication needs but also encourages instantaneity in terms of
response times: to wait, to hesitate, is to miss out. The impact of operating in
'cyber-time', a shortening of temporal distance between events, was exemplified
in the destruction of the World Trade Centre in 2001. Images were transmit-
ted globally almost as it happened (Gere, 2006: 171). The linking factor here
is mediation through a screen: 'it is on screens that life seems most to acceler-
ate, even as speeding images offer manifold reasons for our bodies to stay still'
(Gitlin, 2001: 86).

So how have such technological developments informed cinema? As we have
already seen, cinema emerged from a lineage of optical toys that simulated a
moving image. The public's thirst for visual stimulation and spectacle led to its
early definition as a 'cinema of attractions' (Gunning, 1995). Gunning identifies the appeal as coming from the device itself and its ability to produce the
real, rather than the specific content being screened, even though the audience
knew that what it saw could not be 'real'. By extension, Grusin (2007: 211)
introduces us to the 'digital cinema of interactions' which takes as its starting
point not the Baudrillardian proposition that reality does not exist but rather
'the ways in which we customarily act in a fashion that suggests that digital
media, computer games, or video games, *are* real' (his emphasis). In developing this argument we might propose that the first phase of technology that
informed the recording and reproduction of the moving image was 'mechanical' and was influenced by photography, specifically the work of Marey and
Muybridge who implemented, in rapid succession, the sequential streaming
of still shots to produce before the eye the replication of movement. The next
phase, building on the work of these two noted pioneers, can be defined as
'analogue', comprising continuous magnetic recording technology with images
sequentially reproduced through cathode ray tube (CRT) presentation-video. In
relation to both film and analogue video, what we see on screen is analogous to
how it was originally captured. Finally, we enter the third technological phase
of cinema history, 'the digital age' and the application of computer technologies.
In contrast with analogue, in this third phase, images are recorded as discrete

items of data and, by implication, 'sequentiality is replaced by non-linear code addressing the potential to massively extend the flexibility of data recovery and combination' (Le Grice, 2001: 237). That is to say, it offers spatial rather than temporal data storage. This flexibility emerges from the computer technology that supports digital film-making, allowing visual manipulation and effects that have subsequently informed experimental independent and studio productions alike.

Having established some fundamental characteristics of the digital age, it is now necessary to consider how its inherent temporal sensibilities impact the cinematic experience. From its beginning, cinema pondered the representation of time and used technological developments to inform its response. As the encroachment of capitalism sought to neutralise its impact, to align time of the clock with opportunities for production and profit, so cinema sought to capture its nuances and examine how we inhabit time. Photography captured and fixed time, allowing the ephemeral to remain, to linger, but it could not reveal the passing of time, duration made visible. However as Doane argues, 'the cinema engages multiple temporalities' (2002: 30). Firstly, there is the temporality of the apparatus itself which is characterised as being linear, mechanical and irreversible. Secondly, she documents the temporality of the diegesis, how time is represented on screen. Finally, she notes the temporality of reception which interestingly, she argues, classical cinema tried to tie as tightly as possible to the apparatus and therefore was characterised by linearity and irreversibility. In 'digitime' (Stewart, 2007: 170) these characteristics are fundamentally challenged. In summary, analogue time informs the history of modern temporality: it is linear, presupposes an orderly sequence of events and is underpinned by a sense of rationality, of cause and effect. In contrast, digital time is characterised by rupture and fragmentation; by non-linear models of temporal flow; of multiple renderings and genuflections of temporal experience.

A useful starting point in considering the impact of new digital technologies on film-making practices is provided by Willis (2005) who argues that the essential difference between digital film-making and more traditional methods centres on the concepts of 'transcription' versus 'conversion'. She describes how, in relation to both film and analogue video, the information that we experience in its final form is analogous to the information in its original form. In contrast, information recorded with digital video goes through a process of conversion. That is to say, a digital camera doesn't record an analogue signal of varying voltages but instead a series of zeroes and ones. As Willis extrapolates, '"digital" refers to data that exists as a series of discrete elements, arranged in mathematically determined patterns. As a result, digital information may be endlessly

duplicated, manipulated and transformed without generational loss or degradation of quality' (2005: 6). There are a number of advantages to producing films
digitally rather than in celluloid. Firstly, digital video is cheaper than 35mm
film. Secondly, it is easier to edit. Indeed, since the early 1990s the majority of
Hollywood features shot on 35mm have undergone a digital intermediate process when the film stock is digitised to facilitate the editing process before being
released again on 35mm film. Finally, distribution in the future will become
easier once cinemas adopt the digital video projector. However, it is important
to engage with the different ways in which cinema has embraced the digital
image. For example, films such *Jurassic Park* began a trend whereby a world
could be inserted into a world, offering new possibilities especially in relation
to temporal layering. One of the most interesting studies examining the impact
of computerisation on new forms of cinema is the work of Lev Manovich (2001)
who specifically addresses the temporal structure of film language. Manovich
(2001: 8) raises a question central to this chapter: 'what is unique about how
new media objects create the illusion of reality, address the viewer, and represent
space and time?' In order to respond to this question, Manovich conceptualises
the impact of the computer as having the capacity to 'redefine the very identity
of cinema' (ibid.: 293). One of the ways in which this redefinition is made possible is through the denial that live-action footage is the only possible material
from which a film might be made or, where it is used, is subject to alteration.
In traditional film-making, Manovich argues, editing and special effects were
strictly separate entities but in digital film-making this distinction is removed.
Interestingly, he argues that, as we saw earlier, in this way cinema is drawing
heavily on its pre-history of optical toys, such as the Zoetrope, that required
human intervention in the construction of the image. As a consequence, a 'new
kind of realism' emerges (ibid.: 301).

So we might argue that technology is not only having a significant impact
on film-making as a business but also on the ways in which stories are told.
Cubitt (2002) presents an interesting insight into the possibilities for a new narrative temporal imagination in the digital age. As a starting point, new media's
temporalities offer up the potential to challenge the chronological mode of temporal experience. It is worth citing his position at length:

> The chronological narrative proposes to us a protagonist who always
> occupies a perpetual present (without which such effects as suspense
> and expectation would be impossible) as a point moving along a line
> whose dimensions have however already been mapped: the protagonist
> of the chronological narrative is caught in a story whose beginning and

end have already been determined, and which therefore constructs story time as the unfolding of destiny rather than the passage from past certainty into an uncertain future. This sense of preordination constructs narrative as timeline, as a spatial organisation, and its protagonists as variants moving through rule-governed moves as in a game of chess. (ibid.: 4)

In considering the opportunities for more imaginative forms of storytelling Cubitt provides us with an effective assessment of how we inhabit our lives as temporal beings in the digital age as he describes our experiences of time while surfing the World Wide Web. He argues that: 'we enter a certain, as yet inchoate, mode of time. For all the boasts of instantaneity, our actual relations with one another are mediated and as such subject to delays: slow downloads, periodic crashes, cache clearances and software uploads' (ibid.: 10). As a result, narrative, in mirroring these new temporal relations must embody fragmentation, discontinuity and incomplete resolution. Furthermore, we must consider the way in which data is stored and searched for in the digital age with an emphasis on space over time, as in the example of the database, which is explored through the mechanism of fields allowing us ease of access and retrieval of the data required. On accessing a database we have no conception of a narrative whole; any sense of linear progression consisting of a beginning, middle and end is subsumed in the vastness of the information stored. By extension, nor is it possible 'to imagine the world as already complete and unchangeable' (ibid.: 12). If we reconsider the ways in which time is experienced online and how we access and make sense of virtual information, Cubitt believes we have an excellent vantage point from which to reconsider narrative formations while 'embracing the possibilities of human-computer communication' (ibid.: 8). However, while some critics argue that the relevance of narrative in the digital age remains constant as new media still requires a mechanism to retain a level of coherence, to create connections in its storytelling, others point towards a new star in the ascendant: cinema as spectacle.

We can actually date the impact of the digital on cinema to the special effects of the 1970s (*Star Wars*, in 1977, for example) and it has been making its mark on both production and distribution ever since. The fusion of the Hollywood blockbuster, CGI (computer-generated imagery) and the special effect was seen by many to herald a significant juncture in cinema history whereby the narrative would now be subservient to the spectacle. Viewed negatively, the overt use of the special effect that makes the blockbuster what it is has the potential to disrupt narrative flow through the reaction it produces, disabling, indeed even momentarily freezing, temporal flow: 'the FX overkill sends out a message that has little to do with normal narrative arcs – the basic rationale for it being in the film is: Because We Can' (Roddick, 2010: 46). In contrast, there is a special effect that is much more subtle and informed by the work of Méliès. It functions to 'reinforce, rather than interrupt, the plot's temporal progression' and consequently to 'promote the illusion of cinemato-graphic possibility' (Mak, 2003: 42). Harbord (2006: 265) speaks positively of these changes, positioning digital technology as 'part of the material condition of cinema that affords opportunities for innovation'. Such innovations include the extended potential of the science fiction genre enhanced by the increase of the spectacular, through, for example, the recent reintroduction of 3D. Therefore I would argue that, despite the catalogue of innovations that this chapter has documented, as cinema seeks to map on screen the socio-cultural transformations within which it is situated, this does not represent the end of narrative. So, rather than narrative versus spectacle as opposing positions, should we not recognise 'that narrative and spectacle are inextricably inter-twined' and that 'digital effects therefore have the potential to introduce a dynamism to narrative spaces' (Wood, 2002: 377)?

If narrative provides us with a mechanism by which stories can be told, digital opens up new narrative possibilities. James Cameron, writer, producer and director of *Avatar* (2009), the first full-length feature where a totally CG 3D photo-realistic world was arrived at, highlights this observation. Conceived in the 1990s, the film was put on hold until technology was able to realise its execution, namely, 'performance capture' and 3D. In this technique, the actors are connected to sensors, filmed and then converted via computer into Na'vi. Cameron conceptualises contemporary film-making as follows: '[if] the twen-tieth century was the age of the flat image, the twenty-first must be the age of the deep image' (Appleyard, 2010: 53). The appropriation of new technologies in the making of *Avatar* does not detract from the art of storytelling, indeed, it enhances it in this powerful, highly emotive tale of eco-irresponsibility and the price to be paid for the planet's maltreatment. Cameron rationalises his choice of production technique: 'It is all about immersion and, with competition from computer games and the web, real cinema in real theatres has no choice but to keep up, technology wise'. As a consequence, this is not about the death of traditional cinema in the digital age: rather it is about its re-working, to try to 'reconnect people with that awe and wonder you can only feel in the big-screen group experience' (ibid.: 54). Fabe (2004: 229) supports such a position arguing that the commercial success of digitally animated computer-generated films from *Toy Story* (1995) onwards suggests that digital images trigger strong emotional reactions from the audience if, and only if, the stories themselves are compelling:

> *Toy Story* is, after all, a linear film intended to be viewed in the tradi-
> tional way. It borrows the graphic power of digital media but removes the
> promise (or threat) of interactivity. *Toy Story* shows that 'new' digital film
> can maintain a conventional relationship with its audience – that linear
> media such as film and television can exploit the computer's power to cre-
> ate visually convincing worlds without the troubling notion that the user
> must be in control of these new worlds. (Bolter and Grusin, 1999: 149)

The year 2010 was perhaps the year in which digital cinema truly came of age with the advent of digital 3D. A total of 28 3D films were released in that year, making up 24 per cent of the market share, up from 16 per cent in 2009. Two of the top three highest grossing films in the UK and the Republic of Ireland for 2010 were in 3D: *Toy Story 3* and *Alice in Wonderland*. Despite its release during 'austere times', *Toy Story 3* became the second highest grossing film of all time, behind *Avatar* with earnings of just under £74 million (UK Film Council, 2011). However, in 2011, the form took an unexpected turn, one beyond the exploits of cartoon characters. Moving into the new, unexplored territory of arthouse it simultaneously reminded cinema of its roots in the theatre. Wim Wenders' *Pina* (2011) (Neue Road Movies and Eurowide Film Production) is a documentary dance film that became a tribute to German modern dance choreographer Pina Bausch, who died during filming. Wenders, as director and producer, seeks to capture Bausch's work on film. The first part records her major stage pieces but, in the second part, the performances imaginatively take place outside in Wuppertal, south of the Ruhr. For twenty years Wenders had sought a way to capture her art and 3D is consequently, and indeed unexpectedly, used here to explore theatrical space in a way that had not previously been technically pos-sible. The director refers to 3D as a 'new language ... made to film dance ... the two were made for each other, and that dance could also bring out the best in 3D that was yet uncovered' (Solomons, 2011). Wenders describes the medium as highly immersive, allowing for a new viewing experience in which the audience are placed inside the realm of the dancers in a way that the flatness of 2D could never allow for. As a result he is positive in terms of his assessment of the future of 3D and hints at its evolving potential arguing that 'I think 3D deserves to be taken seriously as a medium – in documentary most of all ... You can take your viewers into the world of your characters in such a complete and immersing way.' For Bausch the legacy is two-fold. Not only is her immortality secured but also the form through which audiences may gain access to work extends beyond the live performance.

In the digital age, it seems we can all be film-makers now, with portable equipment consistently becoming more affordable along with the accessibility of editing software for the home computer and an increasing sense of visual literacy that we absorb from everyday cultural forms. As a result a high degree of creative convergence can be witnessed. Design, advertising, music video production and film all display a high degree of intertextuality of both form and content. This concept of convergence must also be considered in relation to its impact on the viewing experience for, as McQuire (2008: 493) documents, 'in the digital era of convergent media, film content is increasingly imbricated not only with television, video and DVD, but the Internet, video games and mobile devices'. Digital culture heralds a convergence culture bringing about not only a closer proximity between the media producer and the media consumer but also the flow of content across the media platforms on which this relationship is built. We are now at an important juncture in film history whereby 'we can no longer consider the film screened in the theatre as the complete experience' (Grusin, 2007: 213). The opportunities to view extend beyond a succession of visits to the cinema, to include viewing online, on television (including cable and satellite channels), via the DVD, accessing material through the film's website, and interacting through its videogame, if available. This will also impact the speed with which films are consumed beyond their cinema release. As Roddick (2010) has argued, as a consequence of consumer demand films will, in the near future, circulate like any other form of entertainment: a sense of immediacy will bring big screen ticket sales and the ancillary markets closer together. This increasing recognition by the studios of adjunct avenues of revenue-raising potential and the need to overhaul their business models was represented in the response of Odeon cinemas not to screen Tim Burton's *Alice in Wonderland* (2010). This was due to Disney's wish to reduce the period in which the film can be shown only in cinemas from 17 to 12 weeks, thus prompting an earlier release of the DVD. Such a move reflects the way in which audiences, now positioned as consumers, wish to be in control of the media object, to own it and therefore to view it in their own time, in their own way. Each film release in the cinema is simply a starting point to extend the shelf-life and revenue stream beyond the time spent in the box office charts. As a result, the marketing potential of a transmedia film, as pioneered by *The Matrix* series, for example, is exponential.

As with any other brand extension exercise, the studio must be alert to both the creation of strong synergies across all points of interaction that the viewer has with the 'film as brand' but, at the same time, each point of entry must

demonstrate a unique offer at point of sale in order to realise its profit potential. In the case of each film, every offshoot, such as DVD or videogame, must
provide the opportunity to realise a self-contained world that does not require
knowledge or experience from other derivations of the film to produce an enter-
taining experience. However, the more access points that can be engaged with
allow not only the opportunity for extended content but also, within a mass
market context, more intense and indeed personalised readings. Therefore, seeing the film, owning the DVD and playing the videogame will contribute to an
extensive engagement with characters, plot and sub-plots and aesthetics, all of
which in themselves motivate further consumption. Let us return once again to
the film *Donnie Darko*, which exemplifies the multiplicity of ways in which we
can view, interact and construct our own reading of a film through new media
technologies beyond cinema. Both the accompanying website and DVD-release
contain additional information on the film. Accessing one or more of these
divergent sites allows for greater degrees of a personalised reading of the film
and its narrative construction. Therefore, by obtaining extra-diegetic material
such as interviews with the director and cast on the DVD, so their reading of
the film coupled with the viewer's own, allows for polysemic understandings of
what is already a highly complex narrative. As one progresses through the layers and levels of information available, the details gained leads to one's reading
of the film becoming susceptible to change and re-adjustment. Furthermore,
through the interactive capabilities of DVD, a very different cinematic experience can be created by having the opportunity to direct one's own movement through the film, or to freeze each individual crystalline image. With
the introduction of DVD, to watch a film through from beginning to end is
only one option: now we have the capacity to customise what and how we view
and as a consequence we fundamentally alter the visual culture of the moving
image. By extension, the medium we choose has significant implications in
terms of affect. For example, the diverse settings in which a DVD might be
viewed produce local differences of reception. Absorption may now be replaced
by assimilation into a series of co-existing activities.

Convergence may also be considered to influence the ways in which stories
are told or rather narratives are constructed. Cowie (1998: 188) has argued that
one of the reasons for such high degrees of innovation in narrative practice is
purely down to economics. With the decline of the studio system and the emergence of new forms of profit-making institutions that include not just cinema
productions but television, cable and satellite, then narrative cinema 'cannot
be seen as unified as was possible under the old oligopoly'. Intra- and inter-
media competition brings with it constant innovation, frequently feeding off

one another. Picking up on and exemplifying this point, Dowell and Fried (1995: 5) question the originality of *Pulp Fiction*, arguing that indeed its narrative structure 'should be familiar to any television watcher, for it is our psychological accommodations to TV's dramatic shape that Tarantino exploits for his narrative surprises'. Commercial breaks, channel surfing and multi-tasking while watching television all consistently break up any sense of uninterrupted viewing. In this way, we as an audience work at narrative construction, filling in the gaps, as we move between programmes, activities, planned and unplanned interruptions, based on the information that we have available to us. Influenced by TV-viewing practices, the VCR became highly influential here as a technological device that informs our sense of how we view by prioritising the capacity for viewer control based on the ability to pause. Thus, as Deleuze registered how cinematic signs could document our changing relationships to matters temporal, so Tarantino uses *Pulp Fiction* to explore how we experience time through the intervention of other media forms into filmic production and consumption. While now superseded as a technology for both viewing and recording, the VCR is still interesting in terms of what it heralded in relation to changes in viewing practices. Indeed it was positioned as critical to narrative progression in Lynch's *Lost Highway*, as we saw in Chapter 3, functioning in this case, however, to distort rather than clarify the reality of the worlds in which the central characters circulate. New technologies offer up ever changing viewing experiences which in themselves engender new temporal relationships between the viewer and the images on screen. While there is no pause in cinema per se, *Pulp Fiction* creates its own sense of breaks through its continual interruptions and narrative fragmentations. As a result, the film creates a novel and specific appeal for the new media generation. Polan draws attention to the way in which its complicated narrative structure 'is like an electronic work – a video game or a story played out on a computer screen. Its images have a baroque richness, filled up with ever new things to spot, ever new connections to make' (2000: 35). And herein lies the fundamental allure of the film: of the wish to see it again and again, its rich intertextuality allowing the viewer to interact, to play with its content, spotting links which had previously gone unnoticed.

To bring together the series of points made above, it is worth examining in detail a film that exemplifies a number of the trends considered under the heading of 'cinema in the digital age'. Mike Figgis' *Timecode* (2000) could have been positioned in Chapter 1 as an examination of filming in 'real time', as part of the discussion of its infrequent use throughout cinema history. There the problems of real-time filming were noted, encapsulated in the struggles of trying to accurately present time as it is, to try and successfully capture diurnal flow.

As the classical Hollywood narrative developed so a shift took place whereby time was represented rather than presented to counter these challenges, reflecting as a consequence a decision-making process through editing whereby time is rationalised: the non-event stripped away. The move away from 'real time' seemed to suggest that much of the quotidian was mundane and therefore not worthy of recording, as only in scenarios that involve literally 'a race against the clock' does each moment become packed with meaning. Figgis returns to the challenges posed by 'real-time' film-making but charts an innovative course via the concept of temporal simultaneity. It is this specific innovation that allows his work to be positioned here as, in considering filming in real time, he also opens up a series of critical issues pertinent to the themes of this chapter.

The innovative direction he takes with the form encourages a viewing experience based on interactivity and in so doing he implies that 'the diachronic mode of cinema may not be equipped to capture the synchronic, multiple nature of modern urban life' (Cameron, 2008: 161). For the cinematic narrative supported by diachronic montage is always, as noted above, underpinned by selection. But what if that selection process was removed as a requisite of production and repositioned within the context of the viewing experience? In order to facilitate such a transformation, Figgis offers a new temporal model in screen narration as he attempts to consider how we live through time.

Timecode, an example of independent film-making, draws on the grammar of 'simultaneity, the ability to see events, situations and characters impacting on each other' (Harbord, 2006: 269). Figgis fuses real time with a denial of any sense of omission by allowing the viewer, rather than the director, to select what they see. He achieves this through the adoption of the form of synchronic quadrants in what has been described as a 'desktop aesthetic' (Willis, 2005: 39). In this way Figgis realises answers to the issues of real-time film-making discussed in the opening chapter, that technologically, to date, the cinema had not been prepared for. *Timecode* was the first American studio film shot entirely in digital video. Digital technology was necessary because two hours of film can be shot continuously compared with just ten minutes in 35mm film. Underpinned by the concept of synchronicity and using four Sony DSR-1 digital cameras, the film reveals the different sets of actions of the characters or shows one character's actions from four different points of view. During filming all the actors and the four camera operators worked with synchronised watches so that they could, even while improvising, keep in line with key temporal moments in the plot. Indeed, 'the script was "composed" on music paper in a string quartet format (one line for each of the four plot actions) with each bar representing one minute of time' (Fabe, 2004: 230). This does not come without an inherent set of problems. 'One mistaken action in a film shot in real time in long, unbroken takes cannot be corrected unless the entire take is done over' (ibid.). Indeed, extra footage on the DVD reveals that it took Figgis fifteen attempts to get the result he wanted.

Timecode takes as its starting point multiple events happening at the same time; this is achieved by the four main characters each inhabiting one quadrant of the main screen. The setting is the Hollywood of today, specifically the production offices of Red Mullet films. Rose is an aspiring actress and the lover of the highly possessive Lauren. Rose is also having an affair with a director, Alex, who is married to Emma. In revenge, Lauren kills Alex. How these interlinking events can be effectively recorded and represented without the use of editing, is the challenge presented here. As we observed in Chapter 5, Jarmusch chose to represent social time through disparate, unconnected narratives which share in common the same temporal framework of the city. Here, in contrast, the different narrative strands are presented in a more literal fashion as they appear on screen in one of four quarters at the same time throughout the film's 97 minutes. Through this format Figgis seems to be highlighting the complexity of our lives today and as such, the stories we tell require a new mode of realisation. The film introduces the viewer slowly to the idea that independent action is happening in each of the quadrants by opening with an interior shot of a therapy session,

Figure 12. *Timecode* – Screen Gems

taking place in just the top right-hand corner. A few minutes later this is complemented by a second exterior shot in the top left-hand quadrant, of a different
woman walking down some steps to a parked car, the setting for most of the
action in which she will later be involved. She lets the tyres down and the hiss
of the deflation catches our attention and drowns out the sounds of the therapy
session. As a consequence, and with two quadrants present, we become aware of
the deconstruction of sound and image and realise that this film involves choice
at a number of different levels: we can move visually between quadrants or we
can be led by the dominant sound. As the tyres deflate so the third and fourth
quadrants are realised as interior shots of Red Mullett Productions. Within a few
minutes action in all four quadrants has been revealed and our attention has been
drawn to the four main characters in this familiar story based on wrongdoing and
revenge: Emma, Rose, Lauren and Alex.

It is obvious that this director offers a novel approach to the viewing experience but how does he manage to keep the audience effectively orientated?
Firstly, Figgis reminds audiences of the alternative approach adopted in structuring his narrative through the frequent and overt manifestation on screen
of the notion of clock-time. In order that we might be anchored to the narrative unfolding, the familiar sign of the clock, something cinema disavowed
from the outset in the telling of a story, now stabilises our viewing experience at various points in one of the quadrants throughout the film's duration.
Secondly, sound performs several functions in directing the viewer's attention
to important facets of the action. Dialogue is only heard from one quadrant
but at the same time a sound in another quadrant, a phone ringing, for example, acts as a narrative thread across all four and functions to interlink the
actors' responses. Thirdly, four earth tremors (referencing Altman's *Short Cuts*)
happen during the film and their impact is visible simultaneously across each
of the quadrants, evidencing the way in which the characters are all occupying the same local geographical area and temporal moment. As a viewer, it
takes a few minutes to 'learn' to read this film appropriately. We are made
to challenge accepted viewing practices, as the Surrealists had encouraged.
It is surprising, though, how quickly we do adapt, developing our own stra-
tegic response, adjusting between character, quadrant and sound as the film
progresses. Soon we become literate to the connections formed between characters and across quadrants. The opportunity to direct our viewing moment
by moment through this parallel plotting is both empowering and liberating.
Forced constantly to make choices over whom to follow, we are also concurrently left weighing up whether we have made the right choice or if we have
missed important events happening elsewhere.

Figgis himself argued that viewers were now prepared for such a viewing experience, as a constant 'diet of channel-surfing and multi-media has made sophisticates of modern-day filmgoers, equipping them to process a bombardment of information thrown at them on various frequencies' (Brooks, 2000: 36). However, as within consumer culture more generally, choice can become a burden, as Fabe suggests: 'the novelty of the film's experimental form is always something of a distraction, taking precedence over our absorption in the narrative and identification with the characters' (2004: 236). At one extreme *Timecode* can be seen as an exploration in 'thinking beyond narrative's exclusive claim on time' (Cameron, 2008: 168). In a highly self-referential moment towards the end, a film-maker pitches her ideas to the production company. She wishes to make a film in 'real time' that is 'one continuous moment' using four cameras. She challenges the relevance of editing today for 'montage has created a false reality'. Figgis' film offers us alternative codes by which we might navigate our way through the events that unfold on screen and it can be argued that these codes are only a possibility in the twenty-first century owing to both the availability of digital technology and audience familiarity and immersion in this technology. The presentation of simultaneous real-time images is already familiar to the viewer through encounters with CCTV, and the use of diegetic sound, such as mobile phone calls, as a mechanism to form connections between disparate actors, is a scene now visible everyday in any public space. However, experimentation never collapses into chaos for 'in attempting to reconfigure the language of film, *Timecode* bends the rules beautifully. Yet it never quite breaks them' (Brooks, 2000: 37). In September 2010 Mike Figgis performed a live show-and-tell remix of this digital split-screen experiment that is *Timecode*. At this live performance the original method of composition becomes highlighted, namely story composition generated in the same way as a musical score. The second time around, it is possible for a new set of questions to be posed: about the extension of the post-production process, for example. Does it necessarily have to have a finite termination or can it be seen as evolving, transmuting even? The issue of interdisciplinarity of forms also springs to mind, as discussed in *Pina*. On this occasion, the remixed film becomes performance and establishes as a consequence an alternative viewing experience.

In conclusion, I turn to the observations of Mark Cousins (2010: 41) who notes that 'movies are everywhere' so that 'the new question in the twenty-first century is not how to see, but how to choose'. Availability and accessibility make the choice of what to see even more difficult as cinema aligns itself increasingly to the nuances of the mass market. And yet as choice becomes the watchword of cinematic consumption, the premise of cinema as a medium through which stories are told will remain constant for 'stories are basic to all human cultures, the primary means by which we structure, share, and make sense of our common experiences' (Jenkins, 2008: 120). In tune with this recognition, this book has documented how narrative has functioned within cinema's history and in particular how film-makers have sought to present and represent time and to articulate our temporal experiences and revelations. With the films chosen has come a recognition that what exactly time means to us has become increasingly fluid. Therefore its representation more than ever becomes the subject of exciting visual experimentation and innovation, with developments on our small screens influencing future productions on the big screen in terms of both form and content. Figgis' *Timecode* provides an example of this and previews 'one possible way the language of the cinema may evolve in the digital age of the moving image' (Fabe, 2004: 241).

How and where we experience films has changed considerably since its inception. The portability of film means that we can now multi-task, watching on the move as we participate in the daily commute or experience the long-haul flight or the 'non-places' that precede it (Auge, 2009). *Where* and *when* we watch is now marked by endless possibilities. *What* we watch has also been scrutinised by the time-pressured. As the quotation from Douglas Coupland's *Microserfs* at the head of this chapter indicates, to watch a whole film takes time, even on fast forward: hence the new micro trend of 'hyper-editing': five-second movies in which feature films have been edited down to their bare essentials by and for the YouTube generation. Cousins (2010: 41) elaborates on how time scarcity enables new viewing practices as DVD menus allow us to select and watch favourite scenes so that 'cinema nourishes us in a different way'. As a consequence, perhaps, the aura of the cinema visit has lost its glow as more individualistic modes of reception succeed the collective experience of cinema-going. Alternatives to cinema as an institution are obvious, but are we falling out of love with cinema itself as traditionally conceptualised? The UK and Republic of Ireland gross box office for 2010 was up 2 per cent on the previous year (UK Film Council, 2011) demonstrating cinema's resilience 'to weather downturns and generate steady sales increases' (Davoudi, 2011: 13). Choice allows for endless possibilities rather than necessarily an either/or scenario. How we manage our time will inform the choices we make.

BIBLIOGRAPHY

Adam, B. (1990) *Time and Social Theory*, Cambridge: Polity Press.

Ades, D. (1995) 'Dada and Surrealism' in N. Stangos (ed.) *Concepts of Modern Art: From Fauvism to Postmodernism*, London: Thames and Hudson.

Angenot, M. (1979) 'Jules Verne: The last happy Utopianist' in P. Parrinder (ed.) *Science Fiction a Critical Guide*, London: Longman.

Appleyard, B. (2010) 'Beyond the Third Dimension', *Sunday Times Magazine*, 25 April, pp. 50–55.

Artaud, A. (1972) 'Witchcraft and the Cinema' in his *Collected Works*, Volume III, trans. A. Hamilton, London: Calder & Boyars.

Auge, M. (2009) *Non-places: Introduction to an Anthropology of Supermodernity*, London: Verso.

Badder, D. (1978/9) 'An Interview with Michael Powell', *Sight & Sound* 48 (1), pp. 8–12.

Ballard, J.G. (1995) *Crash*, London: Vintage.

—— (1997) *A User's Guide to the Millennium: Essays and Reviews*, London: Flamingo.

Barak, A. (1995) 'Douglas Gordon: The Art of Slowing Down', *Art Press* 208 (December), pp. 45–49.

Barnes, J. (1995) *Dr. Paris's Thaumatrope or Wonder-Turner*, The Projection Box: London.

Barthes, R. (1974) *S/Z*, New York: Hill & Wang.

—— (1977) *Image-Music-Text*, London: Fontana.

Bauso, T.M. (1991) '*Rope*: Hitchcock's Unkindest Cut' in W. Raubicheck and W. Srebnick (eds.) *Hitchcock's Rereleased Films: From 'Rope' to 'Vertigo'*, Detroit: Wayne State University Press.

Beck, J.C. (2004) 'The Concept of Narrative: An analysis of *Requiem for a Dream* (.com) and *Donnie Darko* (.com)', *Convergence*, 10 (3), pp. 55–82.

Benjamin, W. ([1931] 1979) 'A Short History of Photography' in his *One Way Street*, London: New Left Books.

—— ([1935] 1992) 'The Work of Art in the Age of Mechanical Reproduction' in his *Illuminations*, London: Fontana.

Benjamin, M. (1998) *Living at the End of the World*, London: Picador.

Bergson, H. (1911) *Creative Evolution*, trans. A. Mitchell, New York: Henry Holt & Company.

Berman, M. (1991) *All That is Solid Melts into Air*, London: Verso.

Bersmaïa, R. (1990) 'From the Photogram to the Pictogram: On Chris Marker's *La Jetée*', *Camera Obscura* (8), pp. 139–161.

Bertens, H. (1995) *The Idea of the Postmodern: A History*, London: Routledge.

Biodrowski, S. (1991) 'Jacob's Ladder', *Cinefantastique* 21 (4), February, pp. 50–53.

Bloom, C. (ed.) (1998) *Gothic Horror: A Reader's Guide from Poe to King and Beyond*, London: Macmillan.

Bloom, H. (1996) *Omens of Millennium: The Gnosis of Angels, Dreams, and Resurrection*, New York: Riverhead Books.

Bogue, R. (2003) *Deleuze on Cinema*, New York: Routledge.

Bolter, J.D. and Grusin, R. (1999) *Remediation: Understanding new media*, Cambridge, MA: MIT Press.

Bordwell, D. (1982) 'Happily Ever After, Part Two', *The Velvet Light Trap* (19), pp. 2–7.

—— (1995) *Narration in the Fiction Film*, London: Routledge.

Bordwell, D., Staiger, J. and Thompson, K. (1996) *The Classical Hollywood Cinema: Film Style & Mode of Production to 1960*, London: Routledge.

Botting, F. (1996) *Gothic*, London: Routledge.

Bradshaw, P. (2003) *Phone Booth. The Guardian*, 18 April. Accessed at: www.guardian.co.uk/culture/2003/apr/18/artsfeatures2/print

Breton, A. ([1924] 1994) 'The First Manifesto of Surrealism' in C. Harrison and P. Wood (eds.) *Art in Theory: 1900–1990*, Oxford: Blackwell.

Brooker, P. and Brooker, W. (1996) 'Pulpmodernism: Tarantino's Affirmative Action' in D. Cartmell, I.Q. Hunter, H. Kaye and I. Whelehan (eds.) *Pulping Fictions: Consuming Culture across the Literature/Media Divide*, London: Pluto Press.

Brooks, X. (2000) 'California Split', *Sight & Sound* (September), pp. 36–37.

Brown, S. (1997) 'Optimism, Hope and Feelgood Movies: The Capra Connection' in C. Marsh and G. Ortiz (eds.) *Explorations in Theology and Film*, Oxford: Blackwell.

Brunius, J. ([1954] 1978) 'Crossing the Bridge' in P. Hammond (ed.) *The Shadow and its Shadow: Surrealist Writings on Cinema*, London: BFI Publishing.

Buckland, W. (2009) 'Making Sense of *Lost Highway*' in W. Buckland (ed.) *Puzzle Films: Complex storytelling in contemporary cinema*, Oxford: Wiley-Blackwell.

Bufalino, G. (1990) *Night's Lies*, London: Harvill Collins.

Burch, N. (1990) *Life to Those Shadows*, trans. and ed. by B. Brewster, London: BFI.

Button, V. (1996) *The Turner Prize Catalogue – 1997*, London: Tate Gallery Publishing.

Calvino, I ([1979] 1992) *If on a Winter's Night a Traveller*, London: Vintage.

Cameron, A. (2008) *Modular Narratives in Contemporary Cinema*, Basingstoke: Palgrave Macmillan.

Carter, A. (1992) *Expletives Deleted*, London: Vintage.

Celeste, R. (1997) '*Lost Highway:* Unveiling Cinema's Yellow Brick Road', *Cineaction* 43 (July), pp. 32–39.

Chanan, M. (1996) 'The Treats of Trickery' in C. Williams (ed.) *Cinema: the Beginnings and the Future*, London: University of Westminster Press.

Charney, L. (1995) 'In a Moment: Film and the Philosophy of Modernity' in L. Charney and V.R. Schwartz (eds.) *Cinema and the Invention of Modern Life*, Berkeley: University of California Press.

—— (1998) *Empty Moments: Cinema, Modernity and Drift*, Durham, North Carolina: Duke University Press.

Child, H. and Colles, D. (1971) *Christian Symbols: Ancient and Modern*, London: G. Bell & Sons.

Chion, M. (1995) *David Lynch*, London: BFI Publishing.

Chittock, J. (1996) '*Back to the Future:* the Cinema's Lessons of History' in C. Williams (ed.) *Cinema: the Beginnings and the Future*, London: University of Westminster Press.

Christie, I. (1994) *The Last Machine: Early Cinema and the Birth of the Modern World*, London: BFI.

—— (2000) *A Matter of Life and Death*, London: BFI Publishing.

Chumo, P.N. (1996) ' 'The Next Best Thing To A Time Machine': Quentin Tarantino's *Pulp Fiction*', *Post Script* 15 (3), pp. 16–28.

Clarke, I.F. (1979) *The Pattern of Expectation, 1644–2001*, London: Jonathan Cape.

Coe, B. (1992) *Muybridge and the Chronophotographers*, London: BFI.

Colebrook, C. (2006) *Deleuze: A guide for the perplexed*, London: Continuum.

Collins, J. (1987) 'Postmodernism and Cultural Practice: Redefining the Parameters', *Postmodern Screen* 28 (2), pp. 11–26.

Combs, R. (1986) 'High Noon: A review', Monthly Film Bulletin 53 (629), pp. 186–87.

Connor, S. (1996) The English Novel in History: 1950–1995, London: Routledge.

Cook, D.A. (1996) A History of Narrative Film, New York: W.W. Norton and Co.

Copjec, J. (1991) 'Vampires, Breast-Feeding and Anxiety', October (58), pp. 24–43.

Coppola, F.F. and Hart, J.V. (1992) Bram Stoker's Dracula: The Film and the Legend, London: Pan Books.

Coupland, D. (1995) Microserfs, London: Flamingo.

Cousins, M. (2010) 'Overwhelmed by Options', Sight & Sound (February), p. 41.

Cowie, E. (1998) 'Storytelling: Classical Hollywood cinema and classical narrative' in S. Neale and M. Smith (eds.) Contemporary Hollywood Cinema, London: Routledge.

Crary, J. (1993) Techniques of the Observer: On vision and modernity in the nineteenth century, Cambridge, MA: MIT Press.

Cubitt, S. (2002) 'Spreadsheets, Sitemaps and Search Engines' in M. Rieser and A. Zapp (eds.) New Screen Media: Cinema/Art/Narrative, London: BFI.

Currie, G. (1995) Image and Mind: Film, Philosophy and Cognitive Science, Cambridge: Cambridge University Press.

Davidson, G. (1967) A Dictionary of Angels, New York: Free Press.

Davies, P. (1995) About Time: Einstein's Unfinished Revolution, London: Penguin.

—— (2002) How to Build a Time Machine, London: Penguin.

Davoudi, S. (2011) 'Cinemas price seen as fantasy', Financial Times, 23–24 April, p. 13.

Deemer, C. (1997) 'Short Cuts: The Los Angelesation of Raymond Carver', Creative Screenwriting 4 (3), pp. 11–17.

Deleuze, G. (1986) Cinema 1: The Movement-Image, trans. H. Tomlinson and B. Habberjam, Minneapolis: University of Minnesota Press.

—— (1989) Cinema 2: The Time-Image, trans. H. Tomlinson and R. Galeta, London: Athlone Press.

Deleuze, G. and Parnet, C. (1987) Dialogues, London: Athlone Press.

Dipple, E. (1988) The Unresolvable Plot: Reading Contemporary Fiction, London: Routledge.

Doane, M.A. (1996) 'Temporality, Storage, Legibility: Freud, Marey and the Cinema', Critical Inquiry 22 (2) (Winter), pp. 313–43.

Doane, M.A. (2002) The Emergence of Cinematic Time: Modernity, Contingency, the Archive, Cambridge: Mass; Harvard University Press.

Dowell, P. and Fried, J. (1995) 'Pulp Friction: Two Shots at Quentin Tarantino's Pulp Fiction', Cineaste 21 (3), pp. 4–7.

Drummond, P. (1977) 'Textual Space in *Un Chien Andalou*', *Screen* 18 (3), pp. 55–119.

—— (1994) 'Introduction: Surrealism and *Un Chien Andalou*' in L. Bunuel and A. Dali *Un Chien Andalou*. Foreward by J. Vigo, London: Faber & Faber.

Dulac, G. (1988) 'The Expressive Techniques of the Cinema' in R. Abel (ed.) *French Film Theory and Criticism: A History/Anthology, 1907–1939*, Princeton: Princeton University Press.

Durgnat, R. (1978) 'Durgnat on Powell and Pressburger' in I. Christie (ed.) *Powell, Pressburger and Others*, London: BFI.

Dyer, R. (1993) 'Dracula and Desire', *Sight & Sound* 3 (1), pp. 8–12.

Edmundson, M. (1997) *Nightmare on Main Street: Angels, Sadomasochism, and the Culture of Gothic*, Cambridge, MA: Harvard University Press.

Ehrlich, L.C. (1991) 'Meditations of Wim Wenders's *Wings of Desire*', *Literature/Film Quarterly* 19 (4), pp. 242–46.

Eizykman, B. (1985) 'Temporality in Science-Fiction Narrative', *Science-Fiction Studies* 12 (March), pp. 66–87.

Ellis, J. (1978) 'Watching Death at Work' in I. Christie (ed.) *Powell, Pressburger and Others*, London: BFI.

Elsaesser, T. (2009) 'The Mind-Game Film' in W. Buckland (ed.) *Puzzle Films: Complex storytelling in contemporary cinema*, Oxford: Wiley-Blackwell.

Empire (2009) '*The Lovely Bones*', June, pp. 26–30.

Eriksen, T.H. (2007) 'Stacking and Continuity: On temporal regimes in popular culture' in R. Hassan and R.E. Purser (eds.) *24/7: Time and Temporality in the Network Society*, Stanford: Stanford Business Books.

Ermath, E.D. (1992) *Sequel to History: Postmodernism and the Crisis of Representational Time*, Princeton, New Jersey: Princeton University Press.

Ezra, E. (2000) *Georges Méliès: the birth of the auteur*, Manchester: Manchester University Press.

Fabe, M. (2004) *Closely Watched Films: An introduction to the art of narrative film technique*, Berkeley: University of California Press.

Ferraro, M. (1995) 'Beat the Clock', *American Cinematographer* 76 (11), pp. 24–28.

Fielding, R. (1983) 'Hale's Tours: Ultra-Realism in the Pre-1910 Motion Picture' in J. L. Fell (ed.) *Film Before Griffith*, Berkeley: University of California Press.

Finkelstein, H. (1996) 'Dali and *Un Chien andalou:* The Nature of a Collaboration' in R. Kuenzli (ed.) *Dada and Surrealist Film*, Cambridge, MA: MIT Press.

Florida, R. (2002) *The Rise of The Creative Class*, New York: Basic Books.

Foster Wallace, D. (1996) 'David Lynch Keeps His Head', *Premiere* (September), pp. 91–114.

Fotiade, R. (1995) 'The Untamed Eye: Surrealism and Film Theory', *Screen* 36 (4), pp. 394–407.

Franklin, H.B. (1978) *Future Perfect: American Science Fiction of the Nineteenth Century*, London: Oxford University Press.

Frazer, J. (1987/8) 'Cubism and the Cinema of Georges Méliès', *Millennium Film Journal* 19 (Fall/Winter), pp. 94–102.

Freud, S. (1991a) *The Essentials of Psycho-Analysis*, London: Penguin.

—— ([1900] 1991b) *The Interpretation of Dreams: The Penguin Freud Library, 4*, J. Strachey and A. Tyson (ed.), London: Penguin.

—— ([1917] 2006) 'Mourning and Melancholia' in A. Phillips (ed). *The Penguin Freud Reader*, London: Penguin.

Friedberg, A. (1994) *Window Shopping: Cinema and the* Postmodern, Berkeley: University of California Press.

Future Foundation (2005) 'Industry Eye: A Futurologist's Guide to Today's Changing Technology Consumer', November. Accessed at: www.hotwirepr.com

Game, A. (1993) *Undoing the Social: Towards a deconstructive sociology*, Buckingham: Open University Press.

Gaudreault, A. (1983) 'Temporality and Narrativity in Early Cinema, 1895–1908' in J.L. Fell (ed.) *Film Before Griffith*, Berkeley: University of California Press.

—— (1987) 'Theatricality, Narrativity, and Trickality: Revaluating the Cinema of Georges Méliès', *Journal of Popular Film and Television* 15 (3), pp. 110–19.

Gauldie, E. (1992) 'Flights of Angels', *History Today* 42 (December), pp. 13–20.

Gere, C. (2006) *Art, Time and Technology*, Oxford: Berg.

—— (2008) *Digital Culture* (2nd edition), London: Reaktion Books.

Gershuny, J. (2005) 'What do we do in Post-Industrial Society? The nature of work and leisure in the 21st century', *Institute for Social and Economic Research Working Papers*, 2005–7, Colchester, University of Essex.

Gibson, A. (1996) *Towards a Postmodern Theory of Narrative*, Edinburgh: Edinburgh University Press.

Gibbs, N. (1993) 'Angels Among Us', *Time Magazine* vol. 142, no. 27, 27 December, p. 56.

Gitlin, T. (2001) *Media Unlimited: How the torrent of images and sounds overwhelms our lives*, New York: Metropolitan Books.

Gleick, J. (1999) *Faster*, London: Abacus.

Godwin, K.G (1984) '*Eraserhead*: An Appreciation', *Cinefantastique* 14 (4/5), pp. 50–54.

Godwin, M. (1993) *Angels: An Endangered Species*, London: Boxtree.

Gormley, P. (2005) *The New Brutality Film: Race and affect in contemporary Hollywood cinema*, Bristol: Intellect.

Green, A. (2002) *Time in Psychoanalysis*, trans. by A. Weller, London: Free Association Books.

Grusin, R. (2007) 'DVDs, Video Games and the Cinema of Interactions' in J. Lyons and J. Plunkett (eds.) (2007) *Multimedia Histories: From the magic lantern to the internet*, Exeter: University of Exeter Press.

Gunning, T. (1994) 'Primitive Cinema: A Frame-Up? Or The Trick's On Us' in T. Elsaesser (ed.) *Early Cinema: Space, frame, narrative*, London: BFI.

—— (1995) 'An Aesthetic of Astonishment: Early Film and the (In)Credulous Spectator' in L. Williams (ed.) *Viewing Positions: Ways of Seeing Film*, New Brunswick: Rutgers University Press.

—— (1997) 'In Your Face: Physiognomy, Photography, and the Gnostic Mission of Early Film' in *Modernism/Modernity* 4 (1), pp. 1–29.

Hammerton, M. (1995) 'Verne's Amazing Journeys' in D. Seed (ed.) *Anticipations: Essays on Early Science Fiction and its Precursors*, Liverpool: Liverpool University Press.

Hammond, P. (1974) *Marvellous Méliès*, London: Gordon Fraser.

Hammond, P. (ed.) (1978) *The Shadow and its Shadow: Surrealist Writings on Cinema*, London: BFI Publishing.

Hansen, M. (1987) 'Benjamin, Cinema and Experience: "The Blue Flower in the Land of Technology"', *New German Critique* (Winter), pp. 179–224.

Harbord, J. (2006) 'Digital film and "late" capitalism: a cinema of heroes?' in J. Curran and D. Morley (eds.) *Media and Cultural Theory*, Abingdon: Routledge.

Harbord, J. (2007) *The Evolution of Film: Rethinking Film Studies*, Cambridge: Polity.

Harvey, D. (1990) *The Condition of Postmodernity*, Cambridge: Blackwell.

Hassan, R. (2007) 'Network Time' in R. Hassan and R.E. Purser (eds.) (2007) *24/7: Time and Temporality in the Network Society*, Stanford: Stanford Business Books.

Hassan, R. and Purser, R.E. (eds.) (2007) *24/7: Time and Temporality in the Network Society*, Stanford: Stanford Business Books.

Heilbroner, R. (1996) *Visions of the Future*, Oxford: Oxford University Press.

Heise, U.K. (1997) *Chronoschisms: Time, Narrative and Postmodernism*, Cambridge: Cambridge University Press.

Hillier, J. (ed.) (1992) *Cahiers du Cinéma. The 1960s: New Wave, New Cinema, Reevaluating Hollywood*, Cambridge, MA: Harvard University Press.

Honoré, C. (2004) *In Praise of Slow: How a worldwide movement is challenging the cult of speed*, London: Orion Books.

Huyssen, A. (1988) *After the Great Divide: Modernism, Mass Culture and Postmodernism*, London: Macmillan.

Jackson, K. (2009) 'The Vampire Next Door', *Sight & Sound* (November), pp. 41–43.

Jackson, R. (1993) *Fantasy: The Literature of Subversion*, London: Routledge.

Jacobs, M. (1992) *Sigmund Freud*, London: Sage.

James, N. (2011) *Motion Pictures, Sight & Sound* (May), pp. 21–24.

Jencks, C. (1981) *The Language of Postmodern Architecture* (3rd edition), London: Academy.

Jenkins, H. (2008) *Convergence Culture: Where old and new media collide*, New York: New York University Press.

Johnson, W. (1997) 'Enigma Variations: The Elusive Film Blanc', *Film Comment* 33 (6), pp. 70–73.

Kawin, B. (1982) 'Time and Stasis in *La Jetée*', *Film Quarterly* 36 (1), pp. 15–20.

Kelly, R. (2003) *The Donnie Darko Book*, London: Faber & Faber.

Kern, S. (1983) *The Culture of Time and Space: 1880–1918*, Cambridge, MA: Harvard University Press.

King, E.H. (2007) *Dali, Surrealism and Cinema*, Harpenden: Kamera Books.

Kovács, K.S. (1983) 'Georges Méliès and the Feerie' in J.L. Fell (ed.) *Film Before Griffith*, Berkeley: University of California Press.

Kubler, G. (1962) *The Shape of Time: Remarks on the history of things*, New Haven: Yale University Press

Kuhn A. (ed.) (1996) *Alien Zone: Cultural Theory and Contemporary Science Fiction Cinema*, London: Verso.

Lacey, A. R. (1989) *Bergson*, London: Routledge.

Lapsley, S. and Westlake, M. (1992) *Film Theory: An Introduction*, Manchester: Manchester University Press.

Laqueur, W. (1996) 'Fin-de-siècle: Once More with Feeling', *Journal of Contemporary History* 31 (1), pp. 5–47.

Lash, S. and Urry, J. (1994) *Economies of Signs and Space*, London: Sage.

Leccardi, C. (2007) 'New Temporal Perspectives in the 'High-Speed' Society' in R. Hassan and R. E. Purser (eds.) (2007) *24/7: Time and Temporality in the Network Society*, Stanford: Stanford Business Books.

Le Grice, M. (1995) 'Kismet, Protagony and the Zap Splat Syndrome', *Millennium Film Journal* 28 (Spring).

Lewis, D. (1995) 'The Paradoxes of Time Travel' in R. Le Poidevin and M. MacBeath (eds.) *The Philosophy of Time*, Oxford: Oxford University Press.

Lewis, D. and Bridger, D. (2001) *The Soul of the New Consumer*, London: Nicholas Brealey Publishing.

Lynch, D. and Gifford, B. (1997) *Lost Highway: The Screenplay*, London: Faber & Faber.

Lyotard, J. F. ([1979] 1991) *The Postmodern Condition: A Report on Knowledge*, trans. G. Bennington and B. Massumi, Manchester: Manchester University Press.

Macnab, G. (1994) '*Short Cuts*: A Review', *Sight & Sound* 4 (3), pp. 49–50.

Mak, M. (2003) 'Keeping Watch of Time: The Temporal Impact of the Digital in Cinema', *Convergence: The International Journal of Research into New Media Technologies*, vol. 9 (4), pp. 38–47.

Mandelbrote, S. (1996) 'History, Narrative and Time', *History of European Ideas* 22 (5/6), pp. 337–50.

Manovich, L. (2001) *The Language of New Media*, Cambridge, Mass: The MIT Press.

Marker, C. (1992) *La Jetée: ciné-roman*, New York: Zone Books.

Marriott, S. (2007) *Live television: Time, Space and the Broadcast Event*, London: Sage.

McKenna, R. (1999) *Real Time: Preparing for the age of the never satisfied customer*, USA: Harvard Business School.

McQuarrie, C. (1996) *The Usual Suspects: The Screenplay*, London: Faber & Faber.

McQuire, S. (1998) *Visions of Modernity: Representation, Memory, Time and Space in the Age of the Camera*, London: Sage.

—— (2008) 'Film in the Context of Digital Media' in J. Donald and M. Renoir (eds.) *The Sage Book of Film Studies*, London: Sage.

Méliès, G. (1984) 'Cinematographic Views', *October* (29), pp. 23–31.

Morgan, J. (2004) 'Time after Time' in J. Morgan and G. Muir (eds.) (2004) *Time Zones*. An exhibition at Tate Modern, London, October 2004–January 2005, London: Tate Publishing.

Muir, G. (2004) 'Chrono-Chromie' in J. Morgan and G. Muir (eds.) (2004) *Time Zones*. An exhibition at Tate Modern, London, October 2004–January 2005. London: Tate Publishing.

Mulvey, L. (1989) *Visual and Other Pleasures*, London: Macmillan.

—— (2007) 'Foreward' to J. Lyons and J. Plunkett (eds.) (2007) *Multimedia Histories: From the magic lantern to the internet*, Exeter: University of Exeter Press.

Neupert, R. (1995) *The End: Narration and Closure in the Cinema*, Detroit: Wayne State University Press.

Newman, K. (1997) '*Lost Highway:* A Review', *Sight & Sound* 7 (9), pp. 48–9.

Newton, R. (1997) 'Angels', *The North American Review* 282 (3/4), pp. 4–6.

Nietzsche, F. (1989) *Ecce Homo*, New York: Vintage Books.

Nowotny, H. (1994) *Time: The Modern and Postmodern Experience*, trans. N. Plaice, Cambridge: Polity Press.

Odell, C. and Le Blanc, M. (2007) *David Lynch*, Hertfordshire: Kamera Books.

Odih, P. (2007) *Advertising in Modern and Postmodern Times*, Los Angeles: Sage.

O'Malley, M. (1992) 'Standard Time, Narrative Film and American Progressive Politics', *Time and Society* 1 (2), pp. 193–206.

ONS (2008) 'Life Expectancy: Life expectancy continues to rise', Office for National Statistics, 30 October. Accessed at: www.statistics.gov.uk

Orgeron, D. (2008) *Road Movies: From Muybridge and Mélies to Lynch and Kiarostami*, New York: Palgrave Macmillan.

Penley, C. (1989) *The Future of an Illusion: Film, Feminism and Psychoanalysis*, London: Routledge.

Pérez-Reverte, Arturo (1996) *The Dumas Club*, London: The Harvill Press.

Pizzello, S. (1997) 'Highway to Hell', *American Cinematographer* (March), pp. 34–42.

Polan, D. (2000) *Pulp Fiction*, London: BFI.

Powell, A. (2005) *Deleuze and Horror Film*, Edinburgh: Edinburgh University Press.

—— (2007) *Deleuze, Altered States and Film*, Edinburgh: Edinburgh University Press.

Powell, M. (1986) *A Life in Movies: An Autobiography*, London: Heinemann.

Propp, V.I.A. ([1928] 1968) *Morphology of the Folk Tale* (2nd revised edition), Austin, Texas: University of Texas Press.

Ray, R.B. (1985) *A Certain Tendency of the Hollywood Cinema, 1930–1980*, Princeton: Princeton University Press.

—— (1995) *The Avant-Garde Finds Andy Hardy*, Cambridge, MA: Harvard University Press.

Rice, A. (1996) *Interview with the Vampire*, London: Warner.

Richardson, M. (2006) *Surrealism and Cinema*, Oxford: Berg.

Ricoeur, P. (1980) 'Narrative Time', *Critical Inquiry* 7 (1) (Autumn), pp. 169–190.

—— (1984) *Time and Narrative*: Volume I, trans. K. McLaughlin and D. Pellauer, Chicago: University of Chicago Press.

Robbe-Grillet, A. (1965) *Snapshots* and *Towards a New Novel*, trans. B. Wright, London: Calder & Boyars.

Roberts, A. (2005) *The History of Science Fiction*, Basingstoke: Palgrave Macmillan.

Robinson, D. (1993) *Georges Méliès: Father of Film Fantasy*, London: BFI.

Roddick, N. (2010) 'The Medium is the Message', *Sight & Sound*, February, pp. 44–46.

Rodley, C. (ed.) (1997) *Lynch on Lynch*, London: Faber & Faber.

—— (ed.) (2005) *Lynch on Lynch* (revised edition), London: Faber & Faber.

Rodowick, D.N. (1997) *Gilles Deleuze's Time Machine*, Durham, USA: Duke University Press.

Romney, J. (1994) 'In the Time of Earthquakes', *Sight & Sound* 4 (3), pp. 8–11.

—— (2010) 'In Search of Lost Time', *Sight & Sound* (February), p. 43–44.

—— (2011) 'What time is it where?', *Sight & Sound* (May), pp. 30–31.

Salt, B. (1994) 'Film Form, 1900–1906' in T. Elsaesser (ed.) *Early Cinema: Space, frame, narrative*, London: BFI.

Self, R. (1982) 'The Art Cinema and Robert Altman', *The Velvet Light Trap* (19), pp. 30–34.

Sheehan, H. (1993) 'Trust the Teller: An Interview with James V. Hart', *Sight & Sound* 3 (1), p.14.

Short, R. (1991) 'Dada and Surrealism' in M. Bradbury and J. MacFarlane (eds.) *Modernism: A Guide to European Literature*, London: Penguin.

Sinclair, R. (1993) 'Douglas Gordon's *24 Hour Psycho*: A Review', *Art Monthly* (June), pp. 22–23.

Smith, Z. (2011) 'Killing Orson Welles at Midnight', extract from *The New York Review of Books* (April) in *The Guardian: Review*, 16 April, pp. 1–2.

Solnit, R. (2003) *Motion Studies: Time, Space and Eadweard Muybridge*, London: Bloomsbury.

Solomons, J. (2011) 'Wim Wenders discusses *Pina*', *Observer: Film Weekly Podcast*, 24 April, www.guardian.co.uk/filmweekly.

Sopocy, M. (1996) 'The Role of the Intertitle in Film Exhibition: 1904–1910' in C. Williams (ed.) *Cinema: the Beginnings and the Future*, London: University of Westminster Press.

Stafford, B. (1994) *Body Criticism: Imagining the Unseen in Enlightenment Art and Medicine*, Cambridge, MA: MIT Press.

Staller, N. (1989) 'Méliès' Fantastic Cinema and the Origins of Cubism', *Art History* 12 (2), pp. 202–217.

Stewart, G. (2007) *Framed Time: Toward a postfilmic cinema*, Chicago: University of Chicago Press.

Stoker, B. (1993) *Dracula*, London: Penguin.

Sutton, D. (2005) 'Rediagnosing *A Matter of Life and Death*', *Screen* 46 (1), pp. 51–61.

Suvin, D. (1984) 'The Extraordinary Voyage, The Future War, And Bulwer's *The Coming Race:* Three Sub-Genres in British Science Fiction, 1871–1885', *Literature and History* 10 (2), pp. 231–48.

Tarantino, Q. (1996) *Pulp Fiction: The Screenplay*, London: Faber & Faber.

Tarkovsky, A. (1989) *Sculpting in Time: Reflections on the cinema*, London. Faber & Faber.

Taubin, A. (1996) 'Douglas Gordon', *Catalogue of the Spellbound Exhibition*, Hayward Gallery, London, 22 February to 6 May.

—— (2002) 'Bloody Tales' in K. Newman (ed.) *Science Fiction/Horror: A Sight & Sound Reader*, London: BFI.

Thiher, A. (1977) 'Surrealism's Enduring Bite: *Un Chien Andalou*', *Literature & Film Quarterly* 5 (1), p. 38.

Thompson, E.P. ([1967] 1991) 'Time, Work-Discipline and Industrial Capitalism', *Customs in Common*, London: Merlin Press.

Todorov, T. (1971) 'The Two Principles of Narrative', *Diacritics* 1 (1), pp. 37–44.

Tulle, E. (2008) 'The Ageing Body and the Ontology of Ageing: Athletic competence in later life', *Body & Society* 14 (3), pp. 1–19.

Turim, M. (1991) 'Cinemas of Modernity and Postmodernity' in I. Hoesterey (ed.) *Zeitgeist in Babel*, Bloomington: Indiana University Press.

Turner, B.S. (1995) 'Ageing and Identity: Some reflections on the somatization of the self' in M. Featherstone and A. Wernick (eds.) *Images of Ageing: Cultural representations of later life*, London: Routledge.

Turner, B.S. (2006) 'The Body', *Theory, Culture and Society*, 23 (2–3), pp. 223–36.

Twain, M. (1994) *The Adventures of Tom Sawyer*, London: Penguin.

UK Film Council: Research and Statistics Unit (2011) *The UK Box Office in 2010*, 20 January, pp. 1–5.

Usai, P. C. (1991) 'A Trip to the Movies: Georges Méliès, Filmmaker and Magician (1861–1938)', *Image* 34 (3–4), pp. 2–15.

Valenti, P.L. (1978) 'The 'Film Blanc': Suggestions for a Variety of Fantasy, 1940–45', *Journal of Popular Film*, VI (4), pp. 294–304.

Verne, J. (1965) *From the Earth to the Moon*, London: Arco Publications.

Walker, I. (1977–78) 'Bunuel's Half Century', *Sight & Sound* 47 (1), pp. 3–5.

Walters, J. (2008) 'When People Run in Circles: Structures of Time and Memory in *Donnie Darko*' in C. Lee (ed.) *Violating Time: History, Memory and Nostalgia in Cinema*, London: Continuum.

Warner, M. (1993) 'The Uses of Enchantment' in D. Petrie (ed.) *Cinema and the Realms of Enchantment*, London: BFI.

Warner, M. (1997) 'Voodoo Road', *Sight & Sound* 7 (8), pp. 6–10.

—— (2006) *Phantasmagoria: Spirit Visions, Metaphors, and Media into the Twenty-first Century*, Oxford: Oxford University Press.

Waugh, P. (1993) *Metafiction: The Theory and Practice of Self-Conscious Fiction*, London: Routledge.

Whitrow, G. J. (1972) *What is Time?* London: Thames & Hudson.

Wiebenson D. (1969) *Tony Garnier: The Cité Industrielle*, London: Studio Vista.

Williams, L. (1992) *Figures of Desire: A Theory and Analysis of Surrealist Film*, Berkeley: University of California Press.

Williams, M. (2003) 'Real-time Fairy Tales' in A. Everett and J.T. Caldwell (eds.) *New Media: Theories and Practices of Digitextuality*, New York: Routledge.

Willis, D. (1980) 'Modernism! The terror from beyond space', *Film Comment* 16 (1), pp. 9–15.

Willis, H. (2005) *New Digital Cinema: Reinventing the Moving Image*, London: Wallflower.

Wood, A. (2002) 'Timespaces in spectacular cinema: crossing the great divide of spectacle versus narrative', *Screen* 43 (4), Winter, pp. 370–386.

Woolf, V. ([1925] 1966) 'Modern Fiction' in her *Collected Essays: Volume II*, London: Hogarth Press.

Wright, E. (1993) *Psychoanalytic Criticism: Theory in Practice*, London: Routledge.

INDEX